# Take Off into English Tea

Planning to become a secondary English teacher? This must-have guide contains everything you need to know before embarking on your training programme. From your reflections on your chosen course and your preparations for interview to thinking about the demands of school-based training, this book encourages you to engage with the challenges of teaching in a realistic and enthusiastic manner. It aims to answer the question: *What should trainees know, understand and be able to do before they start the training programme?*

Written in a practical, accessible and thought-provoking style, each chapter is packed full of reflective points, discussion questions, and a wealth of activities and examples. It explores key aspects of practice, including target setting and progression, as well as observing and being observed, and offers advice on tricky topics such as how to accept and build upon criticism and how to take responsibility for your professional development. There are numerous opportunities to reflect upon your subject knowledge, in order to help you celebrate what you know already as well as to identify what you still need to find out before you begin. Above all, the book encourages you to think about what English teaching means to *you*. You are invited to engage with core issues related to theory, curriculum and assessment, before exploring these issues in the context of the school.

Although *Take Off into English Teaching!* is written for trainee teachers and teachers of Secondary English, many of the issues it covers will be highly relevant for school and academic staff, trainees and training staff involved in secondary education generally.

**Nicholas McGuinn** has trained teachers of English and Drama for more than twenty years and is an Honorary Fellow in the Department of Education, University of York, UK.

# Take Off into English Teaching!

## How to Prepare for your Secondary Teacher Training Programme

Nicholas McGuinn

Routledge
Taylor & Francis Group

LONDON AND NEW YORK

First published 2018
by Routledge
2 Park Square, Milton Park, Abingdon, Oxon OX14 4RN

and by Routledge
711 Third Avenue, New York, NY 10017

*Routledge is an imprint of the Taylor & Francis Group, an informa business*

*British Library Cataloguing in Publication Data*
A catalogue record for this book is available from the British Library

*Library of Congress Cataloging in Publication Data*
Names: McGuinn, Nicholas, author.
Title: Take off into English teaching! : how to prepare for your
    secondary teacher training programme / Nicholas McGuinn.
Description: Abingdon, Oxon ; New York, NY : Routledge, [2018] |
    Includes bibliographical references
Identifiers: LCCN 2017012188| ISBN 9781138681453 (hbk) |
    ISBN 9781138681460 (pbk) | ISBN 9781315545806 (ebk)
Subjects: LCSH: English language—Study and teaching
    (Secondary)—Great Britain. | English teachers—Training
    of—Great Britain. | English teachers—In-service training—
    Great Britain.
Classification: LCC LB1631 .M3944 2018 | DDC 428.00712—dc23
LC record available at https://lccn.loc.gov/2017012188

ISBN: 978-1-138-68145-3 (hbk)
ISBN: 978-1-138-68146-0 (pbk)
ISBN: 978-1-315-54580-6 (ebk)

Typeset in Sabon LT Std
by Swales & Willis Ltd, Exeter, Devon, UK

For Martha, Jacob and Jacqui

# Contents

# Illustrations

# Acknowledgements

I would like to thank Christine Lewry, Rachel Singleton and all at Swales &
Willis and Taylor & Francis who contributed to the production of this book.
Special thanks to Helen Pritt for her encouragement and support.

# Introduction

Learning to become a teacher can be exhilarating, engaging and, if we are not careful, all-absorbing. Even if we manage to maintain a sense of proportion when training, the experience can still present formidable challenges because it can be so unlike anything else one might have attempted before. People who embark on a training programme straight from higher education have to exchange the life of a student for that of a working professional. People who opt for teaching as a change of career, sometimes resigning from positions of authority to do so, have to learn how to be students and to take instruction again. They may also find that the educational world has changed quite significantly since they left school. Having spent over twenty years watching 'new recruits' engage, sometimes painfully, with the challenges posed by teacher training programmes, it struck me that their lives might be made easier if they could undertake as much focussed pre-course preparation as possible. Above all, this means visiting schools and finding out how they work.

It was these people I had in mind when I first thought about writing this book. As a trainer specialising in secondary English teaching, I was prompted by the following question: *What would I like my trainees to know, understand and be able to do before they start the training programme?* The more I thought about a response to that question, the more I saw the potential audience for the book widening beyond this core group to include trainees already engaged on a course programme as well as newly qualified teachers of English for whom the memory of their own training experience, and the issues it raised, would still be fresh. Trainees and newly qualified teachers from other subject areas could, by exercising a little flexibility, engage with the issues explored in the book and adapt the suggested tasks to meet their own needs. I also felt that the book could be of use to school staff who work with trainees in various capacities while they are on placement in that it might help them appreciate further the kinds of academic, pedagogic and practical challenges faced by trainees from all subject areas. Reflecting on one's own practice and beliefs with someone who is new to the profession can be a thought-provoking, even energising, experience.

The structure and content of the book are informed by a number of key principles. I think it is important that teachers should 'lead by example'. I have therefore, where appropriate, demonstrated how I would respond to a number of the practical or reflective activities which comprise a significant element of each of the ten chapters. For the same reason, I have shared my own reflections on some of the core questions which run through the book: what is the relationship between the teacher of English and the state? What model or models of English should we offer to our pupils? How might theory inform our practice as teachers of English? Can established assessment procedures accommodate the complexities of a subject – if it actually *is* a subject – which encompasses the teaching of fine-motor skills at one level and exploration of the aesthetic domain at the other?

How and what we teach are bound up with who we are and the stories our lives tell. I have tried to demonstrate this by showing how experiences in my own past have shaped my engagement with pedagogic theory. In this context, I should say that the writers cited throughout the book are not meant to represent some definitive course reading list (though I would recommend each one of them heartily). They happen to be some of the thinkers who have helped me become a teacher of English. I hope readers of this book will take pleasure, not only in engaging with these particular texts, but in finding their own guiding spirits.

I would like to conclude by saying something about how you might work with this book. I recommend that you undertake a quick, initial reading of the whole text, so that you get a sense of its overall structure and dynamic. The first part starts with *Helen*, an undergraduate who has just heard that she has been awarded a place on a Secondary English course. How did she achieve this success? How might she best build upon her achievement to prepare herself for the start of the programme? What kinds of evidence collection does a *competence-based* training system require and how can those requirements be accommodated? Part II of the book is more reflective in tone. It provides opportunities to think about the kinds of teachers of English we want to be, as well as to engage with core issues related to theory, curriculum and assessment. The final section of the book considers how issues raised in Parts I and II might be explored within the context of the school.

Once you have an overview of the book's structure and dynamic, you might then like to focus in detail on individual chapters, using your own judgement about which activities – or *cluster* of activities: they are carefully sequenced – would best suit your particular needs, be you an aspiring trainee, a trainee, a newly qualified teacher or an experienced member of staff. Some of the activities are designed for individual engagement. However, as Vygotsky tells us, we *grow into the intellectual life of those around us* (1930/1978: 88). Many of the activities therefore are designed for sharing and exploring with other people, particularly other trainees, qualified teachers and educational professionals working within and beyond school.

# Chapter outlines

## Part I Starting out: planning and preparing for success

### Chapter 1: taking bearings

The opening chapter focuses upon the experience of *Helen*, an undergraduate who, it is imagined, has just been awarded a place on a teacher training programme. The chapter reflects upon Helen's achievement in order to provide guidance and advice to future candidates. It then uses her *personal statement* as a starting point for thinking about how she might begin to develop her potential as a teacher. Opportunities for development are mapped against four core elements of teacher professionalism and a possible *target timeline* is described.

This chapter will be of particular relevance to people who are thinking about applying for a place on a Secondary English training programme or who have already made a successful application. Trainees at the start of their course might also find it particularly beneficial.

### Chapter 2: target setting and progression

Chapter 2 focuses more closely on the challenges facing Helen by suggesting how they might be rationalised through the application of *SMART* target criteria. Bruner's concept of the *spiral curriculum* is invoked in order to offer an alternative to linear *progress narratives* of teacher development. The chapter concludes by providing examples of how a trainee might engage in a *cycle* of *baseline assessments* as a way of tracking their deepening engagement with pedagogy.

Chapter 2 would be particularly relevant to course tutors and school staff tasked with overseeing trainees' professional and pedagogic development. It would also of course be relevant to the trainees themselves.

## Chapter 3: recording evidence

Chapter 3 explores formal and informal approaches to the collection and organisation of evidence. Drawing upon an extract from the current *Teachers' Standards* for England as an example, it describes how the evidence expected from a trainee nearing the end of their course might differ from that expected of a beginner. The reader is encouraged to try their own hand at making evaluative judgements and identifying progress.

Chapter 3 is relevant to the audience identified in Chapters 1 and 2. In addition, it would be useful to newly qualified teachers and others who are required to collect and organise evidence for colleagues in school or in response to outside agencies such as government inspection teams.

## Part II Who we are and where we stand

### Chapter 4: why bother with theory? A closer look at praxis

Chapter 4 challenges the unhelpful binary which is sometimes used to create a rift between *theory* and *practice*. The concept of *praxis* is defined. Readers are challenged to consider how theoretically informed reflection might help them engage with some of the key ethical and pedagogic issues faced by teachers – particularly teachers concerned with the language arts. Reference is made to thinkers such as Althusser and Habermas.

Chapter 4 is relevant to all teachers concerned about the ideological role of the school and about issues of social justice. The exemplar material – particularly the *critical incidents* involving grammar and spelling – are pertinent to teachers of English especially.

### Chapter 5: what kind of English teacher do you want to be?

Drawing upon the work of Bourdieu and Bronfenbrenner particularly, Chapter 5 demonstrates how the application of theory can help us to enrich our understanding, not only of what happens in the classroom, but also of how life experiences can shape our vision of English teaching. The practical activities encourage readers to explore these issues by reflecting in detail upon their experiences as users of language.

Chapter 5 is aimed at all teachers concerned with language arts in general and with English pedagogy in particular. It is especially important that prospective English trainees, and those about to embark on a training programme, undertake the reflective exercises – or some version of them – described in this chapter.

### Chapter 6: thinking about the curriculum

Chapter 6 encourages readers to let the imagination run free by describing their ideal English curriculum. Focussing on the *Cox model* as an example, the chapter then contrasts that ideal with an officially sanctioned alternative. Ideological issues related to the teaching of Shakespeare are explored and these in turn lead into a consideration of arguments which challenge conventional views about what *Subject English* is or should be. *Collection* and *integrated* curriculum models are described, compared and critiqued.

Chapter 6 is relevant to all teachers of English. Again, it is especially important that prospective English trainees, and those about to embark on a training programme, should be able to take an informed theoretical position with regard to the concerns of this chapter.

### Chapter 7: assessment in English: key issues

Chapter 7 argues that English teachers should be practitioners of the arts and skills they profess to teach. To that end, the author opens the chapter by presenting an extract of his own fictional writing for critical scrutiny. This piece of exemplar material is used as a means of engaging with key issues pertinent to the assessment of English in general and writing in particular. Different forms of and purposes for assessment are considered and the uneasy relationship between assessment and the curriculum is explored.

Chapter 7 is relevant to the audience described in Chapter 5. In addition, trainees from other subject areas, particularly those related to English, would find many of the core issues pertinent to their own concerns about assessment.

## Part III Taking praxis into school

### Chapter 8: under the school microscope: observing and being observed

Drawing upon the work of Foucault among others, Chapter 8 considers some of the ideological issues, the tensions and the opportunities, implicit in the act of observation. What sensitivities and issues of etiquette might be brought into play when a trainee asks to observe an experienced teacher at work in the classroom – and what happens when the roles are reversed? What kinds of judgements do we make in these situations and what might their consequences be? How might lesson observations be seen in a positive light? Readers are encouraged to consider the school as a community located within a specific social context. What are the particular needs of the community served by the school? Who within a school community can offer particular assistance to trainees seeking to enrich their understanding of school life in general and classroom practice in particular?

Chapter 8 is geared towards the needs of English trainees. However, it would make useful reading for any of their peers, irrespective of subject area, who undertake a school placement. Chapter 8 would also prove useful not only for school staff tasked with organising and coordinating trainee placements, but also for qualified teachers who have to undergo or undertake lesson observations.

### Chapter 9: classroom observation: the practicalities

Chapter 9 builds on the previous chapter by comparing and contrasting quantitative and qualitative approaches to classroom observation. Exemplar material based on an English lesson is explored. Issues related to the sharing of feedback are considered. The chapter concludes with a detailed aide-memoire designed to help trainees and host school staff to organise lesson observations so that they become mutually beneficial and professionally positive experiences.

The main audience for Chapter 9 is as for Chapter 8.

### Chapter 10: assessment revisited: the school context

Why are issues of *assessment for accountability* so foregrounded in today's school system? Which individuals and social groups claim a right to scrutinise teachers' practice and which of these groups have particular claims to make on the attention of a trainee teacher of English? Building on the discussion initiated in Chapter 7, Chapter 10 describes the various *assessment contracts* (considered in terms of *privileges* and *obligations*) which might exist between these core claimants and a trainee teacher of English. The chapter considers the implications of these *pacts* for the trainee's placement practice. Warning of the dangers of what Ellis (2007:17) calls the *continuity-displacement contradiction*, the chapter and the book conclude with a plea for the maintenance of a strong, international academic presence within the teacher training system.

The main audience for Chapter 10 is as for Chapters 8 and 9.

# Part I

# Starting out

## Planning and preparing for success

# Chapter 1

# Taking bearings

## Section 1: what it takes

How does it – or how did it – feel to win a place on a Secondary English teacher training programme?

That achievement says a lot about you. You must have submitted an application form and personal statement which persuaded a selection panel that you have good academic credentials and a commitment to your chosen teaching subject. Your statement will have declared an interest in working with young people and a fascination with the way that adolescents, particularly, see the world. You have a sense of idealism – a vocation, even – and you recognise that the classroom is an important space in which teachers can have a powerful influence for good.

These qualities – and the testimony of the referees who vouched for them – secured you an interview. From the moment the members of the selection panel first met you on interview day, an important question will have run through their minds: *Can I imagine this person working successfully as a member of a teaching team?* I use the word *team* advisedly. Maverick teachers might make good fictional material; but a flourishing school is one where people work well together: offering each other support, sharing ideas, debating and developing pedagogy.

This is why your interview will probably have included some kind of team exercise. At the institution where I work, for example, we would invite you to explore a poem with the other candidates and discuss together ways in which you might teach it. What we are looking for here is evidence of those human qualities one would hope to find in a good team member: a sense of humour; enthusiasm; flexibility; sensitivity to the needs of others; an awareness of group dynamics; the ability to make – or concede – your point and, if need be, to stand your ground politely but assertively. Your contribution to the discussion will also have reassured the interviewing panel that you have good subject knowledge. In the example cited above, you would have shown not only that you are comfortable with and excited by the language and the possibilities of poetry but also that you have some understanding of how to share that excitement with young people.

Which takes us to what was probably a major component of the interview proceedings: a teaching activity. You might have had to teach the members of the interviewing panel, or you might have been placed in front of a class of pupils you had never met before. This exercise will also have provided opportunities to demonstrate those human qualities and that subject knowledge exhibited during the group task; but this time, particularly if you found yourself in a real classroom, you would also have been expected to show that you are competent in a range of other skills: an understanding of how to translate curriculum requirements into engaging teaching and learning activities; time management; an appreciation of logistics; the ability to 'think on your feet', to respond to a range of different needs and, not least, to demonstrate a capacity for leadership.

The members of the selection panel who observed your teaching will have been looking to see how adept you are at recognising and engaging with what Vygotsky (1986) called the *zone of proximal development (ZPD)*: the opportunity to nurture a pupil's readiness to learn something by providing appropriate teacher intervention. This is one of the most important teaching skills and interviewers are constantly on the alert for it. To cite my own institution again, the members of the selection panel would have assessed your appreciation of the ZPD not only by asking you to teach them something, but also by inviting you to mark a pupil's writing. Marking occupies a considerable amount of an English teacher's time. We will return to this issue in Chapters 7 and 10. However, it is important for interview candidates to appreciate the significance of assessment right from the start. There is a good reason why marking features so prominently in the life of an English teacher. Regular focussed assessment – verbal and written; undertaken during and after a lesson – is the most effective way for teachers to understand what their pupils can do and how they might be helped to develop further.

Effective marking requires sensitivity, skilfulness, subtlety – and staying power (particularly when faced with the task of reading and assessing thirty scripts on the same topic). Should errors be highlighted? Which errors, how and why? Should some spelling and syntactical mistakes, for example, be applauded because they indicate an intelligent and logical attempt to engage with an unfamiliar word or an ambitious sentence construction? If a pupil writes as they speak – perhaps, as in the example explored in Chapter 4, using *we was* instead of *we were* – how should the teacher respond? How does one explain the difference between a comma, a semicolon and a full stop in terms that a pupil in thrall to *comma splicing* can understand? What if the content of the pupil's writing raises issues of pastoral concern? If one has to grade the writing, should effort be awarded as well as attainment? How is technical skill weighted against content? Should the teacher's assessment comment be designed to encourage – or should it provide an unvarnished statement of the pupil's achievement when judged against national criteria?

To win a place on a training programme, you convinced the interviewing panel that you possess the potential to engage with complex issues such as those described above. No wonder congratulations are in order. There will be times during your teaching career when you will feel particularly challenged and your confidence will be shaken. When such moments come, read back over Section 1 and remind yourself of all the skills and the promise that you demonstrated when you submitted your application form and completed a successful interview to secure a place on a training programme.

## Section 2: mapping and personalising your learning – four areas of knowledge

This initial review process needs to go further, however. So far, we have considered some of the *generic* qualities expected of *all* teachers of English. Now we need to begin to focus on what *you as an individual* bring to the profession. This is one of the most important issues (we will explore it again in Chapter 5) which the staff on a teacher training programme have to consider with their trainees so that together they can plan a developmental programme tailored to individual strengths and learning needs.

Ben-Peretz (2011) has provided a useful summary of the extensive literature which, over the past fifty years or more, has attempted to identify just exactly what it is that aspiring teachers need to know and to be able to do. De Corte (2003) argues that one of the characteristics of powerful learning environments is that they provide opportunities for teachers to model the learning expected of their pupils. In the section which follows, I have tried to adhere to De Corte's principle by outlining four of the key areas of knowledge and understanding summarised by Ben-Peretz which have particularly resonated with me. I have also attempted to model how a teacher of English might interpret them.

### Content, curriculum and pedagogic knowledge

This term is particularly associated with the writing of Shulman (1986a). In order to tease out what these words might mean in an actual classroom context, consider the following scenario.

A trainee English teacher has just graduated with a good degree in English literature and thus, quite reasonably, believes she possesses strong *content knowledge* – at least in certain areas of the subject. Perhaps she is particularly proud of the dissertation she wrote on the Gothic novel: does this automatically qualify her to teach Mary Shelley's *Frankenstein* to a class of fifteen-year-olds?

To teach successfully, our candidate needs to have *curriculum knowledge* as well as content knowledge: an understanding – to cite the Mary Shelley example again – of how the study of *Frankenstein* fits into the pupils' overall English learning programme. Exploring issues of curriculum knowledge raises a series of important questions (they are worth keeping in mind as you work through the book and are particularly relevant to Part III):

- What level of textual engagement is it reasonable to expect of fifteen-year-olds?
- If the pupils are to be assessed on their knowledge of *Frankenstein*, what understanding and skills should they be able to demonstrate and how? What influence will assessment requirements have upon teaching approaches?
- What curricular and personal resources can a teacher draw on to support the pupils' learning?

Crucially, if our candidate's teaching is to be effective, she also requires *pedagogic knowledge*. She must try to imagine what it feels like to be fifteen years old and to be encountering a novel like *Frankenstein* for the first time – perhaps as a pupil from a background and with priorities very different from her own. These questions come to mind:

- How can a teacher bring the text alive?
- How can a teacher draw on the pupils' previous learning experiences to help them engage with this particular text?
- How can a teacher do so in a way that caters for different learning needs and behaviours?

## Professional knowledge

Tamir defines *professional knowledge* as 'that body of knowledge and skills which is needed in order to function successfully in a particular profession' (1991: 263). The important word *team* comes into play again here and a third set of powerful questions is raised:

- What behaviours are expected of teachers if they are to become effective members of the school community?
- How do teachers negotiate positive working relationships – sometimes with colleagues they might not necessarily warm to on a personal level?
- Are the school's values, codes and management systems ones teachers feel they can support?
- How might teachers develop their wider professional knowledge beyond the immediate confines of the school – by networking with colleagues on a national level, for example, studying for further qualifications or developing areas of expertise outside their immediate subject area?

One of the ways in which De Corte's concept of teacher modelling has been translated into the classroom is through the creation of what is known in the parlance of pedagogic acronyms as a *WAGOLL (What A Good One Looks Like)*. True to the principles of De Corte, I include below a copy of a personal statement written by a third-year English and Education undergraduate whom I will call Helen. (It is reasonable to assume that Helen's statement is a WAGOLL because it gained her access to at least two successful interviews for a place on secondary English teacher training programmes.)

## OVER TO YOU

### Activity I

- Read Helen's personal statement as if you were a member of a course selection panel. Briefly – we will undertake more detailed work later – analyse the statement in terms of its content knowledge, curriculum knowledge, pedagogic knowledge and professional knowledge. Find **one** example of evidence for each of the four knowledge areas.
- Consider what this personal statement suggests about Helen's potential as a teacher.

## Helen's statement

Teaching English is a demanding profession that requires management of ambiguity surrounding the changes to the curriculum and pedagogical strategies. However, my resilience, confidence and innovativeness in educational contexts have proven that I am just one step closer to embracing these challenges to lead to a successful career as an English teacher. My experience in a variety of educational institutions has enabled me to understand that teaching English can be a powerful and rewarding opportunity. My commitment to English has also shaped my understanding of the subject as a transformative force, which has the power to shape the development of young people not only intellectually, but also personally and socially.

Having volunteered in English classes in two contrasting schools, one being outstanding and the other being in need of improvement, I have had the opportunity to work on creative tasks with pupils with differing academic abilities. I have assisted pupils with learning differences such as dyslexia and Asperger's syndrome who found the subject of English extremely daunting. Through this I was able to learn that teachers need to employ a range of different pedagogical strategies to cater for the diverse needs in the classroom. This may include a range of learning tasks from one-to-one support to collaborative group discussion to stimulate imaginative and creative responses to this fascinating subject.

Naturally, I chose to study English in Education for my undergraduate degree to gain a theoretical grounding in education and the political, social and cultural implications surrounding teaching. My real passion lies in the aesthetic value of English literature and the unlimited boundaries of language, which is justified in my choice of modules, varying from the analysis of poetry to the vast world of children's literature. Reading for pleasure is a routine activity for me, as is brushing my teeth. My dissertation will explore teenage fiction and the everyday pressures of adolescence. My interest in secondary school teaching has stemmed from my degree and my experience in educational settings. At an age when students are developing their skills and gaining a personal identity, I am eager to learn from experienced classroom practitioners how I can influence the lives of young people and contribute to their learning.

Being assessed through oral presentations, group work and independent assignments at university I have demonstrated that I can adapt to different contexts and manage my time and workload effectively. This is highlighted in my academic performance in which I am on track to graduate with a First.

Being the coordinator for a 'Nonsense Language' workshop for a year 7 class has taught me that preparation and innovative ideas are critical factors to ensure that learning takes place in the classroom. Using the poem *Jabberwocky*, I was able to plan a workshop that met the criteria of the National Curriculum and the interests of the pupils. This enabled me to build a strong rapport with the English department at the school and exhibit my interpersonal skills with staff. The activities incorporated a wide range of tasks, such as drama and creativity, to ensure that all students were engaged with the subject in a fun and upbeat way. Through my strong engagement with current affairs in English teaching and my degree I now feel that I am more than prepared to study for my PGCE and fulfil my aspiration of becoming an English teacher with outstanding recognition.

### A worked example

Table 1.1 provides an example of how I attempted a response to Activity 1. To help my thinking, I divided my comments into two areas: strengths and opportunities.

### OVER TO YOU

### Activity 2

- How does your response to Helen's statement compare with mine? Did we choose similar areas of significance?
- What points from this personal statement would you wish to follow up at interview if you were on the selection panel?

Table 1.1 Helen's personal statement tracked against Ben-Peretz's four areas of teacher knowledge

| Knowledge area | Evidence from Helen's statement | Strengths | Opportunities |
|---|---|---|---|
| Content knowledge | *My real passion lies in the aesthetic value of English literature and the unlimited boundaries of language, which is justified in my choice of modules, varying from the analysis of poetry to the vast world of children's literature. Reading for pleasure is a routine activity for me.* | Favours an aesthetic model of English. Appreciates the importance of fictional writing for young people. A committed reader. | Good to have a group member who is enthusiastic about poetry – sometimes an area of concern for beginning teachers. Commitment to other models of English beyond the aesthetic? Familiarity with canonical texts? Shakespeare? Linguistic approaches? |
| Curriculum knowledge | *Naturally, I chose to study English in Education for my undergraduate degree to gain a theoretical grounding of education and the political, social and cultural implications surrounding teaching.*<br>*Using the poem Jabberwocky, I was able to plan a [Year 7] workshop that met the criteria of the National Curriculum [for England].* | Naturally chose a degree course which combined English with Education. Aware of English as an ideological construct. Already has some awareness of what national curricular statements might look like in practice. | Receptive to the concept of theoretically informed educational practice (*praxis*). Able to build on prior knowledge of key educational concepts. Able to work creatively within national curriculum frameworks – and can critique these, too? |
| Pedagogic knowledge | *I have had the opportunity to work on creative tasks with pupils with differing academic abilities. I have assisted pupils with learning differences such as dyslexia and Asperger's syndrome who found the subject of English extremely* | Receptive to issues regarding personalised learning, differentiation and special needs. | Liaison with special needs staff when on school placement? Opportunity to explore issues of differentiation and personalised learning through research for written assignments? |

| | | | |
|---|---|---|---|
| | daunting. Through this I was able to learn that teachers need to employ a range of different pedagogical strategies to cater for the diverse needs in the classroom. This may include a range of learning tasks from one-to-one support to collaborative group discussion to stimulate imaginative and creative responses to this fascinating subject. | Aware that not all students might share her own facility with English; but this has not shaken her own belief in the need to provide imaginative and creative curricular experiences for all pupils. <br> Appreciates that pupils may learn from each other as well as from the teacher. | Potential to engage early with more challenging and diverse classes when on school placement? <br> Lesson planning should show early and increasingly sophisticated engagement with differentiation strategies, including questioning. |
| Professional knowledge | Teaching English is a demanding profession that requires management of ambiguity surrounding the changes to the curriculum and pedagogical strategies. <br> Being assessed through oral presentations, group work and independent assignments at university I have demonstrated that I can adapt to different contexts and manage my time and workload effectively. | Understands that teachers may not necessarily have professional autonomy and that politicians have a major influence on their working lives – but is willing to meet those challenges with creative resilience. <br> Aware that beginning teachers are assessed regularly in a wide range of contexts. <br> Appreciates the importance of time management. | Might bring a positive sense of resolution and determination to a school staffroom, thus counteracting the potential negativity of some established colleagues. <br> Should be able to engage professionally and collaboratively with evaluative feedback, even when it is not entirely positive. Should be expected to meet professional commitments and deadlines, both in and outside school. |

## Activity 3

Now let us shift the focus on to you.

- Read through the application form you completed in order to win your place on a training programme. As well as your personal statement, you might also wish to review other pieces of information provided at the time. Helen's material, for example, included an additional section called *School and Work Experience*, where she described how she had worked as a peer mentor, contributed to her university's Education Society and participated in a Students in Schools initiative.
- Map the information provided with your application against the four areas of knowledge, as I have done in Table 1.1, in terms of strengths and opportunities. This time, try to be as detailed as you can.

How might trainee teachers in English use information of the kind you have explored in the previous activity to help plan for their training course? Training programmes usually begin with an induction meeting held between individual trainees and one or more of the course tutors. The aim of that meeting is to help the trainees compile an audit of the strengths and learning needs which they bring to their training.

Beginning that auditing process as early as possible will put a trainee in a strong position because it will help them to engage confidently, professionally and above all *proactively* in that discussion with their tutors. It is most important to be able to demonstrate, from the start of the course, the ability to be professionally proactive – to demonstrate a capacity to *take charge of one's own learning*. In this, the ultimate goal of teacher trainers is the same as for all committed educators: paradoxically, they want to make themselves redundant by achieving what De Corte (2003) calls *teacher fade*. Teacher fade is achieved when a learner acts autonomously.

## Section 3: planning a target timeline

Target setting plays a significant part in training programmes (see Chapters 2 and 3) so it is important for trainees to start thinking about it as early as possible – and to think about it in such a way that the targets set are professionally useful and, above all, *manageable.*

### A worked example

Please look at the example of target setting which I have modelled in Table 1.2. I have used Helen's exemplar material from Section 2 again and selected as illustration one piece of evidence from each of the four knowledge areas explored there.

Table 1.2 Planning a target timeline for Helen, tracked against the four areas of teacher knowledge

| Knowledge area | Evidence from Helen's statement | Opportunity | Immediate target | Mid-term target | Long-term target | Who or what can help? |
|---|---|---|---|---|---|---|
| Content knowledge | *Naturally, I chose to study English in Education for my undergraduate degree to gain a theoretical grounding of education and the political, social and cultural implications surrounding teaching.* | Receptive to the concept of theoretically informed educational practice (praxis). | Compile a list of essential reading related to general and subject-specific pedagogy **(March)**. | Read and annotate four key texts (two in each area) **by the end of April**. | Continue to extend reading at the same pace until the course begins **(September)**. **Throughout the course,** relate reading to classroom observations, lesson evaluations, written assignments and job application letters. **After the course** – engage in pedagogical debate with colleagues at international, national and regional networking and in-service training events. | Online reading lists provided by a range of training programmes. Resources provided by professional organisations and academic libraries. Tutors and colleagues on the training programme. Host teachers and training consultants in schools In-service programmes. |
| Curriculum knowledge | *Using the poem Jabberwocky, I was able to plan a [Year 7] workshop that met the criteria of the National* | Able to work creatively within national curriculum frameworks – and can | Review and critique the references to poetry in the programmes of study for the National Curriculum for England. | Arrange interviews with the members of the English department of a local secondary school and the teachers responsible for Year 6 English in one of | Helen's statement suggests four particular areas of curricular interest: the place of poetry teaching; the status afforded to works from the literary heritage; the role of | Course reading lists, academic journals and English teachers' websites |

*(continued)*

Table 1.2 (continued)

| Knowledge area | Evidence from Helen's statement | Opportunity | Immediate target | Mid-term target | Long-term target | Who or what can help? |
|---|---|---|---|---|---|---|
| | Curriculum [for England]. | critique these, too? | Consider how poetry is positioned within that curriculum across the age range and the modalities of English. [Speaking, listening, reading and writing – more on this in Chapter 7.] Look for evidence to support the claim that the Jabberwocky workshop plan 'met National Curriculum criteria'. Review and critique the assessment of poetry as revealed in an examination board English specification (**March**). | the school's 'feeder' primaries. Review the Jabberwocky workshop plan with the teachers. Ask them to evaluate the plan and to comment on how it might or might not fit in with their established schemes of work. Compare the responses of the Year 6 and the secondary school teachers and consider any issues of cross-phase transition which might be raised. Ask the teachers for advice on poetry and poetry pedagogy resources. Start to explore these (**April–July**). | fantasy literature; and engagement with language through literary texts. **Throughout the training programme**, she should use the opportunities provided by training sessions, teaching placements, research for written assignments and access to academic libraries to develop an enriched critical understanding of how these four areas are positioned within school and national curricula. **After the course** – engage in pedagogical debate with colleagues at international, national and regional networking and in-service training events. | (national and international). Tutors, teachers, colleagues and consultants (including examination board officers), pupils and their carers. |
| Pedagogic knowledge | I have assisted pupils with learning differences such as dyslexia and Asperger's syndrome. | Receptive to issues regarding special needs. | Review online resources relating to dyslexia and Asperger's syndrome. | Interview professionals working within the special educational needs area. What do they consider the main issues to be? What constitutes best practice? | If the training course is affiliated to a research-active academic institution, **once the course begins**, meet with researchers and teachers working in the area of special educational | A range of professionals working in the area, including tutors, advisors, academics, |

| Professional knowledge | Being assessed through oral presentations, group work and independent assignments at university I have demonstrated that I can adapt to | Aware that student teachers are assessed regularly in a wide range of contexts. Appreciates the importance of time management. | Identify specific training needs. Create a realistic timeline for addressing targets and write the first draft of an agenda for an induction meeting with course tutors (**March**). | Locate these within the wider educational context of special educational needs, including codes of practice, guidelines for teachers and government policy statements (**March**). Arrange to visit teachers and other relevant staff responsible for special needs in a local school. If possible, arrange to 'shadow' a teacher. What core reading would specialist staff recommend? (**April–July**). | Following discussions with teachers [described in the *curriculum knowledge* section earlier], liaise with appropriate staff to plan and teach either part or all of a lesson which builds on the *Jabberwocky* workshop material and which addresses a specific needs. How do their views compare with those of other professionals? Get to know the library's online journals dedicated to special educational needs. Try to read a recently published article once a fortnight. Use the opportunities provided by school placements and written assignments to extend understanding of how special educational needs are catered for in the classroom. **After the course** – as for *content knowledge*. | **Shortly before the course begins**, create a focussed work plan for the programme ahead, identifying potential pressure points (for example, when school placement commitments might clash with written assignment deadlines). | teachers, consultants, researchers and librarians. Colleagues on the training programme. The pupils encountered on school placement (and their carers). The authors of specialist journal articles, books and online material. Extensive literature on teacher training (consult course reading lists and librarians for details). |

*(continued)*

Table 1.2 (continued)

| Knowledge area | Evidence from Helen's statement | Opportunity | Immediate target | Mid-term target | Long-term target | Who or what can help? |
|---|---|---|---|---|---|---|
| | different contexts and manage my time and workload effectively. | | | requirement of the National Curriculum for English. Invite the host teacher to scrutinise the lesson plan before it is taught. Ask the host teacher to observe the lesson. Evaluate it together afterwards, verbally and in writing. If the host school is willing, repeat this process several times and see if it is possible to create a scheme of work based on the topic. Try to establish a habit of engaging professionally with feedback, even when it is not entirely positive **(April–July)**. | Once the course is underway, set up a *reflective learning partnership* with two other colleagues for the purposes of observing and providing feedback on each other's teaching. On school placement, extend this network to include mentors and other relevant school staff. Create a clear line of communication with key staff involved in evaluating progress throughout the course. Clarify exactly what is expected of a trainee and why. | Tutors, host teachers (particularly those who have recently completed their training) and colleagues (particularly *reflective learning partnership* members). Pupils and their carers (encountered at parents evenings and other school open events). |

Helen set herself a tight deadline. She did not apply till February for a training programme starting in September. I have therefore constructed Table 1.2 and Table 2.1 in the next chapter on the basis of a six-month timeline. (Suggested timings are highlighted in bold.)

Note that I have added an additional set of headings relating to *Immediate, Mid-term and Long-term targets*. Bear in mind, too, that by including a series of long-term targets, I wish to make it clear that learning does not end when a training programme finishes. In Chapters 8 and 10, we will consider in more detail how a trainee might use the *Who or what can help?* heading.

Sketching out a plan like the one above can help Helen to orientate herself and to get her bearings so that, by the time she begins her course in September, she will have already proved herself to be organised, forward-thinking and proactively engaged. Chapter 2 will explore ways in which Helen's targets might be configured so that they are practical and manageable.

# Chapter 2

# Target setting and progression

## Section 1: setting SMART targets

During a training programme, trainees are likely to hear much use made of the acronym *SMART* in relation to target setting. SMART stands for *specific, measurable, attainable, relevant* and *time-bound*. In Table 2.1, I have put together, as an example, Helen's mid-term targets from Section 3 of Chapter 1, selected for each of the four areas of knowledge.

### *A worked example*

This is how I might critique Helen's mid-term targets against SMART criteria.

#### *Are the targets specific and relevant?*

I believe I can make a strong case for arguing that these targets meet the *specific* and *relevant* SMART criteria because they have been designed to address particular developmental opportunities identified in Helen's personal statement.

#### *Are the targets time-bound?*

The *time-bound* criterion is a little more problematic. Helen has submitted her application form at what is the busiest period of her degree programme: she has a dissertation to write, final module assignments to submit and an end-of-course exam to sit. Given that she believes she is 'on track to graduate with a First', she might feel the stakes are particularly high and that immediate academic pressures must take precedence over longer-term training considerations. I have tried to take all this into account when constructing a timeline for her mid-term targets. I think it is reasonable to allocate two months to the target of reading and annotating 'four key texts'

Table 2.1 Helen's mid-term targets tracked against the four areas of teacher knowledge

| Content knowledge | Curriculum knowledge | Pedagogic knowledge | Professional knowledge |
|---|---|---|---|
| Read and annotate four key texts (two in each area) **by the end of April.** | Arrange interviews with the members of the English department of a local secondary school and the teachers responsible for Year 6 English in one of the school's 'feeder' primaries.<br><br>Review the *Jabberwocky* workshop plan with the teachers. Ask them to evaluate the plan and to comment on how it might or might not fit in with their established schemes of work.<br><br>Compare the responses of the Year 6 and the secondary school teachers and consider any issues of cross-phase transition which might be raised.<br><br>Ask the teachers for advice on poetry and poetry pedagogy resources. Start to explore these **(April–July).** | Interview professionals working within the special educational needs area. What do they consider the main issues to be? What constitutes best practice?<br><br>Arrange to visit teachers and other relevant staff responsible for special needs in a local school. If possible, arrange to shadow a teacher.<br><br>What core reading texts would specialist staff recommend? **(April–July).** | Following discussions with teachers [described under the *curriculum knowledge* heading], liaise with appropriate staff to plan and teach either part or all of a lesson which builds on the *Jabberwocky* workshop material and which addresses a specific requirement of the National Curriculum for English.<br><br>Invite the host teacher to scrutinise the lesson plan before it is taught.<br><br>Ask the host teacher to observe the lesson and evaluate it together afterwards, verbally and in writing.<br><br>If the host school is willing, repeat this process several times and see if it is possible to create a scheme of work based on the topic.<br><br>Try to establish a habit of engaging professionally with feedback, even when it is not entirely positive **(April–July).**<br><br>In Chapters 7 and 8, we will explore in more details the implications of this target statement. |

in the area of general and subject-specific pedagogy. Rather than being an additional burden at a busy time, if chosen carefully, these works should enrich the final year degree work of an English and Education student (see the reference to Locke later in the chapter).

I have allocated four months to the mid-term targets in the other three knowledge areas because these are logistically more challenging and time-consuming: Helen is dependent here upon the generosity and the calendars of busy teachers and other educational professionals who have their own responsibilities and deadlines to meet. However, phone calls and emails could prepare the ground for the suggested visits while Helen is still working hard towards her degree. Given that her undergraduate course finishes in June, she still has time to undertake those visits before the end of the school term. If it is just not possible to meet 'face-to-face', online interviews might prove a workable solution (though nothing equals the opportunity to get into a school and to talk to teachers within their professional environment).

I have deliberately left August free when constructing my timeline for two reasons. First, it is important that Helen does not move straight from an intensive final undergraduate year into an even more intensive professional training programme. She needs to have a break if possible, in order to recharge and refresh herself. The second reason is to allow some space for slippage – a special educational needs expert, for example, might not have time to meet with Helen during the term, but may have more flexibility in the school holidays.

If I could for a moment address specifically readers who have not yet applied for a place on a training course. One particularly important lesson to take from this exploration of the *time-bound* SMART criterion is that you need to try to submit your application as soon as you reasonably can. The earlier you apply, the more places will be available for you to choose from; and once you have secured that place, you will have more time to undertake the activities described in this book – including planning and addressing your own pre-course SMART targets. Helen has put additional pressure on herself by applying so late on in the academic year. She might have had double the amount of time to prepare, had she come to an earlier decision about wanting to become a teacher of English.

### Are the targets attainable?

The *attainable* criterion also gives pause for thought in terms of manageability. One solution to the challenges it poses is to try to *amalgamate* the targets wherever possible.

The mid-term targets for reading set out under the Content knowledge heading could be linked directly to the work on *Jabberwocky* outlined in the Curriculum knowledge and Professional knowledge sections.

Helen – who has taken undergraduate modules involving 'the analysis of poetry' and an exploration of 'the vast world' of children's literature – could build on this foundation and prepare for the school-based elements of her mid-term targets programme by reading texts which explore praxis specifically related to the teaching of poetry from the *cultural heritage* model of English (for example, as mentioned earlier, Locke: 2015. Models of English will be explored in more detail in Chapter 6). Preparatory reading of this kind will enrich the interviewing, planning and teaching activities which follow and thus make them all the more sharply focussed.

The mid-term targets outlined in the Pedagogic knowledge section can also be linked with the other three. The interview with professionals working in the special educational needs area could, perhaps, include a discussion of how best to teach a poem like *Jabberwocky* so that *all* pupils can access the text. Helen has a declared interest in dyslexia: she might therefore want to include, as one of her interview questions, advice on how to help a dyslexic pupil engage with the unconventional words encountered in *Jabberwocky*.

In the diagram which follows, the mid-term targets for each of the four areas of knowledge 'feed' clockwise and sequentially into one 'blended' target represented by the four quadrants of the circle:

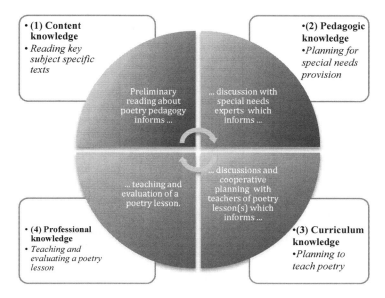

*Figure 2.1* Working 'smartly': blending targets across four areas of knowledge and understanding

*Are the targets measurable?*

This criterion is particularly problematic. Trainees planning, like Helen, to undertake their training within the English secondary education system as it is constituted at the time of writing, will quickly appreciate that the dominant discourse associated with assessment privileges words like *measurement* and *progress*. Chapter 3 will have more to say about these two elusive concepts; but for now I just want to draw attention to the fact that trainees embarking on a training programme within the current English system are judged against specific, criterion-referenced standards. To cite again the example of the system current in England at the time of writing, the following eight headline statements[1] are used to assess trainee teachers:

1   Set high expectations which inspire, motivate and challenge pupils.
2   Promote good progress and outcomes by pupils.
3   Demonstrate good subject and curriculum knowledge.
4   Plan and teach well structured lessons.
5   Adapt teaching to respond to the strengths and needs of all pupils.
6   Make active and productive use of assessment.
7   Manage behaviour effectively to ensure a good and safe learning environment.
8   Fulfil wider professional responsibilities.

In addition, trainee teachers are expected to demonstrate consistently high standards of personal and professional conduct (GOV.UK, 2011: 10–14).

It is not my intention here to critique the current training standards for England; and it would be a strange educator who argued that the eight teaching criteria listed above are not highly valuable and important. I do, however, want to draw upon this set of teaching standards to explore some general issues associated with the SMART criterion of *measurement*. First, like any attempt at codification – in Section 2 and then again in Chapter 6 we will consider the problems involved in attempting to define a 'canon' of English literature – it establishes *boundaries*: some criteria make it inside the boundary, some perhaps are left outside. Second, it creates a questionable sense of security: the implication is that if we address these eight standards, we will have met the criteria which characterise a successful teacher. Is that really the case? If you had been asked to draw up a list of teaching standards, would you have chosen the eight described above? Would you have had more or fewer than eight? Personally, I can think of at least four additional headline statements which come immediately to mind:

1    Demonstrate an ability to engage critically with educational theory and to apply theory to practice.
2    Demonstrate an appreciation of and ability to engage with special educational needs in the classroom.
3    Demonstrate an appreciation of and ability to engage with issues of social justice in the classroom.
4    Demonstrate a commitment to the emotional, mental and moral well-being of all pupils.

I could continue; but I am sure you take the point.

To locate the issue within a broader context, it seems to me that this current foregrounding of criterion-referenced standards in teacher training is linked to the *progress narratives* which, developing during the European Enlightenment, attained their 'high-water mark' in the nineteenth century (Lange: 2011). The French 'Positivist' Auguste Comte – to cite just one example – argued that humanity is engaged on a staged journey from savagery to civilisation. Comte conceded that the journey might be fraught with difficulties and setbacks; but he nevertheless encouraged a sense that the direction of travel is forward and that ultimately humanity is making incremental progress.

We could argue on an existential level whether that kind of progress narrative aligns with the experiences of twentieth-century global history. More specifically: how accurately does it describe the experience of learning to teach? Take another look at the mid-term *content knowledge* target suggested for Helen on page 27. I noted earlier that she might be asked to 'read and annotate four key texts' by the end of April. One of those texts, I suggested, might be Locke's 2015 account of the various ideological models which have informed the teaching of English over the past century or more. Say that Helen addresses this target by reading and annotating Locke's chapter and then using that knowledge to inform her meetings with English teachers – does this mean that the target can be ticked off as completed? The fact that Helen has been set long-term content knowledge goals which extend well beyond the end of the course – in fact, throughout her entire teaching career – suggests that the answer to that question is 'definitely not'. It is no good archiving those initial reflections on Locke's chapter somewhere in a computer file or in an academic essay; they need to be a consistent 'presence' in the classroom; they need to be refreshed, challenged and modified in the light of further readings, teaching experiences, training opportunities, debates and discussions – so that the issues they raise become embedded in Helen's pedagogy.

There will be times, during the course of the training year and beyond, when Helen's apparent progress towards this particular target will seem to be knocked back. Under pressure from other commitments on school placement, for example, she might hurriedly construct a lesson on *Jabberwocky* which fails to take account of the issues raised by a cultural heritage approach to teaching literature. She might find herself on a second, contrasting placement where her English teacher colleagues hold very different views on the teaching of poetry from those she felt comfortable with in her first placement school. She might read a critique of the cultural heritage model which shakes her faith in the educational value of teaching the works of 'canonical' writers. Should student teachers too readily accept a 'Positivist' model of progress – particularly one which employs criterion-referenced grades (see also Chapter 7) to assess achievement – they run the risk of assuming that, if the grades and evaluations they receive are not consistently 'improving', they must be failing in some way. The consequences for morale and self-confidence can be imagined; and it is as well for trainees to be aware of this and to prepare themselves to face the issue before their training programme begins.

## OVER TO YOU

### Activity 1

- Look again at the work you completed for Section 2 Activity 3 of Chapter 1 on page 20. Focus particularly on the Opportunities section. Using the worked example I have provided in Table 2.1 page 27 to guide you, organise the contents of your Opportunities section into immediate, mid-term and long-term targets.

### Activity 2

- Critique these targets according to SMART criteria, using the model I have provided on pages 26–32 as a guide.

### Activity 3

- Tracking backwards from the imagined start date of your selected training programme to today, create **three** tables of SMART targets (one each for immediate, mid-term and long-term).

- Colour-code the targets (a different colour for each of the four areas of knowledge) so that it is possible to see where you could create blended SMART targets. Alternatively, represent the blended SMART targets graphically, as I have done for Figure 2.1 on page 29.
- Set dates in bold for each of the targets.

## Activity 4

Consider the following questions:

- What targets can you **realistically** hope to address by the start of the course?
- If it is just not possible to address all the identified targets in the time available to you, what further action will you take?

## Section 2: a spiral model of progress

The poet T. S. Eliot offers an alternative to Comte's Positivist vision of progress. Towards the end of his poem *Little Gidding*, he describes the goal of exploration as being the ability to return to one's starting point, recognising it as if for the first time. Taking Eliot's lead, I would argue that a more persuasive way to think about progress is to consider it in terms of what Bruner calls a *spiral curriculum* – one which, as it develops: 'should revisit [its] basic ideas repeatedly, building upon them until the student has grasped the full formal apparatus that goes with them' (1960:13).

There are several advantages in thinking about target setting and progress in these terms – though I would want to question Bruner's assertion that we can ever grasp the 'full formal apparatus' of any learning experience. That caveat aside, I would suggest that the image of the spiral is helpful because it reinforces the idea that targets are 'always with us', throughout our careers. The day we declare that we have nothing more to learn is the day we should leave teaching. The image of the spiral can also serve to remind us that striving to reach a target does not have to be a 'zero sum' game which we either win or lose. It is all right to have a go, to take a risk and even to fail – especially, as the playwright Samuel Beckett might put it, if we fail *better*. What matters is that we recognise what we have achieved, what we still need to achieve and what we can learn from the mistakes we make.

Trainees who are sincerely trying to do their best and are able to reflect upon their performance with professional integrity, need to remember to be kind to themselves when, during the course of their training pro-gramme, things seem to go wrong – as they inevitably will. It would do no harm for trainers to bear this in mind, too.

Being compassionate about failure and suspicious of linear progress narratives should not imply some woolly-minded, 'anything goes' approach to target setting and professional development. At the very least, trainees have to remember that the people concerned with their training are required to make frequent, high-stakes judgements about them – judgements which could determine their future as teachers. They may well be involved in a programme which defines starkly their professional competence in terms of words like *good* and *satisfactory* – or, even more bleakly, by allocating them a number. We will return to this issue in Chapters 7 and 8; but for now, we have to face the fact that regular evaluations of practice are a constant in teaching today. It is as well for trainees to come to terms with that reality before the course starts. Even if this were not the case, it is most important for the sake of their wellbeing, sense of professional achievement and self-confidence – and most important above all for the sake of the pupils in their care – that they are prepared to evaluate themselves and to *visualise* what effective work towards a specific target might look like. In the words of Albert Bandura: 'Those who have a high sense of efficacy visualize success scenarios that provide positive guides for performance' (1989: 1176).

To achieve this while remaining true to Bruner's model of progression, we could establish a *baseline assessment* (Lindsay and Desforges: 1998) against which progress along the spiral might be evaluated. Referring to Helen's application form one last time as an example, I want to return to a statement which has already featured significantly in the mid-term target-setting plan outlined earlier in Chapter 1, Section 3 on page 21:

*Using the poem* Jabberwocky, *I was able to plan a [Year 7] workshop*

The *Jabberwocky* workshop plan makes a particularly useful starting point because it represents a first, relatively untrained attempt to engage with the four areas of knowledge introduced in Chapter 1. Helen could *revisit* the plan – to borrow Bruner's term – on completion of each of her four mid-term target tasks, rewriting it in the light of the new learning she has taken from each of those encounters.

In Table 2.2, I have included a heading called *Success criteria* (another phrase encountered frequently in schools and explored later in the book). This section attempts to identify what exactly Helen might actually do at each revisit to show she had successfully used the baseline *Jabberwocky* material to demonstrate an incrementally richer engagement with a specific target.

Table 2.2 Helen's mid-term targets: an example of a spiral model of progression

| Spiral level | Knowledge target addressed | Success criteria | Preparing for next review |
|---|---|---|---|
| **Spiral level 1: Baseline reviewed end of April** | **Content knowledge:** Read and annotate four key texts (two in each area). | *Jabberwocky* workshop plan rewritten. Ideological and pedagogical assumptions behind aims and activities identified and linked explicitly to reading. | When exploring curriculum knowledge target with teachers, make explicit reference to ideological and pedagogical issues arising from reading and subsequently identified in review of original workshop plan. Question staff on their own ideological and pedagogical positions and use this information to inform future planning. |
| **Spiral level 2: Baseline reviewed between April and July** (The chronological sequence for the *Spiral Levels 2 and 3* reviews is dependent upon the availability of teachers and special educational needs professionals). | **Curriculum knowledge:** *Jabberwocky* workshop plan evaluated by primary and secondary teachers within the context of existing schemes of work. | *Jabberwocky* workshop plan recast as a lesson plan which meets the approval of the evaluating teachers. In response to this feedback, provide a brief rationale for the plan which shows how readings and discussions have informed the changes. | Helen completes an analysis of the lesson plan in terms of its accessibility. She prepares a series of questions regarding accessibility which can be asked of special educational needs experts. |
| **Spiral level 3: Baseline reviewed between April and July** | **Pedagogic knowledge:** Discussions with and possible 'shadowing' of special educational needs professionals working within and | *Jabberwocky* lesson plan and rationale revised in the light of discussions and encounters with special educational needs professionals. Issues related to special educational needs | Drawing on the discussions with host teachers undertaken for the *spiral level 2 review* and with the special educational needs professionals for the *spiral level 3 review*, Helen creates a scheme of work which builds on the |

*(continued)*

Table 2.2 (continued)

| Spiral level | Knowledge target addressed | Success criteria | Preparing for next review |
|---|---|---|---|
| | beyond the school context. | are now clearly addressed in the lesson plan. | revised *Jabberwocky* lesson plan. She reflects particularly upon any negative comments which were made and considers how these might be addressed positively and professionally. |
| **Spiral level 4: Baseline reviewed between April and July** | **Professional knowledge:** Helen teaches the *Jabberwocky* lesson in the presence of an observing host teacher. She evaluates the lesson with the observer. Together, they focus upon the extent to which targets have been addressed. | The observing teacher notes that the *Jabberwocky* lesson has been informed by a clear ideological and pedagogical vision and has demonstrated a commitment to inclusiveness. Both parties engage professionally in feedback discussion, identifying positives and negatives and agreeing on practical ideas for improvement. | **Baseline Revisited:** Helen critiques her original *Jabberwocky* workshop plan in the light of her learning during the past four months. She compiles a *recommendations for effective practice* checklist drawn from this critique which she intends to use as a guide during her training programme. |

### Tracking and documenting Helen's deepening engagement

The review points described below could provide opportunities for recording Helen's learning throughout her preparatory year with regards to the specific mid-term targets described in Table 2.2. The final column for *Spiral Level 4: Baseline Reviewed between April and July* (the bottom row of the table) gestures towards the idea of progression as a return to the beginning described in Eliot's poem *Little Gidding*.

---

*Spiral level 1 review*

- *Jabberwocky* workshop plan revised in light of reading.
- Questions prepared for teachers.

*Informs:*

*Spiral level 2 review*

- *Jabberwocky* workshop plan becomes lesson plan drawing on *strengths and opportunities* analysis as well as teachers' responses to questions.
- Questions prepared for Special Education Needs (SEN) professionals.

*Informs:*

*Spiral level 3 review*

- *Jabberwocky* lesson plan revised again in the light of discussions with SEN professionals.
- Scheme of work (see also Chapter 7) demonstrates learning achieved so far and ability to locate individual plan within a larger context.

*Informs:*

*Spiral Level 4 Review*

- Evaluation of *Jabberwocky* lesson, including comments from observing teacher.

*Informs:*

*Spiral level 1 revisited*

- Original *Jabberwocky* workshop plan reviewed in the light of all that has been learned.
- Recommendations for effective practice drawn up.

---

### *What might these baseline review statements look like?*

Helen did not actually undertake the activity which follows, so I am going to have to use a bit of licence and imagine how I might have responded in a similar situation. In the example below, I have accordingly modelled the response I might make for the spiral level 1 baseline review on page 35, conducted at the end of April according to Helen's timeline.

The reflective writing I undertake here needs to demonstrate that I have responded to my reading targets (for the purpose of illustration, I will only refer to Locke's 2015 chapter on 'Paradigms of English' referenced earlier). I then need to show how my original thinking about the *Jabberwocky* workshop has been influenced by this reading. Finally, I have to use that information to inform my subsequent interviews with host teaching staff.

---

## Response to spiral level 1 baseline review

I remember reading *Jabberwocky* at school when I was eleven. They were fun lessons: our teacher encouraged us to think about what the made-up words might mean and then to see if we could create our own poems in a similar style, using our own invented vocabulary. We also had to draw and describe our own mythical monsters for a wall display. I suppose I just automatically assumed that I could do something similar in my workshop and that pupils today would enjoy the poem as much as I did. If I had to sum up the aims of the original workshop, they were to let pupils have fun with language, enjoy the mystery and excitement of a famous and much-loved poem and to let their imaginations run free.

Until I read Locke's chapter, I had not really thought about the ideological implications of choosing a text like *Jabberwocky*. The poem is almost 150 years old: does it still have the power to speak to young people today? If it does, what are its enduring qualities? Carroll is clearly a writer who belongs to the cultural heritage of English Literature. Locke writes:

> This approach asserted that there was a traditional body of knowledge (including a canon of precious texts and specialist literary knowledge) which was to be valued and inculcated as a means of 'rounding out' learners so that they became fully participating and discriminating members of a society or culture.

He also argues that, in the cultural heritage approach to English teaching, there was 'no suggestion that the ordinary reader herself might produce literature'. (2015: 17)

Where do I stand on this? Part of me feels that yes, there is a 'canon of precious texts' which should be passed on to the next generation. Shakespeare's plays might seem like an obvious example. But if we are only considering for the moment canonical poetry, would his sonnets and longer poems be included? What other texts should be granted (or refused) admission to that canon and who decides? I studied Shakespeare and Milton at school; but I never studied Pope – or either of the Shelleys. Why was that? And if Lewis Carroll is on the cultural heritage approval list, is there a place for other writers of so-called 'nonsense verse' like Edward Lear or, moving on a century, Spike Milligan?

Thinking about the cultural heritage model of English in this way has made me examine my motives for selecting a particular writer to share with pupils in the classroom. If I were to rewrite my original aims for the *Jabberwocky* workshop now, would I say that my overriding purpose was to induct pupils into the 'culture'? Whose culture do I mean? Is the term unproblematic? Locke's comments have also made me think about issues of identity, inclusion and value. Is there a place in the poetry canon for writing in English (or translation) from around the world? Are particular voices over- or under-represented? How do we define an 'English' writer? Do Seamus Heaney and Margaret Atwood qualify?

I'm struck by how often I used the phrase *our own* in the opening paragraph. I realise now that my teacher all those years ago did not accept one particular tenet of the cultural heritage model: the idea that 'literature' was not something the 'ordinary reader' could create. The fact that I intended originally to emulate my teacher's creative approach to *Jabberwocky* suggests that I too believe creativity, and the ability to make literature, should be accessible to all pupils. But to return to an earlier question: why this particular poem? Is it simply to provide a springboard for pupils' own imaginative work? What about engaging with the poem *as a poem*? Its sounds, its rhythms, its language? I want my pupils to develop a lifelong love of poetry; and if I were to rewrite my aims for the *Jabberwocky* workshop now, I would include a much closer focus on the music and craft of the text.

*(continued)*

*(continued)*

My reading and reflections have provoked a number of questions I would like to put to the English teachers I meet:

- Where do you stand in terms of the cultural heritage model of English?
- When you select a literary text to work with in the classroom, what criteria do you use and why?
- What do you believe the value of teaching literature to be?
- Is one of your aims as a teacher of literature to encourage your pupils to become 'fully participating and discriminating members of a society or culture'? If so, what do the terms 'society' and 'culture' mean to you in this context?

## OVER TO YOU

### Activity 5

- Reflect upon my attempt at a response to spiral level 1 baseline review above and imagine that Helen had written it. How might she use it to provide evidence that her thinking is developing? What points do you feel Helen should build on and revisit in the baseline review for spiral level 2? What success criteria would you apply to satisfy yourself that the thinking in regard to the selected target has been enriched?

You will at some time – perhaps quite recently – have written a series of reflections upon teaching and learning. The most obvious examples for trainee teachers are the application form and personal statement completed in order to obtain a place on a training programme. What about other pieces of evidence? Perhaps, like Helen, you created an outline for a teaching sequence, maybe in a school or when working with colleagues or young people in a wider context. Perhaps you wrote an essay or dissertation as part of your degree programme in which you explored pedagogic issues related to the teaching of English in some way. Each of these examples of writing has the potential to serve as a baseline assessment document.

### Activity 6

- Select a piece of writing which you feel would make a particularly useful baseline assessment document. Choose a reading target from the list of immediate targets you created as part of the task for Activity 1 in Section 1 on page 32 – either a book or a journal article – preferably one linked to your selected baseline assessment document. For example, if your baseline document is an undergraduate essay which considers young people's attitudes to poetry, you might explore educators' perspectives on the challenges and possibilities poetry teaching offers – see for example Dymoke et al. (2014).

- Write your own version of the response I have modelled for you above. Link it to your baseline assessment document and selected reading.
- Identify the statements which suggest that your thinking has developed as a result.
- Use that information to draw up a series of questions to inform the next stage of the spiral level review.

## Activity 7

- Review the SMART targets you created for the four areas of knowledge (Section 1 Activity 3 on page 32). Decide whether the baseline assessment document you chose for Activity 6 above is a sufficient starting point for charting progress throughout a training year against all the target clusters. If not, what other starting points might be added?

It must be apparent by now that the activities suggested so far in the book – and this is still only the end of Chapter 2 – could have already generated a significant amount of documentation. By my reckoning, this comprises:

- A personal statement
- A section tracking opportunities against immediate, mid-term and long-term targets
- A colour-coded SMART chart, linking immediate, mid-term and long-term targets
- At least one baseline assessment document, reviewed formally four times

Surprising though this may sound, we are not in the business of accumulating material for its own sake. Chapter 3 will explore how we might organise evidence that is fit for its purpose – to help trainees become successful and professionally fulfilled teachers of English.

## Note

1 These headline statements are supplemented by a series of more detailed criteria.

# Chapter 3

# Recording evidence

## Section 1: What? When? Where?

### *Support evidence: the teaching practice folder*

When I visit trainee teachers on school placement, one of the first requests I make is to 'see their teaching practice folder' (or, in the case of most trainee teachers, *folders* plural – more on this later). The teaching practice folder usually takes the form of a large, lever arch file and is a professional working document. One would expect to find in the folder, therefore, material directly related to teaching: schemes of work, lesson plans, examples of marking, evaluations of and reflections upon taught lessons. The role of the teacher extends beyond the immediacy of the classroom into the wider school community; so the teaching folder needs to reflect this by containing policy documents and other pastorally focussed material relating, for example, to pupil safeguarding, provision for special needs or strategies for helping pupils for whom English is not a first language. Moving outwards again beyond the immediate school community, the folder might contain evidence of wider engagement with the pedagogy of English teaching: reviews of key texts; notes on training sessions; links to helpful online resources. Finally, there is a fourth tranche of documentation which it would be easy for a trainee teacher to overlook but which nevertheless merits attention. I would include here any tokens of acknowledgement of the work that they do: texts, pencilled comments and emails from appreciative colleagues; cards from grateful students and their carers; screenshots of clubs, sports and activities they have contributed to – and so on.

I said earlier that this kind of support evidence is intended primarily to help trainees reflect upon their practice (and to remind them, when times seem difficult, of just how much they have achieved). However, that, as my earlier comment about asking to see teaching practice folders suggests, is not entirely accurate. They need to be aware that the teaching practice folder is also a *public* document and they need to get into the habit of thinking that anyone responsible for their training could ask to inspect it at any time. This means – in answer to the *when* question in the section heading above – that the contents of the folder have to be regularly updated and maintained in a state of readiness. They also have to be presented in a *professional, ethical fashion: nothing should be included which might cause the trainee, their colleagues, or their pupils, embarrassment.* It also means that the folder has to be organised in such a way that an outsider – be that a school mentor, a programme tutor, a government inspector or an external examiner – could navigate their way through it without difficulty. Ease of access is one reason why lever arch files are a particularly efficient means of physically organising teaching practice folder material. Much as it pains me to say it in these environmentally conscious times, the need for public access to the folder means that it is probably best to keep it in hard copy form: those whose job it is to read through the folder do not like hearing that the trainee teacher's copy is 'on their computer' or, worse, that the computer is 'at home' or 'not working properly'.

The teaching practice folder is a professional working document so it is important that the trainee organise it in a way that, while being accessible to others, satisfies their particular working and organisational style. One approach which makes sense to me (see Table 3.1) is to divide the folder into four sections corresponding to Ben-Peretz's four areas of teacher knowledge discussed in Chapter 1: content, curriculum, pedagogic, professional. Working within that broad framework, one might wish to create a separate folder for each year group taught; or – thinking of the current education system in England – one might have a folder for each of the three relevant Key Stages (11–14; 14–16; 16–18). If Ben-Peretz's model does not suit, a trainee might choose instead to have a series of folders: one dedicated to assessment, for example; another to pastoral issues; a third to teaching ideas; a fourth to schemes of work and lesson plans; a fifth to English pedagogy. It is up to the individual – as long as the folders are organised in a way that makes sense to those with a professional interest in reading them; and as long, of course, too, that it shows the trainee in their best light as a reflective, committed professional who appreciates just what a wide area of experience a teacher must encompass.

*Table 3.1* A teaching practice folder organised according to the Ben-Peretz model

| Heading | Contents |
| --- | --- |
| Contents section | Explains to the reader how the teaching practice folder is organised. Contains important contact and contextual information (school, training institution) as well as calendars for the placement school year and the training course. Key dates – such as assignment deadlines – are highlighted. |
| Content knowledge section | Contains evidence of engagement with subject English and its pedagogy, such as: an audit of subject knowledge and particular interests; notes on reading and on training experiences; links to key resources and professional institutions. |
| Curriculum knowledge section | Contains information about (inter)national and school-based curricula, including departmental schemes of work, exam board specifications and examiners' reports. Records and examples of marking could be included here as might links to (inter)national assessment databases and reports. |
| Pedagogic knowledge section | Contains evidence of engagement with fundamental pedagogic issues applicable to all teachers: for example, the role of talk in the classroom; behaviour strategies; the teaching of early literacy and numeracy; catering for special educational needs. Material could include references to key readings and training sessions as well as to (inter)national and school policies. *Informed reflections on and evaluations of lessons observed as well as taught will form a key component of this section.* |
| Professional knowledge section | Contains information about trainee's role as a professional member of a school community. This might include for example: school policies on safeguarding and pastoral welfare; information pertaining to role as a form tutor; contributions to school clubs, societies, activities; links to the wider community and to relevant outside agencies; an audit of the qualities and experiences that can contribute to the school as a whole. |

## OVER TO YOU

## Activity 1

Buy or borrow a lever arch folder (!) Read through the examples of evidence you have created in response to the Chapter 1 and Chapter 2 activities described so far.

- Evaluate the example of a teaching practice folder which I have modelled in Table 3.1. Would it work? Is there anything that is misplaced – or missed out? What do you feel, for example, about my decision to locate references to assessment in the Curriculum knowledge section? Are the five sections placed in an appropriate sequence?

- If the model I have created does not work for you, think how it might be modified, or describe a more workable system.
- Does your suggested filing system work smoothly or does it raise issues? For example, you might find that the baseline assessment review you wrote for Activity 6 in Chapter 2 (page 40) provides evidence across several conceptual areas. How will you accommodate this? If you feel you need to devise a cross-referencing system, how will it work?
- Ask a friend to see if they can follow the system you have created: what impression of your development as a teaching professional has your friend gained from reading through the evidence you have assembled? Does your folder system need modifying in the light of this evaluation?

## Activity 2

- Arrange a visit to a school which hosts trainee teachers. Ask staff responsible for teacher training there, and the trainees themselves, to evaluate your suggested teaching practice folder: could they work with it? Are there any changes they might suggest? Compare your folder with the folders used by the trainees at the school and make any adjustments to your own filing system which you feel might be appropriate.

### Formal evidence keeping

Throughout the book, I attempt to highlight key attitudes of mind which trainees need to develop if they are to engage successfully with a secondary English teacher training programme. So far, I have tried to emphasise how important it is that they demonstrate the courage and honesty, not only to reflect upon their own practice, but also to allow others to scrutinise and evaluate that practice – sometimes in ways which might not seem entirely positive (see Chapters 7 and 8 for more on this). Trainee English teachers are often people who are used to academic success – if not always at school, then later in life – and sometimes they do not find it easy to admit that they have made a mistake or to accept criticism.

The second attitude of mind I want to describe now links to the one above. Throughout the world, governments are taking an increasingly interventionist role in education, defining the criteria by which successful teaching is measured and using global data to gauge the perceived efficacy of their teaching forces (see for example OECD: 2016a). This is an issue I will return to in the later chapters of the book; but for now I would like you to reflect upon the extent to which you feel willing to 'do the state's bidding' – to accept its formal criteria for assessing successful teacher training and to be held publicly to account for your ability to meet (or not meet) the criteria it sets.

As an illustration, I want to return to the Teachers' Standards currently in use for schools in England. I noted on page 30 of Chapter 2 that behind each of the 'headline' statements, there is a series of bullet points which tease out that statement in more detail. Here are the bullet points for an area of experience which trainee teachers find particularly challenging – Standard 7: Manage behaviour effectively to ensure a good and safe learning environment:

- Have clear rules and routines for behaviour in classrooms, and take responsibility for promoting good and courteous behaviour both in classrooms and around the school, in accordance with the school's behaviour policy.
- Have high expectations of behaviour, and establish a framework for discipline with a range of strategies, using praise, sanctions and rewards consistently and fairly.
- Manage classes effectively, using approaches which are appropriate to pupils' needs in order to involve and motivate them.
- Maintain good relationships with pupils, exercise appropriate authority, and act decisively when necessary.

(GOV.UK 2011: 12)

As soon as criteria like these are written down, a series of semantic and pedagogic questions arise. The headline statement, alone, is problematic. What do complex evaluative abstract words like *effectively* and *good* mean in a classroom context? Is behaviour something which is, as the headline statement puts it, *managed?* In some classrooms, behaviour might be *imposed* while in others it might even perhaps be *negotiated*. Would the same behaviour criteria apply in a library lesson as in a Drama improvisation? What is *a safe learning environment*: a Science laboratory where there are clear guidelines for the use of potentially dangerous equipment? Or a Science laboratory in which every pupil can expect to have their voice and opinion respected? This is not mere wordplay. These statements represent the criteria against which, the state decrees, trainee teachers currently training in England are to be judged. It is *essential* therefore that both trainees and the people who evaluate their performance have a shared understanding of what these statements actually mean.

## OVER TO YOU

### Activity 3

- Reread carefully the first bullet point statement related to Standard 7 on page 46 above. Underline the key words.
- Make a table consisting of two columns. In the first column, note the keyword statements. In the second, write examples of the successful strategies you would expect to see if this particular criterion were being addressed effectively.
- When you have finished, compare your completed table with the worked example provided in Table 3.2. How consistent are our interpretations of the criteria? If there are any discrepancies in our approaches, how might we address these?

### A worked example (1)

*Table 3.2* Identifying successful practice for a trainee teacher at the end of their school placement

| Criteria | What successful practice might look like |
|---|---|
| Have clear rules and routines for behaviour in classrooms. | When first meeting the class, teacher explains clearly and authoritatively what is expected from the pupils in terms of behaviour. These expectations are reinforced – and respected – in this and subsequent lessons. A list of behaviour rules is prominently displayed on a classroom wall and referred to by the teacher and pupils as appropriate. Clear guidelines regarding key routines are established from the start: for example, entering and exiting the classroom; taking the register; managing talk; setting and collecting homework. A cheerful, well-ordered and working atmosphere prevails throughout lessons. Potential disruption is dealt with quickly before it can develop. Transitions between lesson activities take place smoothly and efficiently. |
| Take responsibility for promoting good and courteous behaviour both in classrooms and around the school ... | Teachers and pupils talk and listen to each other politely. The clear rules for the management of talk are adhered to. There is no place in the classroom for abusive language or behaviour of any kind. The teacher models the behaviour expected of the pupils. In dining areas and other spaces around the school where pupils congregate in numbers, the teacher takes the opportunity to get to know pupils as individuals as well as to help ensure orderly and good-natured behaviour. At school gatherings like assemblies, the teacher either participates actively or models the behaviour expected of a member of the school audience. |

*(continued)*

*Table 3.2  (continued)*

| Criteria | What successful practice might look like |
|---|---|
| ... in accordance with the school's behaviour policy. | References to behavioural issues in the classroom are explicitly linked to the school behaviour policy. Where appropriate, sanctions and rewards are applied according to school guidelines. Outside the classroom, teacher reinforces school policy by, for example, reminding pupils of rules about uniform or about movement in the corridors. Teacher volunteers to help organise school outings and other events provided as a reward for good behaviour. |

I alluded in Chapter 2 to the problematic word *progression*; here again it emerges to complicate matters. It does this in three ways. The first question it raises for me is: would it be fair to expect a trainee at the start of their training to meet the Standard 7 criteria at the same level as someone coming to the end of their programme? If the answer to that question is 'yes', then why bother with a training programme at all? More realistically, the criteria need to be interpreted in such a way that, when assessing a beginner, an evaluator is particularly concerned with *potential* and when assessing a more experienced trainee, they are particularly concerned with *efficacy*.

A second complicating factor, then, is the issue of *weightings* (see also Chapter 7). The evaluative stakes are raised even higher here by the fact that, as I hinted on page 34 of Chapter 2, training programmes like the current English model fine-tune their assessment procedures so that it is not enough simply to pass the course: one must be graded as either *satisfactory* (a word I used to regard as representing something positive but which now – as we shall see in Chapter 8 – seems to have acquired negative connotations), *good* or *outstanding*. As a trainee progresses from beginner to more experienced practitioner, how and when do the criteria tilt from potential to efficacy, from satisfactory to good – and perhaps even to outstanding performance?

Consider as an example the first set of criteria described in Table 3.2 above. I can imagine a beginner explaining to the class what they expect of pupils in terms of behaviour and routines. I can imagine them, too, putting a set of rules on the classroom wall and drawing the pupils' attention to them. They might even try to reinforce their expectations and to show that they are capable of organising transitions or dealing with misbehaviour. However, qualities like *authority* and *respect* are hard won. They are achieved *over time* as relationships between pupils and teacher develop. It would be unrealistic to expect a beginner to be able to walk into a classroom and demonstrate them straightaway. Conversely, if trainees were still unable to command authority and respect by the end of the training programme, one would have serious doubts about their ability to pass the course.

Taking these issues of progression into account, I might reconfigure the worked example for the first set of criteria described above so that it is weighted more heavily towards potential. (Note the title and contents of the added third column below.)

## A worked example (2)

Table 3.3 Identifying successful practice for a trainee teacher at the start of their school placement

| Criteria | What successful practice might look like | Response to challenges and setbacks |
| --- | --- | --- |
| Have clear rules and routines for behaviour in classrooms. | At the introductory meeting with the class, teacher makes a sustained attempt to create a positive first impression through choice of body and verbal language, posture and voice projection. Teacher explains clearly and sincerely what is expected from the pupils in terms of behaviour. If challenged, sustained attempts are made to reinforce these expectations in this and subsequent lessons. A list of behaviour rules is prominently displayed on a classroom wall and referred to by the teacher (and possibly pupils) as appropriate. Teacher makes a sustained effort to establish clear guidelines regarding key routines from the start: for example, entering and exiting the classroom; taking the register; the management of talk; the setting and collecting of homework. Teacher tries hard to create a cheerful, well-ordered working atmosphere in lessons. Teacher tries to address potential disruption quickly before it can develop. Teacher's lesson plans show that thought has been given to how transitions between lesson activities might be effected smoothly and efficiently. | Teacher responds to disruption in lessons by reviewing reading and training materials on behaviour management in an attempt to identify what went wrong. Having reflected on this material, teacher writes an evaluation of the lesson. Pastoral and other staff with experience of teaching this particular class are consulted for advice on behaviour management strategies. Prior to subsequent lessons, plans are discussed with and checked by training staff to see if potential weaknesses have been identified and addressed. Teacher arranges for training staff to observe a lesson with the class and asks the observers to focus in their evaluations upon Standard 7. |

When training courses fine-tune their assessment procedures to include grades and numbers, they inevitably invite a consideration of *threshold descriptors*: those key words which indicate that a trainee's practice has moved from one level to another (ideally, upwards – but as I noted on page 32 of Chapter 2, not necessarily so). Look at the worked example modified for a trainee teacher at the start of their school practice (above), which is weighted towards *potential* rather than *efficacy*. Consider the phrases in italics. Notice how often words like *tries* or *makes an effort* feature here. In the third column – if I can return to my Samuel Beckett reference from Chapter 2 – the trainee is rewarded, not for making mistakes, but for how they reflect upon and then take action in response to those mistakes.

## OVER TO YOU

### Activity 4

Tables 3.2 and 3.3 above are designed to show what successful practice might look like at both ends of the scale from beginner (potential) to experienced trainee teacher (efficacy).

- Underline the words in both tables which you would consider to be *threshold descriptors* for the criterion *Have clear rules and routines for behaviour in classrooms.*
- Imagine this trainee is now ten weeks into their placement and is still teaching this particular class. Create a **third table** for the criterion *Have clear rules and routines for behaviour in classrooms.* How would the weightings be balanced now between potential and efficacy? What threshold descriptors would appear in column 2 and what would you expect to see in column 3?

### Activity 5

- Ask some current trainee teachers to show you how their host training institution has attempted to map threshold descriptors and examples of successful practice against externally imposed criteria for teacher training. How do the trainees themselves engage with this material and what formal evidence do they collect at different stages of their programme to demonstrate that they have met those criteria? What issues have they faced and how have they addressed them?

## Activity 6

This is a long-term activity; but if you feel you can take it on, you will find it invaluable preparation for your training year.

- Review the assessment criteria for the training programme you will be following (it may be the current Teachers' Standards for England or it may be a different assessment system). For each of the criteria, try to imagine what evidence of successful practice would look like and what the key threshold descriptors might be.
- If you are ready for an even greater challenge, tease out that evidence and those descriptors for trainees at beginning, intermediate and experienced level.

## Section 2: presenting formal evidence

A useful analogy is to think of the record of support evidence (the teaching practice folder) as a *book* and the record of formal evidence as a *table of contents*. In other words, the latter is a quick and accessible reference guide which indicates to the reader the level of progress the trainee has made in addressing the Teachers' Standards criteria and which also shows where the evidence for that progress can be located. While the support evidence is best collected as hard copy, the formal record is usually maintained digitally for several reasons. First – and here I return to my point about the need for trainees to be accepting of public scrutiny and accountability – many host institutions now construct their formal evidence documents in such a way that tutors and other relevant training staff can access (and comment upon) their trainees' copies online at any time. Orwellian though this seems, it emphasises the need for trainees to maintain their evidence bases in a constant state of readiness. Following on from that point, presenting formal evidence digitally means that it is far easier to update entries regularly, and to use the affordances of a computer – different fonts and graphics, access to colour coding, tracked changes, the addition of hyperlinks and so on – to map progress against the teaching standards criteria.

Trainees need to be aware that, while they might be afforded professional autonomy with regards to the organisation of their teaching practice folders, the format and conventions of formal evidence documentation are usually imposed by the host training institution.

I am going to use again as an example Standard 7 from the current Teachers' Standards for England. A formal online evidence document might look something like Table 3.4 (I am imagining that this document

*Table 3.4* Tracking evidence against a teaching standard at the start of a school placement

*Standard 7:* Manage behaviour effectively to ensure a good and safe learning environment

| Bullet point | Evidence | Location of evidence in teaching practice folder (Ben-Peretz model) |
|---|---|---|
| *Have clear rules and routines for behaviour in classrooms.* | Discussed school behaviour policy and the particular needs of Class X with my mentor and their regular teacher of English. (4 November). | Reflective journal for week beginning 31 October. *Pedagogic Knowledge* section. |
| *Take responsibility for promoting good and courteous behaviour both in classrooms and around the school . . .* | Shadowed form tutor Y on bus duty. (2 November) | Email from Y praising my attempts to get to know some of the pupils from my form (see *email* sub-section of *Professional Knowledge* section). |
| *. . . in accordance with the school's behaviour policy.* | Attended a meeting for trainees on school behaviour policy organised by member of the senior management team. (8 November) | Highlighted and annotated copy of the school behaviour policy document (see *policy documents* sub-section in *Professional Knowledge* section). |

belongs to a trainee at the beginning of a first school placement which began at the start of November).

Just a week into the placement, this trainee has already collected significant evidence of engagement with Standard 7 at a level appropriate for a beginner. Similar amounts of evidence will be available for the other standards, too. It is important to note the range of evidence used here: it would be very easy to overlook, for example, the seemingly mundane experience of bus duty without realising what an opportunity it provided for professional development (more on this when we consider the *silent music* of school in Chapter 4). In other words, there should be no reason why a trainee should ever feel at a loss with regards to finding material to address teaching standards criteria. As Chapter 4 will demonstrate, it is a question of knowing where and how to look and being receptive to the opportunities which present themselves.

Trainees should not be daunted by the judgemental overtones of the formal evidence document. It also serves two other purposes: to help them argue their case and to celebrate their achievements. In terms of the former, it might be helpful to think of the book and table of contents analogy again and note how, in the example above, the third column is used to identify exactly where the teaching practice folder evidence needed to support the assertions made in the formal document is to be found. Adding dates for the support evidence (see column 2) not only eases the process of locating the relevant material but also provides a useful chronological record of the trainee's professional development.

I noted in Chapter 1 that one of a trainee's professional goals during their training programme should be to achieve what Erik De Corte called *teacher fade*: the capacity to act as an autonomous learner. Support and formal evidence documents give them the opportunity to do this. When they meet with training staff to come to a decision about their progress towards qualified teacher status, they should arrive at the meeting with their evidence assembled and their case prepared. This means that a decision about their current level of achievement can be decided through professional dialogue rather than through imposed judgement.

Finally: celebration. Table 3.5 shows what the (digitally updated) formal evidence entry for Standard 7 might look like on completion of the training programme (which I am imagining occurs at the end of June). I have included

*Table 3.5* Tracking evidence against a teaching standard at the end of a school placement

*Standard 7:* Manage behaviour effectively to ensure a good and safe learning environment

| Bullet Point | Evidence | Location of evidence in teaching practice folder (Ben-Peretz model) |
| --- | --- | --- |
| *Have clear rules and routines for behaviour in classrooms.* | I was asked if I would take over the teaching of Class Y, regarded as a particularly challenging group in the school. (24 April) | External examiner observed me teaching this class and complimented me afterwards on my management skills (see dated report in *lesson evaluations* subsection of *Pedagogic Knowledge* section – cross-referenced to *Content Knowledge* section for Standard 3). |

*(continued)*

Table 3.5  (continued)

| Bullet Point | Evidence | Location of evidence in teaching practice folder (Ben-Peretz model) |
|---|---|---|
| Take responsibility for promoting good and courteous behaviour both in classrooms and around the school... | Throughout the summer term, I organised and ran a Drama Club for younger pupils. We concentrated on team- and confidence-building skills. | Thank You card signed by all the members of the Drama Club; note from three form tutors commenting on how much their pupils had enjoyed the club (see *miscellaneous* and *email* subsections respectively in the *Professional Knowledge* section). |
| ...in accordance with the school's behaviour policy. | Invited by training institution tutor to lead a seminar with next year's recruits on behaviour management policies and their implementation in schools (scheduled for September). | Emails from training institution tutor and head teacher of my new school, respectively confirming the invitation and granting permission to run the session (see *email* subsection in the *Professional Knowledge* section). |

in this version an example of cross-referencing (Standard 3 requires trainees to demonstrate good curriculum and subject knowledge). Once again, think about the range, date and type of evidence provided here.

## OVER TO YOU

### Activity 7

- Review the documentary evidence collected so far. Map it against the eight Teachers' Standards headline statements on page 30, using Tables 3.4 and 3.5 above as a guide.
- Invite a teacher to help you review the evidence you have prepared. Can you together come to a consensus about what has been achieved and what might be attempted next? How well are you able to use the evidence to argue your case?

# Part II

# Who we are and where we stand

# Chapter 4

# Why bother with theory?
## A closer look at praxis

## Section 1: what is it that is going on here?

Some years ago, I worked at an institution where trainee teachers were asked to write a number of 'academic' assignments as part of the course requirements. On the front cover of each, the trainees had to explain how the assignment had helped their professional development. One trainee wrote: 'As if we haven't enough to do, without this lot as well!'

I felt some sympathy. The deadline for the particular assignment which had caused this trainee so much exasperation fell in the middle of a school placement when she was preoccupied with a daily round of planning, teaching, marking and pastoral work. The last thing she felt like doing at the time was writing an essay for her university tutors.

I felt some sympathy – but only to a certain extent; and I think this anecdote is worth reporting here because it raises several important issues. First of all, the trainee *chose* to accept a place on this particular programme, knowing that essay writing was a course requirement. She was also given a calendar, explaining clearly when the essays were due. I am saying this here to emphasise two important points which have already been made in earlier chapters: if you are a reader who is still thinking about what training programme to apply for, be sure that you are clear about the course requirements and be sure to select a course which suits your particular learning preferences. If you are a reader who has already secured a place or has begun your training programme, you must plan ahead so that you can anticipate 'pinch points' in the programme and be prepared for them well in advance.

In the opening paragraph, I put the word *academic* in speech marks; and this leads me from logistical considerations to a more philosophical issue. The 'academic' essay my trainee was asked to write required her to engage with a concept which was mentioned briefly in the opening chapter of the book: theoretically informed practice or praxis. The assignment task was to reflect upon a practical teaching activity within the context of key writings on learning theories. In other words, it attempted to create a conceptual bridge between the day-to-day business of the classroom and the global heritage of thinking about teaching and learning. There are some in the educational world who would share this trainee's impatience with praxis. As Calderhead observes: 'Staffroom folklore, for instance, commonly purports that one learns to teach by being thrown in at the deep end and learning for oneself' (1989: 49). Indeed, when I trained over forty years ago, it was still possible to obtain a teaching post merely on possession of an undergraduate degree – a situation not unlike that pertaining to the current *Teach First* initiative in England.

The philosophical question provoked by my trainee's exasperated comments about essay writing has already been raised on page 46 of Chapter 3: how willing should a teacher be to conform to and be judged against a set of externally imposed criteria? To rephrase the question in more ethical terms: how willing should teachers be to regard themselves as 'servants of the state'? It may be that you are one of those people who would sympathise with the trainee's comments and that you also regard 'this lot' of formal theoretical reflection as a distracting irritant which interferes with classroom practice. Perhaps you would prefer to concentrate on the *how* of teaching, leaving the *what* and *why* for somebody else to decide for you. To what extent would you be prepared to defend that position?

## OVER TO YOU

### Activity 1

Here are three examples of how, over the past eighty years, the *what* and *why* of teaching have been imposed on teachers. Each has a particular resonance for English practitioners.

- Read the extracts in turn and consider to what extent you regard them as acceptable.

---

### Extract one

From the windows the swastika flags wave.... In the shop windows stand pictures of the Fuehrer.... The boys climb up trees.... When a flag-bearer passes, Klaus raises his right arm in salute.

All at once Klaus hears heil salutes from afar. The shouts sound ever nearer. And then Klaus sees the Fuehrer. He stands in the car and waves in a friendly manner. Heil! Heil! calls Klaus, as loud as he can. What a pity, the Fuehrer is already past! But Klaus continually calls: Heil Hitler! Heil Hitler!

(Blackburn, 1985: 42)

## Extract two

*Prohibition on promoting homosexuality by teaching or by publishing material*

(1) A local authority shall not—

(a) intentionally promote homosexuality or publish material with the intention of promoting homosexuality;
(b) promote the teaching in any maintained school of the acceptability of homosexuality as a pretended family relationship.

(Legislation.gov.uk: 1988)

## Extract three

*Reading*

Pupils should be taught to:

• develop an appreciation and love of reading, and read increasingly challenging material independently through:

reading a wide range of fiction and non-fiction, including . . . high-quality works from English literature, both pre-1914 and contemporary, including prose, poetry and drama; Shakespeare (2 plays) and seminal world literature.

(DfE: 2014)

Extract One is a translation from a German early-reading primer (Börner, Groh and Schnabel, 1938), published shortly before the Second World War and designed to instil in young children feelings of veneration for Adolf Hitler.

Perhaps you feel that an example taken from an almost eighty-year old textbook is too far removed from present-day experience. Extract Two is

Section 28 of the 1988 *Local Government Act*, which was not repealed until the early years of this century. Imagine that you were working in a school during this period and that you wanted to teach Sarah Waters' prize-winning 1998 novel *Tipping the Velvet*, which contains explicit descriptions of lesbian sexuality. Would you have given up the idea altogether, or would you have constrained your teaching of the novel in order to comply with Section 28 of the Act?

Extract Three brings the issue into the contemporary classroom in that it is an excerpt from the current version of the English National Curriculum for Key Stage 3. To what extent would you be prepared to accept an externally determined definition of the words *high quality* and *seminal?* When charged with the task of constructing the first version of the English National Curriculum, Brian Cox declared confidently: 'almost everyone agrees that [Shakespeare's] work should be represented' and that 'even those who deny his universality agree on his cultural importance' (Cox 1991: 82). Forty years on, Shakespeare remains 'the ultimate citadel to be protected' (Burnett 2007: 16). Do you agree? Should all National Curriculum Key Stage 3 pupils *read* – and that in itself is an interesting word to use about a dramatist – two plays by Shakespeare? If you are obliged by law to teach Shakespeare's plays, which ones would you choose and why? Would you include *The Merchant of Venice* or *Romeo and Juliet*, for example? If so, how would you engage with the anti-Semitism depicted in the former and the sexual activity of a thirteen-year-old depicted in the latter?

### A worked example

I included in the chapter title the question: *Why bother with theory?* I hope by now you are getting a clear idea of where I stand on this. I believe that it is difficult to engage effectively with any of the extracts above unless one has a very clear, theoretically informed vision of what English teaching should be. Take Extract One as perhaps the most extreme of the three examples. The only way I can hope to engage with this text effectively is by bringing to bear all my theoretical grounding in deconstruction, textual politics and media awareness. To help me, I might turn – citing just one example out of the many available to choose from – to a theoretical work like Erving Goffman's seminal *Frame Analysis*. Goffman notes that 'events' incorporating 'the will, aim, and controlling effort of an intelligence' – such as the creation of Extract One – involve 'motive and intent'. If we are to understand what those motivations and intentions are, we should ask a key question: 'What is it that's going on here?' In order to find answers to that question, Goffman suggests, we need to place a series of 'social frame-works' around the 'event' under scrutiny (1974/1986: 24, 27, 24).

The first social frame I might apply to Extract One is a *textual-political* frame. How does this text wish to position the reader ideologically? Clearly, the kind of ideal reader the authors (three people cooperated on the primer) envisage is a devotee of Adolf Hitler. I am not prepared to accept that position, so I therefore have to read *against* the text. To help me do this, I might draw upon my understanding of media theory and put a second, *connotative* 'frame' around the extract so that I can consider how images of domestic normality – shop windows, boys climbing trees, a friendly wave from a passing car – are intertwined with Nazi iconography. Drawing upon media theory again, I could apply a *cinematic* frame and consider how the episode might appear on film. Viewed from this perspective, I notice how cleverly the authors have appealed to the senses of hearing and sight: waving flags echo the wave from the Führer and the arms raised in the Nazi salute; with subtle use of tempo, the 'soundscape' of the passage builds to a crescendo of voices and then fades until we are left with only Klaus's small, child's voice repeating the key message of the whole passage. On what images would the camera linger? At what points might the shots be fast-edited to heighten a sense of tension and excitement? If a musical soundtrack were to be added to the film, what might it be and why?

By attempting to answer the question 'What is it that's going on here?', Goffman writes, 'one has a means of distinguishing types of answers to that question that was not quite available before' (1974/1986: 27, 46). The 'means' I have employed in the previous paragraph have helped me in the task of 'distinguishing types of answers' that the authors of the extract would certainly not have wished to hear. 'More is involved' in an analysis of this kind, Goffman adds, however, 'than merely a matter of variation in focus' (1974/1986: 46). It is by resorting to a forensic, theoretically informed decon-struction of the extract that its grubby 'motive and intent' can be fully exposed.

## OVER TO YOU

### Activity 2

- Select a theoretical text from your past educational experience which you have found particularly helpful and insightful. Use the procedures described in that text to deconstruct Extract Three.
- Consider how this exercise has helped you to explore your own beliefs about English teaching.

## Section 2: human agency

In order to strengthen the case for praxis, I want to revisit a quotation from Albert Bandura cited on page 34 of Chapter 2: 'Those who have a high sense of efficacy visualize success scenarios that provide positive guides for performance'. Section 2 of that chapter explored ways in which a spiral model of progression might help reflective practitioners establish and review 'positive guides for performance'. Now, though, I want to focus on the quotation's use of the word *efficacy* and link it to another key term which features in the title of the paper by Bandura cited in Chapter 2: *human agency*.

Bandura refuses to dismiss human beings as nothing more than 'neurophysiological computational machines' – mere 'mechanical conveyors of animating environmental influences'. On the contrary, he argues, 'the capacity to exercise control over one's own thought processes, motivation, and action is a distinctively human characteristic'. The stronger a person's belief in their powers of 'personal agency' and 'perceived self-efficacy', Bandura continues, 'the greater and more persistent are their efforts' and their concomitant 'performance accomplishments'. Conversely, those who are 'beset by self-doubts about their capabilities slacken their efforts or abort their attempts prematurely and quickly settle for mediocre solutions'. Two key characteristics of powerful personal agency are the capacity for 'forethought' and for 'perseverant effort' – a person's willingness to face the challenges of life with resilience and a 'firm belief in the worth of what they are doing' (1989: 1175, 1176, 1179, 1176).

When I listed the achievements of a successful interviewee at the start of Chapter 1, I was in effect praising you, whether you be a trainee or an established teacher, for having convinced your interviewers that you possess a strong sense of personal agency. All the activities described in this book are predicated on the belief that successful trainees will respond to the challenges posed by their training courses with a self-efficacy founded – certainly – on 'perseverant effort'; but just as importantly on 'forethought'.

Bandura defines forethought as the 'capacity to extrapolate future consequences from known facts' and thus 'take corrective actions to avert disastrous futures'. He continues: 'In acting as agents over themselves, people monitor their actions and enlist *cognitive guides* [my italics] and self-incentives to produce desired personal changes' (1989: 1181). Let me tease out Bandura's ideas in the context of Extract One. I was able to apply 'forethought' to that adulatory account of Hitler by drawing upon 'known facts' (about the rise of Nazism and the consequences of the Second World War) and then enlisting the 'cognitive guides' of critical literacy to help me read against the text. Without recourse to such theoretical knowl-edge, I would not have had the weapons with which to fight against this insidious example of Fascist propaganda and I would have been incapable of demonstrating personal agency. Praxis, however, consists of theoreti-cally informed *practice*. Theory must be translated into action. There are two particularly uncomfortable phrases in Bandura's account of personal agency which have to be confronted. People who 'act as agents over them-selves', he argues, 'take corrective actions . . . to produce desired personal changes'. It is easy enough for me, writing eighty years after the event from the security of my study in a Western democracy, to deconstruct and denounce Extract One. Would I have had the courage to 'take cor-rective actions' if I had been a teacher in Germany at the time? Leonore Goldschmidt did. Dismissed from her official teaching post, in 1935 she defied the Nazis by opening in Berlin of all places a private Jewish school which survived for four years until she was forced to flee to England. In Poland, Antoni Dobrowolski was sent to Auschwitz for his efforts to pre-serve Polish education during the Nazi occupation.

I hope your praxis is never put to a test as extreme as those faced by Goldschmidt or Dobrowolski; but, as Extract Two suggests, even teach-ers working within a twenty-first-century democratic society have faced substantial challenges to their core beliefs about the nature and purpose of education. It may be that you are never faced with a similar challenge; but, as I hope Activity 3 will demonstrate, you still need to prepare yourself for that eventuality with forethought and perseverance.

Returning to Extract Two, I noted earlier that Section 28 was repealed in the early years of this century – 2003, in fact. This does not mean, however, that the issues it raised simply disappeared. In 2012, Stonewall – an organisation created to campaign against Section 28 – published an update of its 2007 report into the experiences of gay young people in British schools. Reflecting on that first report, Chief Executive Ben Summerskill noted in the Introduction: 'Although the last version of this study was conducted four years after the repeal of Section 28, its shadow continued to loom large.' He continued: 'many teachers not only lacked the confidence and skills to tackle homophobic bullying, but weren't even sure that they were allowed to do so.' The situation described in the 2012 report seems no better:

- More than half (55 per cent) of lesbian, gay and bisexual young people experience homophobic bullying in Britain's schools.
- Ninety-six per cent of gay pupils hear homophobic remarks such as 'poof' or 'lezza' used in schools.

- Almost all (99 per cent) lesbian, gay and bisexual young people hear phrases such as 'that's so gay' or 'you're so gay' in school.
- More than half (53 per cent) of gay pupils experience verbal homophobic bullying, almost a quarter (23 per cent) experience cyberbullying and one in six (16 per cent) gay pupils experience physical abuse.
- Six per cent of lesbian, gay and bisexual pupils are subjected to death threats.

(Guasp et al., 2012: 4)

## OVER TO YOU

### Activity 3

- Reread Extract Two in the context of Summerskill's comments and the headline statistics from the 2012 report above.
- How might you, as an English teacher, demonstrate personal agency to challenge the homophobia described here?

## Section 3: listening to silent music

The examples explored so far have considered how personal agency, mediated through praxis, can be brought to bear upon major existential issues which test our core beliefs as English teachers. It would be tempting to conclude that the deployment of praxis is something to be 'held in reserve' for those 'big' occasions. This is not the case. The Marxist philosopher Louis Althusser – for whom schools, as constituted within 'the capitalist social formation', represent the 'dominant ideological State apparatus' by which the ruling class replicates its power structures – argues that these value systems 'are so integrated into our everyday "consciousness"' that we no longer notice them. 'This is the School' [sic], Althusser writes, 'though hardly anyone lends an ear to its music: it is so silent!' (1971: 148, 145, 146).

Whether one accepts Althusser's critique of the 'capitalist' education system or not, his point about the *silent music* of the school is important. *Critical incidents* – educational encounters which offer opportunities for exploring and refining our thinking about English pedagogy – can occur at any time in school, within and beyond the classroom. We need to have our ears tuned to that silent music.

**OVER TO YOU**

## Activity 4

On page 13 of Chapter 1, I noted that one of the issues I might raise with interview candidates is to ask them how they would respond if a pupil wrote *we was* instead of *we were* in a piece of fictional writing.

- Imagine that an interview candidate answers by saying that they would put a line through the word was and write were above it instead, in the hope that the pupil would understand the teacher's response and not make the same error again.
- Consider this response in the light of Althusser's critique of the school system below (he was writing within the context of mid-twentieth-century France):

> It takes children from every class at infant-school age, and then for years, the years in which the child is most 'vulnerable', squeezed between the family State apparatus and the educational State apparatus, it drums into them, whether it uses new or old methods, a certain amount of 'know-how' wrapped in the ruling ideology (French, arithmetic, natural history, the sciences, literature) or simply the ruling ideology in its pure state (ethics, civic instruction, philosophy).
> (Althusser, 1971: 147)

- How might the imagined candidate's answer to the *we was/we were* question be interpreted as an example of a teacher dispensing 'know-how' 'wrapped' in a 'ruling ideology'?

### A worked example

This is how I would respond to Activity 4 if I were to critique that critical incident from Althusser's perspective. Should a teacher choose to answer the question by suggesting they would simply correct the grammatical error in writing and expect the correction to be acted upon without any further intervention, they would be transmitting a powerful ideological message to the pupil. Such an approach speaks to something which the pioneering Drama practitioner Peter Slade, selecting a more violent metaphor than that employed by Althusser above, describes as the 'bashing-in method of teaching' (1954: 98) in which – to change analogy and cite a much quoted phrase from Plutarch – 'the mind' requires 'filling like a bottle' (Babbitt, 1927: 259). The writer is positioned as deficient in some way and thus requiring correction by a more knowledgeable other.

To respond in the monologic, authoritarian manner described above is to close down the discourse space in which it is possible to talk about language – a particularly unfortunate consequence in this case, given that the writer of the piece in question is someone whose mother tongue is English and who has been speaking the language fluently all her life. It also suggests that grammatical rules – and by extension all rules – have to be accepted without question simply on the basis that a more powerful other has said they have to be obeyed. One has only to recall Extract One to imagine where this might lead.

The negative ramifications go further. The writer of this piece comes from a community where, in oral speech, *we was* is consistently used instead of *we were*. If a teacher strikes through the phrase *we was* to signify that it is incorrect, what message does that action send to the writer in terms of family and identity? 'Know-how' might indeed be transmitted when the teacher substitutes *we were* for *we was*; but, 'wrapped' in such a 'ruling ideology' – at what cost? A cost borne not only by the pupil but also, as the next part of this worked example will explain, by the teacher as well.

### We was/we were: an alternative response

A very different way of engaging with the *we was/we were* question might be guided by the theories of a near contemporary of Althusser who, like him, had direct experience of the Second World War: Jürgen Habermas. Having spent his early years under Nazi rule, Habermas appreciated only too well the malign influences of an authoritarian educational system driven by the kind of propaganda described in Extract One. In proposing an alternative, critical pedagogy, Habermas argued that a 'commitment to consider all individuals as potential participants in discourse presupposes a universalistic commitment to the potential equality, autonomy, and rationality of individuals' (1982: 252). The role of the teacher is not to be Plutarch's bottle filler but a 'transformative intellectual' (Aronowitz and Giroux 1986/2003: 23) who – to borrow and redirect Goffman's question – works alongside pupils in order to help them learn how to ask 'What is it that's going on here?' and thus to identify and engage with Althusser's silent music for themselves. A third element is added to the concept of praxis, therefore: 'action that is informed by reflection *with the aim to emancipate*' [my italics] (Morrison 2001: 218).

A Habermasian response to the *we was/we were* question would thus be predicated on the belief that the writer is already a practised 'participant in discourse' – a sophisticated and autonomous user of language who is not only capable of entering but also morally and ideologically entitled to enter into dialogue with the teacher about the kinds of answers to Goffman's question which might be prompted by this particular critical incident. The discussion could range over such issues as: the differences between spoken and written forms of language; the rationale behind grammatical rules regarding singular and plural verb forms; the historical and political reasons why some dialects (such as Standard English) seem to have acquired more status and power than others; the influence of context, register, repertoire and audience on language use; the relationship between language and identity.

I noted earlier that choosing the monologic, authoritarian response to the *we was/we were* question is harmful to the teacher as well as the pupil concerned. Bluntly, that approach can be summarised as meaning: 'You will do this because I tell you to.' The implication is that, if the pupil does not comply, then the teacher will invoke the force of the state for which he or she is, in this instance, merely a mouthpiece. The consequences of non-compliance by the pupil are not good. To quote Althusser again, she will join the 'huge mass of children' who, 'around the age of sixteen' are 'ejected "into production"'. In mid-twentieth-century France, this might mean joining the ranks of 'the workers or small peasants' (1971: 147). In our current age of austerity and bleak acronyms, it is just as likely to mean that the young writer becomes what in contemporary England is called a *NEET*: someone *not in education, employment or training*.

Compared with using Nazi propaganda as a literacy primer or complying with Clause 28's strictures against 'the acceptability of homosexuality as a pretended family relationship', striking a line through and correcting a grammatical error might seem a small matter; but the way in which you choose to respond to the *we was/we were* question actually says much about the kind of English teacher you want to be. To decline a Habermasian-style response to the question is to decline the opportunity to demonstrate personal agency and thus to come perilously close to being classed as one of Bandura's 'neurophysiological computational machines'. That might seem an overly dramatic way of putting it, but educationalists have been alerting us to these dangers for years. Writing thirty years ago and not long before the implementation of the National Curriculum in

England, Aronowitz and Giroux, for example, could see which way the wind was blowing. Their prophetic words are worth quoting at length.

## OVER TO YOU

### Activity 5

- Read the extract from Aronowitz and Giroux's 1986 publication *Education Under Siege* below:

It is important to stress that teachers must take active responsibility for raising serious questions about what they teach, how they are to teach it, and what the larger goals are for which they are striving. This means that they must take a responsible role in shaping the purposes and conditions of schooling. Such a task is impossible within a division of labor where teachers have little influence over the ideological and economic conditions of their work. There is also a growing political and ideological tendency as expressed in the current debates on educational reform, to remove teachers and students from their histories and cultural experiences in the name of pedagogical approaches that will make school more instrumental. These approaches generally mean that teachers and students alike are 'situated' within curricula approaches and instructional management schemes that reduce their roles to either implementing or receiving the goals and objectives of publishers, outside experts, and others far removed from the specificities of daily classroom life. This issue becomes all the more important when seen as part of the growing objectification of human life in general. The concept of teacher as intellectual[1] provides the theoretical posture to fight against this type of ideological and pedagogical imposition.

(1986/2003: 31)

- Discuss this quotation with English teachers and students currently in training. Does it still ring true today, thirty years after it was written?
- What do current teachers and trainees think about the 'teacher as intellectual' or 'teacher as proletarian' distinction?
- What steps can you take, during your training year and beyond, to preserve your professional integrity and human agency in the current educational climate?

## Activity 6

Here is a final example of how and why we need to attune our ears to Althusser's silent music, one to try for yourself.

The young author who wrote *we was* for *we were* spelled *guaranteed* as *garanteed* in the same piece of writing.

- Consider the ideological issues at play here and, in the light of these, construct a Habermasian-style response to this critical incident which enables the teacher (and the pupil) to demonstrate human agency and encourage *emancipatory* praxis.

Here are some questions to explore as you shape your response:

- Rather than focussing on deficiencies, think about the phonic and lexical skills evident in this misspelling of *guaranteed*.
- If the meaning of the word *garanteed* is perfectly intelligible to the reader, does it matter that the author has left out the letter *u*?
- What is the etymology of the word *guaranteed*? Why do we spell it with a letter *u* and why is that letter silent?
- Do you think Althusser would have been concerned whether *guaranteed* was spelt correctly or not? (You may need to do some additional reading here!)
- What can you find out about current theories regarding the teaching of spelling and how might these influence your response to the critical incident described in Activity 6?

## Note

1 In proposing the concept of 'teacher as intellectual', Aronowitz and Giroux were attempting to counter what Giroux described as the 'growing proletarianization and deskilling of teacher work' (1985: 21).

# Chapter 5

# What kind of English teacher do you want to be?

## Section 1: what is the language using us for?

The four chapters of the book so far have emphasised the importance of personal agency and praxis. By doing so, they have invited you to reflect upon and to apply your own experience and expertise as a proficient user and potential teacher of English. Chapter 4 brought those reflections into particularly sharp focus; and now I want to encourage you to look even more closely and also more formally.

I need to explain the choice of subheading for Section 1. In the opening paragraph, I employed the term 'user' of English; but I want to turn that idea around by borrowing and slightly rephrasing – with the addition of italics and a change of pronoun – the title of the poem by W. S. Graham referenced above in order to ask: 'What is the language *using you* for?' How have your encounters with *language* – and it may be that your linguistic expertise runs wider than English – brought you to a position where you want to dedicate your professional life to sharing your passion for words with school pupils? What kind of English teacher do you want to be and why?

Remaining true to the principle of praxis, I want to use a theoretical lens through which to explore and make sense of those practical experiences; and remaining true, also, to the principle that teachers should lead by example, I am going to model how I might respond to what is in effect a very personal – even in some ways confessional – task. When in Chapter 4 I drew upon the theories of Erving Goffman to help me deconstruct the extract from a Nazi reading primer, I emphasised the fact that Goffman was just one of many possible theorists to whom I might have turned for help. I chose *Frame Analysis* because this is a text which has influenced my own praxis as an English teacher. You might share my enthusiasm for Goffman's work – or you might not. Whatever theoretical writings about English pedagogy you choose, the important point is that you have chosen *something* that you find thought-provoking and that your classroom work demonstrates a carefully considered, practical response to your reading.

With this proviso in mind, the first theorist I have chosen to guide me into Chapter 5 is Pierre Bourdieu. Given the nature of the question posed by W. S. Graham above, I have decided to choose Bourdieu because, although his ideas are by no means uncontroversial (see for example Goldthorpe: 2007) he has enriched my thinking about human agency by exploring the ways in which individuals shape and are shaped by the society in which they find themselves. I am particularly interested in the way that Bourdieu has developed the venerable concept (Nash: 1999, Reay: 2004, Wacquant, 2005) of *habitus* to 'revoke the common-sense duality between the individual and the social' and to provide instead an account of how:

> society becomes deposited in persons in the form of lasting *dispositions*, or trained capacities and structured propensities to think, feel, and act in determinate ways, which then guide them in their creative responses to the constraints and solicitations of their extant milieu.
>
> (Wacquant, 2005: 317)

A Bourdieusian response to the Nazi reading primer exercise might differ from one influenced by the thinking of, for example, Bandura (as described on page 62 of Chapter 4) by focussing not so much on *how* but on *why* personal agency is deployed in *that* instance in *that* particular way. For Bourdieu, 'practice' is not 'the mechanical precipitate of structural dictates' (Bandura would approve); but nor is it (and here Bandura would be less enthusiastic) 'the result of the intentional pursuit of goals by individuals' (Wacquant, 2005: 318). Rather, Bourdieu writes, practice is 'constituted' in a 'dialectical relationship' between 'a habitus' and 'an *objective event*' (original emphasis). I responded to the 'conditional stimulation' of the Nazi reading primer in the way that I did because my habitus – 'a *matrix of perceptions, appreciations, and actions*' (Bourdieu, 1977: 83, original emphasis) drawn from my personal history embedded within a particular social context, 'endowed' me with 'a determinate type of dispositions' (Bourdieu, 1977: 83).

## Section 2: reclaiming our histories – applying theory to personal experience

### A worked example

Why do these particular ideas resonate with me? On page 68 of Chapter 4, I noted the warning voiced thirty years ago by Aronowitz and Giroux in *Education Under Siege* (but sadly just as apposite today) that:

There is also a growing political and ideological tendency as expressed in the current debates on educational reform, to remove teachers and students from their histories and cultural experiences in the name of pedagogical approaches that will make school more instrumental.

One of the reasons I looked to Bourdieu for guidance at the start of Chapter 5 is that I believe that his account of practice and personal agency invites teachers to reclaim their 'histories and cultural experiences' – not out of some sense of personal indulgence but as a matter of professional obligation. In order to create an informed Bourdieusian response to the Nazi reading primer, I have to interrogate my history and cultural experience – those intersections between my individual 'trajectory', as Reay puts it, and the 'collective trajectories' of the society in which I am situated (2004: 434). What 'dispositions' embedded in my habitus caused me to find that fascist text so abhorrent? A sense of basic, common humanity, I hope; but other particular and more personal 'perceptions, appreciations and actions' too. For example, I was born only four years after the end of the Second World War when rationing was still in force, and I grew up in industrial Lancashire, where memories of suffering and loss remained strong. I saw for myself the crematoria and mass graves of Holocaust victims when I visited Dachau concentration camp at the age of fourteen. As an academic, I researched and contributed a chapter to a book called *Teaching the Holocaust*. There were less obvious influences, too. I call to mind for example the propaganda disseminated by the war comics and films I devoured as a boy, with their celebration of British heroism and their caricatures of German soldiers called Hans or Fritz begging for mercy in heavily accented English. To think like this about practice and human agency is to engage in something more nuanced, more deeply personal, than Bandura's relatively straightforward account of 'a capacity to extrapolate future consequences from known facts'.

Clearly, emotion played a significant part in shaping my response to the Nazi reading primer – revulsion at what I witnessed during my visit to Dachau, for example or, yes, excitement when exposed to those atavistic war films and comics. A second element of Bourdieu's thinking which attracts me to his work, therefore, is his appreciation of the powerful ways in which the *affective dimension* influences the habitus: 'nothing', he writes, 'is more serious than emotion, which touches the depth of our organic being' (Bourdieu, 2000: 140). When the emotions are positive and the 'habitus encounters a social world of which it is the product, it is like a "fish in water": it does not feel the weight of the water and it takes the world about itself for granted' (Bourdieu and Wacquant, 1992: 127).

However, 'when habitus encounters a field with which it is not familiar', Reay comments, 'the resulting disjunctures can generate change and trans-formation' (2004: 436). For Jerome Bruner, what Reay calls 'disjuncture' is an essential stimulus to learning:

> There is compelling evidence that so long as the environment con-forms to the expected patterns within reasonable limits, alerting mechanisms in the brain are quietened. But once expectancy is vio-lated, once the world ceases strikingly to correspond to our models of it ... then all the alarms go off and we are at full alertness.
>
> (1971: 5)

Bourdieu would concur. 'We are disposed', he writes, 'because we are exposed.' He regards vulnerability as an essential driver of change and growth because it enables us to 'acquire dispositions that are themselves an openness to the world' (Bourdieu, 2000: 140–141). Applying these theories to my childhood experience of post-war Germany, the most pow-erful instance of 'disjuncture' I encountered was at Dachau; but there were other occasions where I was moved and challenged by less momentous and harrowing experiences too; and I am sure you will understand if I say these are the ones I would prefer to share in a public space like this book. I remember for example that we stopped once at a service station and struck up a friendly conversation with a waiter who spoke good English. When we complimented him on his language skills, he gave a wry smile and said: 'Yes, I was your best prisoner.'

In Bourdieusian terms, I could say that this experience brought me into an unfamiliar *field* or 'particular sector of [the] world' (Bourdieu, 1998: 81) – an encounter with a real, rather than a fictionalised, German former soldier. Equipped with 'long-lasting dispositions' or *'embodied'* 'cultural capital' (Bourdieu, 1997: 47, original emphasis) – specifically, a head stuffed full of wartime propaganda mediated through popular culture – I was obliged to speak to a former 'enemy' as one human being to another; and I discovered that he was as far removed as it is possible to be from the comic book caricatures I was used to. Wacquant writes that 'dispositions are socially mounted and can be eroded, countered or even dismantled by exposure to novel external forces' (2005: 319). I do not want to exaggerate the significance of what was a casual conversation in a service station on the German autobahn, particularly when compared with the experience of visiting Dachau; but looking back now over fifty years later, it seems to me that this meeting created for me a sense of 'destabilised habitus' (Bourdieu, 2000: 160) so that I experienced what Bourdieu calls 'critical moments of perplexity and discrepancy' (In Wacquant, 2005: 320). Reay comments: 'Bourdieu argues that those who occupy awkward positions are more likely to bring to consciousness that which, for others, is taken for granted, because they are forced to "keep watch on themselves"' (2015: 14). By exploring the 'apparently subjective tensions and contradictions' thus revealed, Bourdieu writes, an individual can gain a sense of purchase on 'the deepest structures of the social world and their contradictions' (In Reay, 2015: 21). Discovering that our friendly, bantering waiter had been a soldier and prisoner of war – a human being very different from the caricatures I had read about in comics or watched on the screen – obliged me to confront 'subjective tensions and contradictions' and to 'keep watch' on myself – to treat any future caricatures and stereotypes I might encounter with suspicion. It caused me, also, to think about 'the deepest structures of the social world': how could it be that such seemingly 'normal' people as this waiter could fight and suffer imprisonment on behalf of the regime which had created Dachau?

I have tried, in the section above, to lead by example: to share with you aspects of my early life in order to demonstrate how I might make use of a theoretical lens to reflect upon personal educational experiences – in this particular instance, an experience which took place outside the traditional 'field' of the classroom. In order to fulfil the declared aims of Chapter 5, it is necessary to add to the concept of praxis the Habermasian element described on page 67 of Chapter 4: 'action that is informed by reflection with the aim to emancipate'. In terms of my professional development, the anecdote I shared only has real value if it helps me to enrich my practice so that I am better able to inspire and support the learning of the pupils in my care. Making explicit links, therefore, between the service station encounter and English pedagogy, I might, for example, reflect upon the powerful hold which war comics and films exercised over my youthful imagination. What was it about the combination of drawings and text in the one medium and of moving image and sound in the other, which drew me in? What ideological forces were at work here and how were they trying to position me as reader and viewer? Is there a place for the study of popular media such as comics and film (or their modern-day digital equivalents) in the English classroom – and if there is, should pupils be encouraged to create as well as respond to media artefacts? (It is only twenty years since a Prime Minister of the United Kingdom promised his party's supporters at a national conference that he would never countenance the study of television soap opera as part of the English national curriculum.) When exploring difficult issues through literature in the classroom, to what extent should a teacher acknowledge alternative voices and viewpoints?

If I choose to read *Goodbye to All That* – Robert Graves' account of his experiences in the First World War – should I not grant equal space to an equivalent German text, such as Erich Maria Remarque's *All Quiet on the Western Front?*

For Reay, the 'subjective tensions and contradictions' I experienced in that service-station encounter could be described as a mild manifestation of *cleft habitus.* In her own research work – an area of study particularly pertinent for readers of this book – she demonstrates how extreme instances of cleft habitus far more serious than the personal example I have described above can exert 'heavy psychic costs' on those involved. She cites the example of a schoolboy who is loaded with 'an intolerable burden of psychic reparative work' (2015: 13) as he attempts to reconcile his academic ambitions with his deeply felt need to remain loyal to peers who do not share his commitment to the existing educational system.

## Section 3: sharpening the theoretical focus

Urie Bronfenbrenner's *ecological systems theory* has helped me sharpen the focus on the relationship between habitus and field described in the personal account I gave in Section 2 above by foregrounding the latter through a 'systematic description and analysis of the settings in which development takes place'. The *'ecological environment'*, Bronfenbrenner writes, 'is conceived . . . as a nested arrangement of concentric circles, each contained within the next'. Radiating outwards from the individual at the centre, the various circles represent, respectively, *'micro-, meso-, exo-,* and *macrosystems'* (1981: 169, 22, original emphasis).

I would like to return to the story of my visit to post-war Germany, this time mapping it against Bronfenbrenner's four 'concentric circles'. My aim here is to show, not only how the application of ecological systems theory can further enrich the Bourdieusian interpretation of the critical incident recorded in Section 2, but also how it can address the emancipatory element of praxis by offering powerful insights into our practice as teachers.

I want to begin my reappraisal of the critical incident by thinking about it on a *microsystemic* level. Bronfenbrenner defines the microsystem as 'a pattern of activities, roles and interpersonal relations experienced by the developing person in a given setting with particular physical and material characteristics'. Citing the relationship between mother and baby as a fundamental example, he describes the 'dyad' – an encounter between two human beings – as the 'basic building block of the microsystem'. Dyads can be 'observational' (one person watches another doing something) or they can involve both parties working at the same activity. Of particular relevance to us as teachers is Bronfenbrenner's suggestion that these 'joint activity' dyads are 'especially well suited to [the] developmental process' because they 'stimulate the child to conceptualize and cope with power relations' while at the same time providing 'an ideal opportunity for effecting a gradual transfer of power' (1981: 22, 56, 57, 57, 58).

I can see how Bronfenbrenner's comment about power relationships could apply to my conversation with the German former soldier turned waiter. Did my family and I hold all the cards here? We were affluent tourists visiting the man's country scarcely twenty years since its defeat, expecting not only service from this former soldier and prisoner but also conducting the exchange in our first language, not his. Did the 'joint activity' dyad provide 'an ideal opportunity for effecting a gradual transfer of power'? Maybe not an 'ideal opportunity', but an opportunity none the less. The fact that our conversation took place 'in a given setting with particular physical and material characteristics' which felt familiar to me – a motorway service station in one country is similar to a motorway service station in another – created a context which immediately challenged my stereotypical views of Germany. The language the former soldier and I used contributed to the process, too. There was no comic-book *achtung*, no *Gott in Himmel* – just a conversation about holidays and weather and families which allowed us to engage with each other as human beings.

Reflecting upon the encounter in terms of Bronfenbrenner's 'joint activity' dyad has enriched my practice as an English teacher by making me more sensitive to the power relationships which, as we saw in Chapter 4, can be at play in language exchanges – not least in the classroom where one party possesses so much more officially sanctioned authority than the other. The suggestion that a 'joint activity' dyad can help effect a 'gradual transfer of power' also makes sense to me because it recalls the reference to Erik De Corte on page 20 of Chapter 1 and the idea that a key aim of education is to effect teacher fade to such a degree that the learner becomes autonomous. The service-station encounter helped me to 'keep watch' on myself, as Reay puts it, rather than relying on someone else to do it for me. I started to take responsibility for my comic-book prejudices and also to question 'those deepest structures of the social world and their contradictions' described in Section 2. And who was the teacher in this case? Another important aspect of a dyadic relationship, Bronfenbrenner writes, is that it is 'characterized by *reciprocity*' (original emphasis): by which he means that 'if one member of the pair undergoes a process of development, the other does also'. I appreciate how the exchange influenced my development; but what kind of impact did it have on the former soldier?

'[W]hat matters for behavior and development', Bronfenbrenner writes, 'is the environment as it is *perceived* rather than as it may exist in "objective" reality'. As a teacher of English, I need to appreciate how the principle of reciprocity might operate in my classroom, not only by trying to under-stand how my practice is perceived by my pupils but also by being willing to scrutinise and if necessary change that practice in response to those per-ceptions (1981: 22, 4, 4, original emphasis).

Bronfenbrenner describes the next two outer 'circles' of his ecological system thus:

> The principle of interconnectedness is seen as applying not only within settings but with equal force and consequence to linkages between settings, both those in which the developing person actually participates and those that he may never enter but in which events occur that affect what happens in the person's immediate environ-ment. The former constitute what I shall call *mesosystems*, and the latter *exosystems*.
>
> (1981: 7–8, original emphasis)

Exploring my critical incident from a mesosystemic perspective, I can see how my experience at the service station informed and was informed by other 'settings' in which I 'actually' participated – for example, the visit to Dachau, my reading of war comics, school History lessons, a subsequent conversation, several years later, with a fellow factory worker who told me about his war experiences in the Western Desert – and so on. The use of speech marks round the word 'actually' in the previous sentence is significant because it emphasises the difference between mesosystem and exosystem. Bronfenbrenner describes the latter as a network of settings which can exert a profound influence on the 'developing person' – even though that person might not be physically present. As for a setting, so for a dyad. The relationship can continue to exist 'phenomenologically for both participants', Bronfenbrenner writes, 'even when they are not together' – I am demonstrating this by writing here about a conversation with a stranger held fifty years ago.

The idea that a powerful dyadic relationship can be conducted with a participant who is not physically present encourages me to think about people, living or dead, from my past who influenced the way I responded to the encounter in the service station, not only when it actually took place but also now that I am reflecting on it again fifty years later. These 'partic-ipants' might be relatives or friends or teachers (inspirational, indifferent, intimidating) – but they could also include 'participants' from the cultural

heritage of the world – writers, film-makers, politicians, journalists, musi-
cians and so on – with whom I have had a lifelong 'dyadic' relationship
through a whole range of media. To think about dyadic relationships at
this global level is to advance into Bronfenbrenner's outermost circle, the
macrosystem, which references the 'overarching patterns of ideology and
organization of the social institutions common to a particular culture
or subculture' (1981: 58, 8). How did the interplay of historical, geo-
political and cultural forces influence the service-station encounter? What
about issues of class, gender and ethnicity? Is it significant, for example,
that my parents came from a country which had remained neutral during
the Second World War – and if it is, how did they (and how do I, now)
respond to the pronoun chosen by the German former soldier when he
said he was 'your' best prisoner?

There are many implications here for my praxis as an English teacher.
Thinking about the microsystem reminds me how subtly enmeshed are
my pupils' individual habitus and the 'collective trajectories' in which
they are socially situated. As their teacher, I represent just one of what
is for each of them a complex network of dyadic relationships radiating across Bronfenbrenner's four circles. If my work is to have any
positive effect at all, it must try to take some account of those relationships by challenging what might be called *deficit* models of learning and
appreciating instead the rich life and language experiences which each
pupil brings to the classroom. Thinking about Bronfenbrenner's three
outer circles helps me to understand how my English classroom can be
similarly conceived as lying at the heart of 'a nested arrangement of
concentric circles': the work I do within it must relate to the work undertaken by the pupils' previous and future teachers of English, as well
as to the work they undertake with colleagues in other academic and
pastoral contexts within and even beyond the school. Bronfenbrenner's
account of the macrosystem obliges me to confront again an issue which
has emerged in several earlier chapters of the book: the ethical relationship between teacher and State. What ideological model of English do I
present to my pupils? What kind of dyadic relationships – including relationships with home, regional, national and international culture – do I
encourage? How and why?

In a passage which is particularly pertinent to teachers, Bronfenbrenner
writes that the effectiveness of dyadic relationships is 'crucially dependent
on the presence and participation of third parties'. Using the image of a
broken 'three-legged stool', he warns that if 'such third parties are absent,
or if they play a disruptive rather than a supportive role, the developmental
process, considered as a system, breaks down' (1981: 5). Teachers – and

perhaps teachers of English particularly – are 'third parties' *par excellence*. We act as gatekeepers to culture, to life chances, to emotional wellbeing. It is an awesome responsibility.

'Habitus', Reay observes, 'is a way of looking at data which renders the "taken-for-granted" problematic' by, for example, encouraging responses to such questions as 'How well adapted is the individual to the context they find themselves in?' or 'How does personal history shape [an individual's] response to the contemporary setting?' (2004: 437) In the section above, I have tried to reclaim my history and cultural experiences by showing how I might bring theory to bear on a personal language encounter, the better to enrich my future practice as an English teacher. Now it is your turn.

When selecting which elements of my childhood experience of post-war Germany to reflect upon, I deliberately chose not to include in a public space like this book my response to the Dachau visit. You of course do not have to share any of the work which arises from the following activities. Nevertheless, when thinking about the 'cleft habitus' exercise below, please do not choose memories which you find too painful to revisit.

## OVER TO YOU

### Activity I

- Consider the following key points from the reading of Bourdieu in Section 2 and Bronfenbrenner in Section 3. Try for each one to find an example from your own linguistic history and cultural experience.
- Do **not** feel that you have to record your response in writing unless you would find that particularly beneficial: the important point is that you are able to recognise, just by reflecting about it if you like, some connection between the idea and your particular story.
- The 'language encounters' you choose to consider can be taken from any of the modalities of English: speaking, listening (as in my worked example), reading or writing.
- For each example, think about Habermas' conception of praxis as being concerned with emancipation and consider how your reflections might enrich your future practice as an English teacher.

Key terms are in italics. (Three of them – *role expectations*, *chronosystem* and *ecological transitions* – have not been referenced in the chapter so far but the accompanying definitions should make their meanings clear.)

## A fish in water

Reflect upon a language encounter where you felt confident and in control.

- What made this experience so positive?
- Thinking about Bourdieusian concepts of *capital* (cultural or otherwise), consider the assets which you brought to that encounter: how did they contribute to your experience?
- Did the *field* or *setting* help to shape the success of the encounter? If so, how and why?
- Thinking in terms of Bronfenbrenner's *ecological systems theory*, try to identify some of the influences beyond the immediate setting of the specific language experience you are exploring which helped to shape the encounter.

## Cleft habitus

Think about a language encounter which subjected your sense of *habitus* to 'disjunctures'.

- What made the experience challenging?
- Was part of the problem that you were unclear about your *role expectations* – defined by Bronfenbrenner as the 'set of activities and relations expected of a person occupying a particular position in society' (1981: 86, 85)?

For example, I was once reprimanded in primary school for staring out of the window lost in thought while our English teacher was reading the class a story. Apparently, the role I was expected to play here was that of the visibly attentive pupil, sitting up, arms folded on desk, gazing studiously at the teacher as he read.

- What effect did your experience of *cleft habitus* have on you emotionally?
- Did the 'resulting disjunctures . . . generate change and transformation' as Reay suggests? If so, how and why/why not?
- If you feel that you did gain something from the experience, did the positives outweigh the negatives and was it worth it?

## The three-legged stool

Reflecting now specifically within a school *setting* about the influence of *'third parties'* on a *dyadic relationship*, think about a teacher of English whose practice had a particular influence upon your attitudes to the subject – ideally (but not necessarily) in a positive, even inspirational way.

- What was it about this person's practice which made it so memorable?
- Thinking back to the work we have covered in Chapters 1 to 4 (including your responses to the various activities), are you in a position now to say whether this teacher was committed to a particular model of English teaching? If so, which model is it and how were you able to identify it? (In Chapter 6, we will consider in more detail possible models of English teaching.)
- In terms of *reciprocity*, how do you feel your contribution to this *dyadic relationship* might have influenced the practice of your teacher?

## Reciprocity

- Bronfenbrenner says that a *dyadic relationship* can exist 'for . . . participants even when they are not together' and that 'if one member of the pair undergoes a process of development, the other does also'.
- Which encounters with the global heritage of culture have had a particular impact on you and why?
- Which of these encounters would you most like to share with pupils in the classroom and why?
- Thinking in terms of *reciprocity*, how would you work with your chosen cultural encounter so that you might become an effective *third party* in helping your pupils share that same sense of engagement, excitement and pleasure that you experienced?

## Chronosystem

Bronfenbrenner defines the *chronosystem* as a 'research model that makes possible examining the influence on the person's development

*(continued)*

*(continued)*

of changes (and continuities) over time in the environments in which the person is living' (1986: 724).

- Thinking again about *reciprocity*, consider which of your language practices – and those of the environments in which you have lived – have remained constant or have changed with time.
- Do you welcome or regret all or some of these changes? Why?
- How might your experiences differ from those of the pupils you will teach and what might be the implications for the classroom of the future?

### Ecological transitions

'An ecological transition', Bronfenbrenner writes, 'occurs whenever a person's position in the ecological environment is altered as the result of a change in role, setting, or both' (1981: 26).

- What experiences of *transition* have led you to the point where you wish to train as a teacher of English?

## Activity 2

Wacquant traces the roots of the word *habitus* to 'Aristotle's notion of *hexis* . . . meaning an acquired yet entrenched state of moral character that orients our feelings and desires in a situation, and thence our actions'. He continues: '[t]he term was translated into Latin as *habitus* (past participle of the verb *habere*, to have or hold), in the thirteenth century by Thomas Aquinas . . . in which it acquired the added sense of ability for growth through activity, or durable disposition suspended midway between potency and purposeful action' (2005: 317–318).

Having invited you, in Activity 1, to consider in a theoretically informed manner how your life experiences might have helped to influence your decision to become a teacher of English, I would like you now to think about Wacquant's use of the words 'entrenched' and 'to have or hold'. What are your core beliefs about English teaching?

Either:

- Reflect upon the thinking you undertook for Activity 1 and write down **ten words or phrases** which sum up your core beliefs about English teaching.

Alternatively:

- Represent those beliefs visually by creating a collage of key images and words.

Or:

- Choose a song or piece of instrumental music which you find particularly moving and apposite. Create a short film which, when the music is added as a soundtrack, represents what English teaching means to you.

## Activity 3

- Having completed Activity 2, review your responses to any of the activities undertaken in the previous four chapters which required you to think in some way about teaching English.
- Do any patterns of response emerge? Are there particular ideals, practices or texts which feature regularly in those responses? What can you learn from that?
- Are there some aspects of English pedagogy which you have thought or read about or discussed with other teachers – but which seem to be missing from your activity responses? Is this something which should concern you or not? If so, what action should you take?

## Activity 4

- Thinking particularly about the previous bullet point, share the reflections prompted by Activity 3 with a current teacher or trainee teacher of English.
- Which theorists have helped them to reflect upon their practice and why?
- What advice can they give you about making good any perceived gaps in your thinking about the teaching of English?

## Activity 5

- On no more than **two sides of A4,** write your manifesto of English teaching. As well as drawing upon the reflections prompted by the previous activities, be sure to make explicit references to your own history as a language user across all four modalities of English.

# Chapter 6

# Thinking about the curriculum

## Section 1: autonomy or direction?

It is a bright September morning in 1977: the first day of the school year. A fresh-faced, newly qualified teacher of English is reporting for duty to his Head of Department – who shows him the stock cupboard, wishes him good luck and leaves him to it. That was my introduction to full-time secondary English teaching. No schemes of work, no syllabus to follow. No National Curriculum to tell me under pain of legal sanction what – or how – I should teach. No regular national assessment procedures to hold me or the school publicly to account until the pupils – at least, those who were not euphemistically described as 'Easter Leavers' – sat their carefully segregated Certificate of Secondary Education or General Certificate of Education examinations aged sixteen.

Times change.

How would you feel if that had been you reporting for duty in 1977? Basically, you have been told that you could teach English in whatever way you like. Thinking back on all the work we have covered together in the first five chapters of the book and in Part II particularly, I hope you would respond to the challenge positively. I hope you feel by now that you are developing a very clear sense of the kind of teacher of English you want to be. I hope, too, that your thinking about this subject has been informed by the quotations from Althusser and from Aronowitz and Giroux on pages 64, 65 and 68 of Chapter 4. In most of the Anglophone world, teachers of English no longer enjoy the professional freedom I describe in the opening paragraph of this chapter. If you are to have a happy and fulfilled career, it is therefore most important that you come to some accommodation with one of the key issues which has made its presence felt throughout the book: the relationship – perhaps *tension* is a more appropriate word – between a teacher's professional autonomy and the demands of the society which that teacher serves.

Chapter 6 brings this issue starkly to the fore. Readers planning to work within the state system – to take England as an example – will know that in many schools curriculum content is imposed on the teaching staff by law (more on this later in the chapter). One response might be to follow the lead of the exasperated trainee I described at the start of Chapter 4, who felt that teaching the curriculum was quite enough and left her no time to worry about whether or not it aligned with her own vision of English. If you feel like that – even having undertaken Chapter 4's activities – then this book has failed to achieve one of its main aims. I am going to repeat now something I have said several times already: it is most important that you bring to the English classroom a clear, principled, theoretically informed sense of praxis. Even if you find on completion of your training course that you are required to teach a legally enforceable curriculum which you have had no say in designing, you *must* still be prepared to assess that curriculum critically, measuring it, for example, against the criteria of the English 'manifesto' you created for Activity 5 in Chapter 5.

When considering issues of progression in Chapter 2, we explored the ways in which a baseline assessment document (see the example on pages 38–40) might be used as a yardstick with which to measure professional development. I recommend that you use the same strategy when confronted by any English curriculum – legally enforceable or not – which you did not help to design. In the first of this chapter's activities, therefore, I want you to create another 'baseline' document. Let your imagination run free in response to this question: *what do I hope pupils who had been taught English by me would be able to know, understand and do by the time they left school?*

## OVER TO YOU

### Activity 1

- Reread the 'manifesto' for English you completed for Activity 5 of Chapter 5.
- Bearing in mind those three verbs I used in my question above – 'know', 'understand' and 'do' – draw upon the criteria described in your 'manifesto' to create a pen portrait of the pupils who would emerge as school leavers having experienced your 'ideal' English curriculum.

## A worked example

Here is my attempt at the same exercise.

The pupils are able to listen sensitively and to speak fluently, tactfully and confidently in a range of repertoires, whether enjoying a night out with friends or responding to questions at a job interview. Although adept users of keyboards on phone, tablet or computer, they have also developed legible and efficient handwriting styles of which they feel particularly proud. Their fascination for how words work and for what they can do has helped them become not only confident spellers and users of punctuation but also young people who relish encounters with language of all kinds and who are always eager to enrich their own vocabulary.

The pupils are confident and enthusiastic readers and writers in a range of genres. They are, for example, assured and sensitive users of social media, creating positive, supportive digital communities, sharing ideas and information and reaching out in friendship and solidarity to people around the world. They blog and they participate in writers' and readers' groups online. They know how to edit and upload still and moving images. Enthusiastic champions of the arts, they keep up to date with developments in literature, media, theatre and film. They appreciate the rich literary heritage of the British Isles and the Anglophone world; but they are also keen to engage with literature written in other languages. They take civic pride in supporting (inter)national and community initiatives including, for example, literary awards, festivals, museum and gallery exhibitions, local libraries and educational outreach programmes.

The pupils' encounters with literature, media, film and drama in education have encouraged them to be sensitive and compassionate in the judgements they make about other people. Their experiences of poetry, particularly, have helped them to engage confidently with ambiguity and with the idea that there might be many ways of 'reading' an event or situation. They appreciate difference and are willing to learn from it. They understand the closeness of the links between language and identity and they show respect for languages and language practices different from their own. This respect and willingness to engage extends to their encounters with the world's cultures and peoples.

The pupils are looking forward to playing a full part in society at all levels, from local to global. They have been fully trained in the skills of close reading and are alert to the idea that all *texts* – written, audial, visual and multi-modal – have agendas and that all texts, including this one, wish to position the reader in some way. They are able to make fully informed decisions about how they might choose to respond to a textual agenda, be it an advert, a social media meme or a carefully crafted political speech. Their work on grammar and punctuation has encouraged them to expect to know why rules exist, rather than just to accept that they do. They bring this capacity for critical thinking to all aspects of their lives as citizens of a pluralist democracy.

The pupils appreciate that they have acquired a range of transferable skills which they can apply to other life experiences, be they social, educational or vocational. Drama, discussion and debate, for example, have given them the confidence to make a sensitive and effective contribution to teamwork, or to argue a case politely but assertively. They can make informed decisions about what they want to do with the rest of their lives. Those lives could extend well into the latter end of the twenty-first century – a world inconceivable to someone like myself who was born when television was in its infancy and who has lived to witness the possibility of interplanetary travel. Of all the *desiderata* I could wish for my sixteen-year-old pupils, perhaps the most important is that they never lose their fascination for language in all its forms, their willingness to face change with confidence and their commitment to compassion, community, creativity and the transformative powers of the imagination.

Well, I invited you to 'nail your colours to the mast' and I have done the same. With praxis in mind, I want to locate our respective pen portraits within a theoretical context by drawing, first, upon some recent comparative research into global curricula. David Scott, the author of the research, argues that one of the key components of curricula around the world is that they describe 'a set of curriculum standards which articulate the intended student achievements (what they know, what they can do and what dispositions they have acquired)' (2016: 46).

The purpose of the next activity is to tease out the curriculum standards implied by our respective pen portraits.

## OVER TO YOU

### Activity 2

- Compare your pen portrait with mine. What curriculum standards are implied by our respective descriptions of 'intended student achievements'? Are they broadly similar or are there significant differences? If there are differences, what do you feel about this?
- In the light of this review, is there anything you would change about your pen portrait? Is there anything you think I should change about mine? (Think here about the fact that Scott substitutes the noun 'dispositions' for my use of the verb 'understand'.)
- Having compared our pen portraits, do you think we could work together as part of an English-teaching team? (Think back here to the professional knowledge questions posed in Section 2 of Chapter 1.) Are there any accommodations or compromises we would need to make in order for that team to work effectively?

## Section 2: engaging with a prescribed curriculum – the Cox model as an example

My freedom to teach more or less what and how I liked lasted for a decade. In 1988, the then Secretary of State for Education, the Conservative politician Kenneth Baker, established an *English Working Group* under the chairmanship of Brian Cox from Manchester University. The task of this group was to create a legally binding National Curriculum which would prescribe what should be taught as well as how and when that curriculum content should be assessed. 'Despite . . . criticisms from both left and right', Bethan Marshall notes in her account of the creation of the first National Curriculum some twenty years after its inception, 'the Cox curriculum [*sic*] proved popular with teachers' (2011a: 190), not least because, as Cox himself argued, in proposing 'five different views of the purpose of teaching English' he and his colleagues felt that they were offering 'a broad approach to the curriculum which can unite the profession' (1991: 21). For these reasons, Cox's conceptual model has been frequently cited and it is worth describing again here. (We have already encountered the cultural heritage view in Chapter 2.)

The five views are as follows:

a) a 'personal growth' view focuses on the child: it emphasises the relationship between language and learning in the individual child, and the role of literature in developing children's imaginative and aesthetic lives;

b) a 'cross-curricular' view focuses on the school: it emphasises that all teachers (of English and of other subjects) have a responsibility to help children with the language demands of different subjects on the school curriculum: otherwise areas of the curriculum may be closed to them. In England, English is different from other school subjects, in that it is both a subject and a medium of instruction for other subjects;

c) an 'adult needs' view focuses on communication outside the school: it emphasises the responsibility of English teachers to prepare children for the language demands of adult life, including the workplace, in a fast-changing world. Children need to learn to deal with the day-to-day demands of spoken language and of print; they also need to be able to write clearly, appropriately and effectively;

d) a 'cultural heritage' view emphasises the responsibility of schools to lead children to an appreciation of those works of literature that have been widely regarded as amongst the finest in the language;

e) a 'cultural analysis' view emphasises the role of English in helping children towards a critical understanding of the world and cultural environment in which they live. Children should know about the processes by which meanings are conveyed, and about the ways in which print and other media carry values.

(Cox, 1991: 21–22)

Following the recommendation I made in Section 1 of this chapter, I attempted to 'map' the five Cox models against a 'baseline' document – the pen portrait I created in response to Activity 1. Before asking you to do the same, I thought it would be useful to show you how I did it.

*A worked example*

Working on screen, I used blocks of coloured font coded against the five Cox models of English to see if I could map particular statements in my pen portrait against the various categories such as personal growth, cultural heritage and so on. Here are some examples to give you the general idea:

---

### Personal growth

- The pupils' encounters with literature, media, film and drama in education have encouraged them to be sensitive and compassionate in the judgements they make about other people.

### Cross-curricular

- The pupils are . . . young people who relish encounters with language of all kinds and who are always eager to enrich their own vocabulary.

### Adult needs

- The pupils are able to listen sensitively and to speak fluently, tactfully and confidently in a range of repertoires, whether enjoying a night out with friends or responding to questions at a job interview.

### Cultural heritage

- They appreciate the rich literary heritage of the British Isles and the Anglophone world.

### Cultural analysis

- They have been fully trained in the skills of close reading and are alert to the idea that all *texts* – written, audial, visual and multimodal – have agendas and that all texts, including this one, wish to position the reader in some way.

---

## OVER TO YOU

### Activity 3

- Map your pen portrait against the five Cox models of English. In the worked example above, I have only provided, as illustration, one pen portrait statement for each model. When I completed the actual colour-coded exercise, I allocated all my statements to the various models and I would like you to do the same.
- What does the distribution pattern look like? Do you seem to favour certain models over others? What does this say about your particular vision of English teaching?
- If one or more of the five models were under-represented in your mapping exercise (or even barely featured at all), what do you feel about this?
- Did you find it actually impossible to find 'a home' for some of your pen portrait statements? If so, what conclusions do you draw? How might this influence your vision of English teaching and your feelings about working with a statutory curriculum?
- Do you feel that the five Cox models are compatible with twenty-first-century teaching of English?
- If you feel that some or all of the models need updating, how and why would you change them?

## Section 3: issues in curriculum design – two approaches to teaching Shakespeare

When I completed the mapping exercise and considered which blocks of colour dominated my pen portrait, I found that personal growth and cultural analysis statements were almost equally prominent, followed closely by adult needs. Cross-curricular and cultural heritage references hardly featured. Had I experienced no hesitation in allocating my pen portrait statements to the five Cox models, this might have given me pause for thought: why did I seem to be uninspired by those two particular approaches to English teaching? However, I actually found the mapping task problematic. It was difficult for me to decide where to place the majority of my pen portrait statements. To take just one example, I decided to locate the ability to be 'able to listen sensitively and to speak fluently, tactfully and confidently in a range of repertoires' (we will revisit this particular statement in Chapter 7) within the adult needs category – but one could argue convincingly that sensitive listening and speaking are equally important to each of the other four as well, not least the cross-curricular and cultural heritage models.

As you might suspect, given my response to the same issue when it arose in relation to the Teachers' Standards for England (described on page 30 of Chapter 2 and page 46 of Chapter 3), I am actually encouraged by the fact that I found the Cox model mapping exercise problematic; and if you experienced the same difficulty with Activity 3 above, I think you should feel encouraged as well. To explain why, I want to begin by quoting again from Scott's recent article. 'Labelling', he writes, 'acts as a way of establishing strong insulations between people, roles and functions, institutions and human activities' (2016: 47).

The English Working Group's positioning of Shakespeare within the National Curriculum provides a particularly powerful illustration of Scott's argument – and offers an opportunity, thinking of Bruner's spiral curriculum again, to revisit ideological issues which we began to explore in Section 1 of Chapter 2. Given Shakespeare's talismanic status as a national icon, study of his plays and poetry might seem to be most easily accommodated by the cultural heritage model. If a cultural heritage model of English is concerned, as Cox puts it, with 'an appreciation of those works of literature that have been widely regarded as amongst the finest in the language', then, the argument goes, Shakespeare represents the best of the best. 'Many teachers', Cox writes in justification of the decision to make the study of this author compulsory on pain of legal sanction, 'believe that Shakespeare's work conveys universal values, and that his language expresses rich and subtle meanings *beyond that of any other English writer*' [my italics] (1991: 82). The consequences of such insulation through labelling are far-reaching. If Shakespeare's works are the finest – and I am prepared to give Cox the benefit of the doubt by assuming that when he used the adjective *English* in the previous quotation he was referring to the language rather than the country – then all other Anglophone literature, irrespective of genre or nationality, must be considered inferior to them in some way. It does not take too much of a conceptual leap to move from this position to the one adopted by a recent *English* – I do mean the country this time – Secretary of State for Education, Michael Gove, who reportedly declared '*our* [my italics] literature' to be 'the best in the world' (In Marshall, 2011a: 193), rather in the manner of a child who boasts to another that *my toys are better than your toys*. There cannot be many more graphic educational examples of how labelling might establish 'strong insulations between people' than to set up such a cultural and nationalistic binary as *ours* (best) against *yours* (not quite as good).

There are serious pedagogic consequences to consider too. Drawing upon imagery similar to that employed by Scott, Bernstein describes curricular designs where 'the contents are clearly bounded and insulated from each other' as *collection* models. Labelling, or 'classification' as Bernstein calls it, focuses our attention 'upon boundary strength as the critical distinguishing feature of the division of labour of educational knowledge'. The stronger the boundary between – and, I would add, bearing in mind the five Cox models of English, *within* – subjects, the stronger 'the teacher's power in the pedagogical relationship' and the weaker 'the power of the pupil over what, when and how he [*sic*] receives knowledge' (1971/2003: 158, 80, 159). To establish such 'boundary strength' around Shakespeare's work by presenting his plays as the jewels in the cultural heritage crown; to insist by force of law that pupils must be assessed, nationally, on those plays (as is the case with the current GCSE provision in England), is to risk diminishing rather than enhancing their capacity to move, delight or inspire. They are in danger of being regarded either as museum artefacts to be approached in hushed reverence or as an initiation test which must be passed in order to obtain what Burnett describes as a 'passport' to 'assimilation' (2007: 12, 11). Bernstein's use of the phrase 'the division of labour of educational knowledge' quoted earlier in the paragraph is particularly apt here because it draws attention to the ideological as well as the pedagogic consequences of such attempts at 'labelling' or 'classification'. Both the museum artefact and initiation test approach encourage the same unequal distribution of power in the classroom: museums need expert guides and interpreters; high stakes examinations need expert coaches. Confronted by such authority, it would be exceptional pupils indeed who trusted their voices, experiences and judgements enough to believe that they had something valuable and legitimate to say about a literary icon of Shakespeare's stature – and by extension, about the culture which is meant to be their 'heritage'. 'The governing myth of the nation', Bell warns, 'usually gains its ascendancy at the expense of other dissident voices' (2003: 73, 74). It is particularly ironic that Shakespeare, an artist who 'wrote to ask questions' (Irish, 2011: 7), should be considered in that way. The ways in which we choose to organise 'the formal transmission of educational knowledge and sensitivities', as Bernstein (1971/2003: 77) puts it, have profound implications for our pupils in terms of experience, identity and relationships.

**OVER TO YOU**

## Activity 4

- Look again at the work you undertook for Activity 3 and focus particularly on your response to the five Cox models, bearing in mind what Scott and Bernstein say above about labelling and classification.
- Select one of the five models – it could be my choice of cultural heritage or something different – which you feel has the potential to raise ideological and pedagogic issues of the kind described in the Shakespeare example above. If I were to do the exercise again, I might think, for instance, about the implications of assigning a label like *personal growth* to certain kinds of engagement with literature; or classifying all 'communication outside the school' as adult needs (including talk between siblings and friends or parents and children in the home?).
- What ideological and pedagogic issues are raised and how might you as a teacher respond to them?
- Invite a teacher to reflect and comment on your response to Activity 4.

Rough and ready though it was, my attempt to map my 'baseline' pen portrait against the five models of the Cox curriculum helped me to examine more deeply some of my core principles regarding the teaching of English. Despite what I said earlier about the difficulty of allocating categories, the mapping exercise still prompted me to wonder why my first instinct had been to associate so few of the pen portrait statements with the cultural heritage model. This in turn helped me to identify the cause of my unease about that particular Cox approach. Here, then, is an example of what I meant when I wrote again in Section 1 about the tension between personal belief and state obligation. This particular version of a statutory curriculum might instruct teachers to acknowledge the importance of a cultural heritage approach to English and that Shakespeare is the jewel in the cultural heritage crown, but it does not order them *how* to teach – a point to bear in mind when you read the next section of the chapter. Knowing about and being able to apply different approaches to curriculum design within the classroom offers a means of reconciling what I described in the first subheading of this chapter as autonomy and direction.

As an alternative to the labelling and classification associated with the collection curriculum model described above, Bernstein describes an *integrated* approach, in which 'the various contents do not go their own separate ways' but instead 'stand in an open relation to each other' (1971/2003: 72). To be fair to the members of Cox's English Working Group, they did acknowledge that their 'five different views of the purpose of teaching English' were 'not to be seen as sharply distinguishable, and certainly not mutually exclusive' (Cox, 1991: 21). Taking my cue from this concession, I want now to consider how an integrated curricular approach can challenge the 'boundary strength' of the cultural heritage model by opening Shakespeare's work to all five of Cox's approaches to English; thus recalibrating 'the division of labour of educational knowledge' in ways which assert Habermasian principles by valuing pupils as active learners with important things to say. I am choosing as exemplar text *King Lear*, a play I grew to love at school – not least because I was introduced to it by an inspirational teacher of English. In the section below, I have taken each of the five Cox models in turn and set out in bullet points examples of the kinds of teaching and learning activities each approach might encourage.

## A worked example

### Personal growth

- The play provides a safe fictional space in which to explore issues regarding, for example: family relationships, particularly those between parents and children; mental health; loyalty, gratitude and obligation; justice and vengeance.

### Cross-curricular

Subject-specific links with:

- History to illuminate the early seventeenth-century political and social context of *King Lear*.
- Media, Geography and Languages to explore international film versions of the play, such as the Russian director Grigori Kozintsev's 1971 *Король Лир* or Wu Hsing-kuo's 2001 Mandarin Chinese *Li'er zaici*.

*(continued)*

*(continued)*

- Drama, Art and Design, Textiles and Physics to study seventeenth-century as well as contemporary approaches to stage, lighting, costume, make-up and set design – and to experiment with different interpretations of the play through improvisation as well as more formal presentations.
- Biology to research the significance of the many references to flora and fauna in *King Lear*.
- Citizenship to consider the concept of 'strong government' and the ways in which the duties of a 'subject' might differ from those of a 'citizen'.

## Adult needs

- Transferable skills are enhanced in all four modalities of English by providing pupils with a range of opportunities not only to read the play but also to speak and write about it in a number of different genres and registers.
- Visit to a local theatre (organised jointly with teachers responsible for vocational and careers advice) offers alternative professional insights into *King Lear*. The visit also helps to develop pupils' understanding of how a contemporary theatre company devises and implements a business strategy – and this in turn can be compared with how Shakespeare's own acting companies might have faced similar or different challenges.
- Research and note-taking skills honed by study of the play's critical reception and by investigation of the historical, political and social context in which *King Lear* was first performed.
- Thinking and writing skills developed by having to present and defend an argument in essay form or through classroom debate.
- Group improvisations, presentations and seminar-style discussions provide confidence and team-building opportunities.
- Talks from visiting experts (for example, lecturers from a local university's Literature Department, professional actors or theatre directors) enrich the pupils' understanding of the play and provide further opportunities to gain experience of the world of higher education and of other *lifecourse* possibilities beyond school.

## Cultural heritage

- Pupils are encouraged to engage directly with the poetry of *King Lear* by undertaking a series of practical, drama-based language activities which require them to think about sound, imagery, intonation and dramatic context: who is speaking and listening to whom? How and why?
- Pupils are encouraged to appreciate the aesthetic power of *King Lear* by acting out key scenes from the play, exploring how dramatic elements such as spectacle, contrast, tension, climax and anti-climax are employed by Shakespeare to create memorable theatre experiences for an audience.
- Pupils explore the reception of *King Lear* from the seventeenth century onwards (drawing where available on filmed evidence) to consider how attitudes and interpretations have changed and to come to an understanding as to why Shakespeare remains such a cultural icon today.
- Pupils use this evidence to argue for or against Brian Cox's assertion that 'Shakespeare's work conveys universal values, and that his language expresses rich and subtle meanings beyond that of any other English writer'.
- Pupils conduct online research into *King Lear* (for example, via the website *globalshakespeares.mit.edu*) to consider Shakespeare's contribution to the cultural heritage of the world.

## Cultural analysis

- Pupils compare different performances of *King Lear* (for example, the film versions by Peter Brook and Grigori Kozintsev which both appeared in 1971) to consider how the same text can be interpreted in radically different ways.
- Close analysis of key scenes from the play encourages appreciation of symbolic resonances, multiple readings and a consideration of how the meanings of words can change in use and significance over time.
- Pupils invited to direct, or to describe how they would direct, a scene from the play. In this context, they are invited to consider the semiotics of theatre: how language and silence, sound, gesture, lighting, props, make-up and costume combine to create a richly polysemic text.

*(continued)*

*(continued)*

- Research into the historical, political and social context in which *King Lear* was first performed (see *Adult needs* section above) encourages an exploration of the relationship between the artist and society – in Shakespeare's day and now.
- Comparison of scenes from the play written in verse with those written in prose provides an opportunity for a consideration of the links between language, identity and power. (The *Edgar/ Poor Tom* relationship is particularly significant here.)
- Pupils are encouraged to explore the political and social themes of *King Lear*, considering their relevance to contemporary society.
- Pupils compare Shakespeare's *King Lear* with Jane Smiley's retelling of the story in her novel *A Thousand Acres* in order to explore issues of gender politics and patriarchy.
- Pupils extend the work above to compare the ways in which a seventeenth-century English play and a twentieth-century American novel tell the story of King Lear and his family.

Bernstein has shown me how I might fulfil my statutory obligations to Shakespeare and the cultural heritage model while at the same time teaching in a way that I find exciting and which remains true to the principles implied by my pen portrait statements.

Applying the integrated curricular approach to *King Lear* described above encouraged me to use my imagination and to think creatively. Considering for example adult needs or a cross-curricular perspective on teaching Shakespeare offered a bracing alternative to the conventional responses associated with a cultural heritage view caricatured mischievously by Hoffman as the 'tyranny of the "Hey Nonny Nonny" Elizabethan cliché' (In Burnett 2007: 36). Adopting this integrated approach made me take an overview of the Cox models as one *holistic text* rather than as five separate entities. This helped me to notice – in a way which might not have been possible had I considered each model as a discrete statement – how much of Cox's language positions pupils grammatically as the objects rather than the subjects of sentences. For example, it is 'literature' which has a 'role . . . in developing children's imaginative and aesthetic lives'; 'all teachers' who have a responsibility to 'help' or 'prepare' children to face 'language demands'; 'schools' which must 'lead children to an appreciation of . . . literature' – and so on.

Having the pen portrait I completed for Activity 1 to compare with the five Cox models proved invaluable here. The comparison threw into sharp relief our very different uses of language: where Cox positions pupils as *receivers* (and as a consequence comes perilously close to advocating a deficit model of learning), my pen portrait casts them as *initiators* capable of – and here comes a key phrase again – personal agency. Another powerful strategy for reconciling tensions between *autonomy* and *direction*, then, is for teachers to take control of curriculum discourse. We might not be able to write the official, governmental documentation; but we can ensure that the language we use in our school-based schemes of work and lesson plans or when speaking to colleagues, pupils, carers and the wider public, avoids where possible the passive voice and instead positions pupils as the subjects, not the objects of sentences – sentences which contain verbs of action and cognition.

## OVER TO YOU

### Activity 5

- Reread the worked example above, noting the use of verbs and syntax – specifically, in this case, the use of subject and object in each sentence.
- What model of teaching and learning is presented here?
- To what extent do the statements in the worked example represent a practical, classroom application of the 'intended student achievements' described in my pen portrait response to Activity 1?

For Activity 6, below, I am going to ask you to have a go at creating your own worked example modelled on the one I have presented above. Before you attempt the activity, it might be useful to offer you some additional guidance, especially as you may wish to choose an alternative to the cultural heritage model on which I based my response. I mentioned in Activity 4 that other problematic areas I might choose to explore are personal growth and adult needs. How might pupils' engagement with both these models be enriched if they are introduced to them in the context of an *integrated* curriculum design which draws upon all five Cox models? For example, if a pupil gained in self-confidence as a result of a successful mock interview, one could argue that their personal growth had been enriched by a learning experience grounded in the adult needs model.

## Activity 6

- Look again at the work you undertook for Activity 4. If you were able to discuss your responses with a teacher, so much the better.
- Take the element of the Cox models which you found problematic and see if you can devise an integrated curriculum plan (as I did for Shakespeare in my worked example) which proposes a sequence of teaching and learning activities drawn from each of the five models.
- If you really do want to base your work for this activity on the cultural heritage model – and if you really want to select Shakespeare as your example – please make sure that the teaching and learning strategies you choose are different from mine.
- When you have completed your list of possible teaching and learning activities, compare them with the pen portrait you wrote in response to Activity 1. To what extent have you managed to translate your 'intended student achievements' into practical classroom activities?

## Section 4: the case against an integrated English curriculum

Clearly, there are many pedagogic advantages in choosing an integrated curriculum approach to the teaching of English. It makes sense for practical reasons, too. A recent international survey suggested that 'the average number of instruction days per year' for pupils receiving compulsory general education at lower secondary level in OECD countries is 184 – approximately half a year. Only 14 per cent of this time is allocated to '[r]eading, writing and literature' (OECD, 2016a: 391, 393). If teachers did not resort to an integrated approach, it would prove impossible, in the time provided, to offer their pupils the breadth, balance and relevance which are regarded as essential elements of effective curriculum provision (DES, 1985).

Having devoted a considerable amount of space in this chapter to extolling the benefits of an integrated curriculum approach to the teaching of English, I now need to add a note of caution. Hirst and Peters famously argued that the curriculum could be divided into four conceptual areas: *Logic/mathematics*, *Science*, *Personal Knowledge* and, grouped together as a trio, *Morality, aesthetics and religion* (1970/2012). Even a brief scan of my attempt in Section 3 to map a sequence of teaching and learning activities against the five models of the Cox curriculum should be enough to demonstrate how work in 'English' draws upon all four of these areas. Logic is needed to construct carefully crafted arguments about *King Lear*; the mechanics of stage production and research into the play's references to plants require understanding of Science in the form of Physics and Biology respectively; pupils bring personal knowledge to bear when they relate Shakespeare's exploration of family relationships to their own lives; questions of morality and religion are central to the play; and the pupils' engagement with the power and beauty of Shakespearian blank verse, together with their experience of *King Lear* as dramatic spectacle, provide opportunities for memorable aesthetic experiences. Hirst and Peters recognise the protean qualities of English. Anticipating by some twenty years the five Cox models (and using a metaphor which should be familiar by this stage of the chapter), they write: 'Under the label of English . . . it is now not uncommon to find concern for an understanding of other persons and of moral matters, as much as **aesthetic** and linguistic elements' (1970/2012: 71, emphasis in original).

I put speech marks around the word *English* in the previous paragraph because a logical conclusion to draw from its propensity for shape-shifting might be to decide that it can no longer claim to be regarded as an autonomous curriculum subject – 'moral matters' and 'linguistic elements' may sound like strange if not incompatible bedfellows. Leaving aside the fact that Section 3's teaching and learning activities can be accommodated comfortably within Hirst and Peters' four-part structure, those activities themselves assume knowledge, skill and understanding associated with subject areas beyond English – and not only in the cross-curricular section. Two obvious examples are the references to improvisation and theatre production (Drama) or the interpretation of film (Media Studies). I will return to this point later.

A particularly powerful challenge to the autonomy of English as a subject discipline was mounted in the final decade of the last century by the New London Group – a collection of academics from the Anglophone world who met at New London, New Hampshire in the United States in 1994. They argued that dramatic developments in communications technology, together with increasing global linguistic and cultural diversity, necessitated a radical rethinking of literacy. The members of the group declared their aims in an important position paper published three years after the original conference. The 'key concept' informing their rethinking of literacy was 'Design' – in which, they argue, 'we are both inheritors of patterns and conventions of meaning and at the same time active designers of meaning'. The position paper identifies:

six design elements in the meaning-making process: those of Linguistic Meaning, Visual Meaning, Audio Meaning, Gestural Meaning, Spatial Meaning, and the Multimodal patterns of meaning that relate the first five modes of meaning to each other.

(Cazden et al., 1996: 65)

English is not, of course, the only traditional curriculum discipline to be absorbed by this all-embracing term; but a word like *design* – with its *atelier* connotations of structure and construction – gestures towards a shift in focus which is particularly concerning for teachers committed to a personal growth model. Instead of asking – to continue with Shakespeare as an example – *why does the play* King Lear *speak to me?* the question becomes: *how does the play* King Lear *speak to me?* And from there it might not be such a major leap to a radically reframed question which asks: *why should* King Lear *claim a particular right to speak to me when there are so many other texts making pressing demands on my time?* Consider this quotation from a leading member of the New London Group, writing in the year of the New Hampshire conference:

How many school-leavers will be called on to become 'creative' users of language? How many will be called on to become creative users of the genres which are most highly valued in the school, the 'poetic' or literary genres? One might reset the aims of language education more modestly, more realistically and more usefully to give students skills in the use and manipulation of language, to give them a fuller understanding of the manifold meanings of language and of the genres with which they will come into contact.

(Kress, 1994: 126)

## OVER TO YOU

### Activity 7

- Think about the English lessons you have observed recently, in the light of the quotation from Gunther Kress above. His statement is now over twenty years old. Do you feel that the situation he described in 1994 still holds good today? Are 'poetic and literary genres' the 'most highly valued in school'? Should they be?
- When I did my training forty years ago, the personal growth model of English was very much in the ascendant. One of its champions

was David Holbrook who argued that the role of the teacher was to 'nourish the progress of each pupil as he [*sic*] strives towards insight' (1968: 13) through a process which has been described memorably as 'gently shaping' (Westbrook, 2009: 67). If Holbrook were to observe a contemporary English lesson, do you think he would be pleased by what he saw?

* Do you agree with Kress's questioning of 'creativity' in English and his suggestion that we should 'reset the aims of language education more modestly, more realistically and more usefully'? What do you think those three adverbs mean in the context of English teaching?

If you responded to the activities above by suggesting that 'poetic and literary genres' have given ground in school or that Holbrook would have emerged from a contemporary English classroom looking bemused and even unhappy, then you have borne testimony to the far-reaching influence of the New London Group. Taking the context of England as an example: the group's ideas came to powerful fruition when the New (*new* was a popular word towards the end of the last century) Labour government of 1997 expanded the outgoing Conservative's National Literacy Project into a Strategy, first for primary and then, in 2001, for secondary schools. At the heart of this strategy lay a belief in the principle that, to cite an even earlier quotation from Kress, 'knowledge of genre is an indispensable prerequisite for effective participation in social life' (1985: 99). The supremacy of 'narrative . . . as the orthodoxy at the foundation of English work in schools' (Andrews, 2001: 45) was to be challenged by the explicit teaching of so-called 'non-fiction text types' such as *information, recount, explanation, instructions, persuasion* and *discursive writing.*

I used the term *explicit teaching* advisedly in the last paragraph. In Section 3 of the chapter, I suggested that one of the saving graces of the original Cox curriculum was that it did not tell teachers how to do their job. The same cannot be said about the National Literacy Strategy which became, as Westbrook notes, 'the de facto curriculum in many schools'. Strategy consultants were 'armed with huge numbers of English training materials' designed not only to tell teachers in minute detail what but also how they should teach. (2009: 64). Thus was born the so-called *four part lesson,* organised into carefully timed sequences of *starter activity, teacher introduction, development* and *plenary,* each section characterised by 'fast pace and strong focus' (DfEE, 2001: 16).

It is not my aim here to write a history of the National Literacy Strategy, fascinating though that might be. I wanted to use the Strategy as a particularly graphic example of how an integrated curricular approach can pose existential challenges to the concept of subject autonomy. English is particularly vulnerable here, not least because of its status as one of the 'serving competences' – subjects which are 'prerequisites for moving into the knowledge and understanding of the rest of the curriculum' (Beck, 2000: 18). If literacy is the responsibility of *all* teachers – something we have been told since at least the publication of the landmark Bullock Report of 1975 – then why not just let the Strategy consultants and their training materials loose on the entire teaching profession so that this long-held aspiration becomes at last a reality? And while we are about it, why not abolish the school subject currently known as 'English' and replace it with 'Literacy' – or, if you are persuaded by the arguments of the New London Group – something called 'Design' or even 'Semiotics'?

## OVER TO YOU

References to Shakespeare's *King Lear* have run through this chapter. I want to cite the play again one last time here. In Act II, Scene iv, Lear's two eldest daughters, Goneril and Regan, with remorseless logic argue away their father's entitlement to keep even one of the hundred retainers which are the last physical manifestation of his former kingly power.

Imagine that Goneril and Regan are Literacy Strategy consultants arguing away the autonomy of 'subject English'. You, as Lear, are trying to defend it.

## Activity 8

- Why should 'English' not be replaced on the school curriculum by 'Literacy', 'Design', or 'Semiotics'? (Perhaps you feel it should!)
- Share your thoughts with English teachers and current English trainees in school – what are their views?
- Discuss the issues with staff in school responsible for language policies across the curriculum and for curriculum planning.

You will have realised, I hope, from what I wrote in the pen portraits from Section 1 and the attempt to map a sequence of Shakespeare teaching activities against the five Cox models in Section 3, that I believe strongly in the aesthetic, affective, humane and imaginative possibilities afforded by 'subject English' – possibilities which are richer than the somewhat bleak instrumentalism of a 'Literacy' curriculum. I trust that the whole tone of the book so far has made that clear.

For Gunther Kress, statements of belief like the one I have issued in the paragraph above would be just what could be expected of a teacher wedded to what he calls the 'ideology of Romantic individualism' which – writing at a time when I was enjoying the last of my professional independence as a teacher – he described as 'the established discipline of "English"' (1989: 10). However, as I noted in Chapter 2 with regards to target setting and professional development, an appreciation of pedagogic nuance and ambiguity does not have to imply some kind of woolly-minded 'anything goes' liberalism. I want now therefore to issue three 'hard-nosed' challenges to the integrated curriculum approach.

To illustrate the first challenge, I need to return to that sequence of Shakespeare teaching activities which so enthused me in Section 3. I will just take the cultural analysis references on pages 97–98 as an example. Each of those eight bullet-pointed statements assumes that the pupils (notice that I did not specify any particular age or ability level) already possess a significant amount of knowledge and understanding – those key curricular terms again – as well as the ability to apply previously acquired skills in a new context. For instance, to compare a Russian and English film of *King Lear* is no small task. It assumes that the pupils not only already know how to 'read' film but also understand that the medium itself possesses a long, rich and culturally diverse history (the Brook and Kozintsev versions are both over forty years old). The same points about interpretation and heritage apply to the suggestion that the pupils will 'consider the semiotics of theatre' – and I could go on through all eight bullet points in turn, teasing out the assumptions about knowledge, understanding and application embedded in each. The danger of an integrated curricular approach, then, is that if we just 'dip in' to particular elements of the curriculum on an 'as and when' basis, we run the risk of offering our pupils a very patchy, incoherent set of experiences from which many important, if not essential, elements may be missing. One of the advantages of applying the alternative, *collection* model, is that it would help me to identify various *strands* running through, for example, my cultural analysis approach to Shakespeare, and to give those strands titles such as *reading film, engaging with theatre, language and power, interpreting comparative literature* and so on. Establishing 'boundary strength' around each of these strands means that they are taken seriously as academic disciplines in their own right, rather than being regarded as 'service subjects' which are only to be deemed worthy of a classroom summons when they can be put to work on behalf of a 'higher' need – in this case, engagement with Shakespeare. Taking a subject strand seriously means plotting a coherent, rigorous, incremental and progressive pathway through it so that pupils – from the start of primary to the end of secondary level – do not miss out on its key elements and so that they engage with those elements through a range of activities which are appropriate to both 'age' and 'stage' of learning.

## OVER TO YOU

### Activity 9

- Share the issues described in the paragraph above with the members of the school community you worked with for Activity 8.
- Is the curriculum in their school based on a collection or an integrated model? Is it a mixture of both? What is the thinking behind the chosen approach?
- Are particular strands of learning threaded through the school's English curriculum? If so, what are they and how do English teaching staff identify the key elements of learning for each strand? How do they cater for issues of coherence, continuity and progression not only within the school, but also in terms of the English curriculum experienced at their 'feeder' primary schools?

Opting for 'boundary strength', as the quotation from Bernstein on page 93 of this chapter noted, privileges 'the teacher's power in the pedagogical relationship' over that of the pupil. It would be easy to assume that a collection curriculum model was particularly favoured by the political Right, for whom it might form part of a general narrative of what Beck calls 'cultural restoration': a reinstatement of 'orthodox Christian belief, respect for traditional values and institutions, and a stronger emphasis on Britain's cultural heritage' (2000: 17). In fact, 'boundary strength' also has strong advocates on the political Left. My second challenge to the integrated curriculum model, then, begins with a quotation from two other prominent members of the New London Group, Bill Cope and Mary Kalantzis. They criticise the personal growth model – one of the key elements of the Cox curriculum and a major influence on my own training as a teacher – for being 'culture bound' and elitist:

> the progressivist mold with its prescriptions for individual control, student-centered learning, student motivation, purposeful writing, individual ownership, the power of voice matches the moral temper and cultural aspirations of middle-class households.
>
> (Cope and Kalantzis, 1993: 6)

Pupils who do not experience the sense of cleft habitus described by Reay on page 75 of Chapter 5, may well feel – to continue the Bourdieusian analogy from that chapter – like 'fish in water' within a school community which is itself orientated, Cope and Kalantzis argue, towards middle-class modes of discourse and behaviour. Their main concern, however, is for the underachievers who feel decidedly like fish *out* of water when in school. Despite all the resources that have been channelled into education in, for example, England over the past twenty years, the problem, particularly amongst white working-class children, remains 'real and persistent' (House of Commons Education Committee, 2014: 3). Recent published findings from the global surveys involving 510,000 fifteen-year olds from 65 'countries and economies' conducted by the Programme for International Student Assessment (PISA), reveal that the 'United Kingdom performs around the average in . . . reading' and, perhaps more depressingly, that 'there has been no change in performance' when compared with the findings for 2006 (Bradshaw, 2013: 7). If this situation is to be turned around, Cope and Kalantzis argue, underachieving pupils need rigorous, structured, explicit teaching provided by subject experts. The final part of that last sentence contains my third argument against the integrated curriculum and brings to mind again Bernstein's point about how collection curriculum models assert 'the teacher's power in the pedagogical relationship'. Initiatives like the National Literacy Strategy suggest that any teacher – irrespective of subject discipline – can, if suitably drilled by consultants, teach 'literacy'. Cope and Kalantzis mount a left- rather than the traditional right-wing challenge to that position by demanding that underachieving working-class children, particularly, need to be *taught* – I use the word advisedly – a structured curriculum by professionals who are experts in their respective subject disciplines.

## Section 5: a teacher-proof curriculum?

Clearly, both the collection and the integrated approach to curriculum provision have advantages and disadvantages. The philosopher John Wilson put the matter starkly when he said that curriculum designers face a choice between either 'being nice' to children or attempting something 'we could seriously call educating' (In Pollard, 2002: 150). By this he means that we can either place the individual pupil at the heart of the curriculum and then tailor the learning opportunities to that individual's specific interests as and when they feel moved to act on them – or we can locate the subject discipline at the centre and induct pupils into its skills and knowledge contents systematically and rigorously, much as a medieval guild master might have inducted his apprentices. The pupil-centred extreme raises formidable logistical issues of differentiation, certainly within school classrooms as they are currently constituted; the 'guild mastery' extreme will only work if the pupils themselves are committed to the process and believe in its relevance and value. Recent developments in metacognition have served to make these curricular choices even more complex. The psychologist Robert Bjork's work is a case in point. He argues that *interleaving* learning activities is far more effective in the long term than focussing for a block of time on one specific activity. So, to take my worked example of Shakespeare activities in Section 3 (pages 95 to 98) as an illustration, my pupils would learn far more efficiently, the thinking goes, if they were to *combine* a cross-curricular activity such as researching Jacobean theatre *with* a cultural heritage activity, such as acting out a scene from *King Lear*, rather than engaging with each as a sustained and discrete area of study for a block of time. This approach would seem to favour an integrated curriculum model. However, Bjork's theory of *desirable difficulties* (1994, 2016) appears to be more closely aligned to a collection model because it suggests that curricula which focus, in Wilson's words, on 'being nice' – by courting pupil popularity or making learning challenges too easy – achieve poor long-term outcomes.

It would be tempting to respond to these complexities by echoing the words of the trainee I quoted at the start of Chapter 4: 'as if we haven't enough to do without this lot as well!' In other words, leave curriculum planning to the government experts. After all, you may well find yourself working in an education system where the curriculum is enforced by law and you just have to accept it, no matter what your personal reservations. Such a response is not good enough. Leaving aside the ethical implications explored in Chapter 4, we as individual teachers or teams of teaching colleagues still have choices to make about how the curriculum is mediated within our classrooms. Crucially, within those individual classrooms, we still retain responsibility for what Shulman, expanding on the work of Joseph Schwab (1978) describes as the 'syntactic structure' of a subject discipline:

> the set of rules for determining what is legitimate to say in a disciplinary domain and what 'breaks' the rules.
>
> (Shulman, 1986b: 152, 153)

At the very least: within my classroom or team of teaching colleagues, I can still make decisions about how, when and why my mediation of the curriculum might incline towards a collection or an integrated approach (most curricula are a mix of both). I can challenge the discourse of deficit model curriculum-planning by using language which privileges discovery and active meaning-making.

Most important of all, I can stop treating nationally imposed curricula as if they were some counsel of perfection. Towards the end of Activity 3 in Section 2 of this chapter (page 91), I asked you to consider whether or not you felt the five Cox models of English were lacking in any way or required updating. When I tried this exercise myself (mapping the five models again against my pen portrait statements on pages 86–87), I was struck by how inward-looking and insular those five models now seem. The series of Shakespeare activities I subsequently mapped against the five models represented a deliberate attempt to address those perceived deficiencies and to recognise the status of English as a global language by, for example, expanding the concept of cultural heritage to include the whole world, or by referencing international film and prose fiction in the cultural analysis and cross-curricular sections. In other words, I took the five Cox models as a *starting* rather than a *finishing* point and attempted to reach beyond them to an educational provision which might not only enrich my pupils' experience but also enable me to remain true to the vision for English described in my pen portraits. 'Different discourses of English', Terry Locke writes, 'tell different stories about what it means to be an English teacher. In the context of the classroom, these discourses are instantiated in a range of pedagogical practices' (2015:16). Chapter 5 asked you to think about the kind of English teacher you want to be. The answer to that question will be demonstrated in your classroom. To decline the curricular challenge, to say 'as if we haven't enough to do without this lot as well', is to invite the kind of 'teacher proof curriculum' (Eisner, 1984: 201) represented by the worst excesses of National Literacy Strategy pedagogy. And if we do that, we can say goodbye to the concept of professional autonomy.

## OVER TO YOU

### Activity 10

The final activity in this chapter is designed to help you consolidate and apply your thinking about curricular issues.

- Take a look online at the English curricula for three different Anglophone countries.
- Compare the three curricula. The following prompt questions might prove useful:

  o   What balance do they strike between an integrated and a collection curriculum model?

  o   To what extent do they or do they not align with the five Cox models? What do you feel about this?

  o   How do they engage with some of the controversial issues explored in this chapter (for example, attitudes towards cultural heritage)?

  o   How do their approaches to the four modalities of English compare? (Are still and moving images, for instance, included as examples of Reading?)

  o   Which of the three is most sympathetic to your own beliefs as a teacher of English?

  o   Taking your favourite as a starting point, how and why might you wish to develop and enrich it?

# Chapter 7

# Assessment in English
## Key issues

## Section 1: establishing assessment credentials

Before Part III of the book takes us back into schools, I would like to close Part II with a chapter designed to help prepare our thinking for the assessment issues we will encounter in English classrooms.

Consider this piece of writing.

Why did it happen? I remember hearing once about a fire sermon preached by a wandering priest on the banks of the Indus. This priest would have said that it was desire which impelled me to the market place at Venta Icenorum on that hot summer afternoon; but I prefer to think that the spinning sisters had decided to amuse themselves – whether from boredom or from malice I cannot tell – with a fateful act of weaving.

Philo was an old rogue, but he was a Greek rogue who, in his own way, shared my loyalty to Aglibol – or 'Baal's Calf', as he insisted on calling the deity in order to bait me. So long a traveller through the rain and fog of Britain, I found it a comfort sometimes to speak my second tongue and to share the faith of my childhood, even with one so disreputable. Our talk sparked memories which consoled me.

We greeted each other with the sign of the horned moon. 'Ah, Brother!' he cried, snaking a conspiratorial arm around my neck and steering me into the shadows of a colonnade. His familiar stink of stale garlic and rotting teeth made my stomach heave; but I needed to hear what I hoped he had to tell me, so I forced a smile of acknowledgement and inclined my head.

What do you make of this? I expect that you realised fairly rapidly that it is a piece of narrative fiction written in the first person. Those of you who know something about the place names of Roman Britain will have deduced from the reference to *Venta Icenorum* that the extract belongs to the genre of historical fiction and is probably located within the period of the Roman occupation of Britain. Having established the context of the narrative, we could dig deeper for further textual clues: references to a cosmopolitan range of ancient religious practices and beliefs, to oral hygiene in the days before modern dentistry – and so on. Something you will not be able to identify so far, however, is the name of the author responsible for this previously unpublished piece of writing – me.

I have chosen to open Chapter 7 in this way in order to make two immediate points about assessment and the teaching of English. First, I want to draw attention to Stevens' observation that despite a 'huge emphasis in recent years on speaking and listening and on officially sponsored improvements of reading standards', the 'main emphasis in much of the commentary on assessment in English is on the assessment of *writing*' [original italics] (2012: 98). One of the reasons for this is because commentators realise that the assessment of writing in all its many draft and polished variants occupies a substantial amount of every English teacher's time. I know the seventh chapter of this book might seem like rather a strange place to say what comes next; but, bluntly, if you feel daunted by the prospect of reading and responding to a multitude of written scripts on a relentlessly regular basis during term time – then perhaps you had better think again about a career as a teacher of English.

Why should the modality of writing dominate the English curriculum in this way? Modern technologies have posed radical challenges to what Kress and Bezemer describe as the 'previous grooved routines' of written communication (2009: 171). For example, the concept of 'transduction' – which is concerned with the translation of online written text into visual and aural forms (McGuinn, 2014: 8) – has given renewed impetus to Socrates' famous assertion that the face-to-face immediacy of spoken communication is far more powerful and effective than the page-bound written word (Mengham: 1993, Harris, 2009). Nevertheless, certainly within the current educational system in England, writing remains the dominant medium through which pupils are assessed in schools – usually through handwritten responses to examination questions produced under timed pressure 'as the pen flies'. It is important for teachers of English particularly to remember this. Not only do we have a responsibility to help our pupils develop their skills, knowledge and understanding of the language and its literature as *desiderata* in their own right; we also have an obligation to equip those pupils with the requisite skills needed to create fluently crafted, effective written responses to assessment questions across the entire subject range – in Biology, say, or History. This is one reason why *A Language for Life*, the ground-breaking report which helped to shape my early thinking about English, stressed the importance of *literacy across the curriculum* (HMSO: 1975) – a concept reaffirmed by the Cox models of cross-curricular and adult needs English.

The second reason why I opened the chapter with an extract of writing – and specifically an example of personal writing – is because I think it is essential that teachers should practise what they profess to teach. Unfortunately, as Robinson and Ellis observe, most teachers of English are 'more confident readers than writers' (In Stevens, 2012: 107). This perceived imbalance between the roles of *receiver* and *transmitter* of texts has significant implications for pedagogy and assessment.

## OVER TO YOU

### Activity I

If I am to entrust an extract from my attempt at narrative fiction to you for scrutiny and evaluation, I have to feel confident that you will have something useful and important to tell me about it. Please understand that I am not trying to be arrogant in saying that – far from it, as I hope will soon become clear.

Before you attempt the activity, I should explain that the extract I want you to consider consists of the opening three paragraphs of my attempt at a historical novel.

- Tell me what qualifies you to make an informed and authoritative judgement about the piece of writing included at the start of this chapter.

If Robinson and Ellis's assertion is correct, your first response to this request might well have been to cite your *receptive* skills as an experienced reader of texts. Perhaps you are a voracious consumer of narrative fiction and therefore feel well practised in recognising what might or might not make an effective opening to a story, irrespective of its genre. That is fine – as far as it goes. However, I am writing a *historical* novel. No problem, you might respond: you are a fan of Hilary Mantel or C .J. Sansom's fictional accounts of Tudor England. Fair enough again; but my story takes place in early third-century Roman Britain. I need to be reassured that you have sufficient expertise to tell me, for example, whether you feel that my historical references are accurate. Would it have been possible for a third-century Romano-Briton to have known of the Buddha's *Fire Sermon* or to have practised a Middle Eastern religion? There is a wealth of novels set in the Roman period and written by authors as diverse as Gordon Doherty, Robert Graves, Robert Harris, Rosemary Sutcliff and Marguerite Yourcenar, and I think it is reasonable to expect you to have some familiarity with this subgenre of historical writing if you are to make an informed and authoritative evaluation of the extract I have presented here.

Dymoke locates this issue in the school context by focussing specifically upon the teaching and assessment of poetry. Noting that 'a pupil's ability to make an independent choice of genre' is a 'key element of progression', she warns that unless teachers are able to help those pupils engage with (and by implication, I would add, *come to informed evaluative decisions about*) a wide range of poetry, opportunities for 'high level performance' are in danger of being 'undermined' (2003:149). If teachers are to prevent such undermining, they need to be familiar with and to feel confident about teaching poetic genres which extend far beyond the normal school diet of lyrics about death and nature to include, for example, nonsense verse, political satire and epic poetry. But leaving aside formal assessment considerations of 'high level performance', there is a more pressing, human reason for teachers of English to possess this breadth of knowledge. 'People who are good at English', Bethan Marshall writes, '*judge* or assess almost everything' (2011b: 11). One of the most important assessment skills teachers of English need to be 'good at' is to have the capacity to realise when a pupil has reached a critical stage of readiness – readiness not only to enhance their learning in terms of Vygotsky's zone of proximal development (page 12, Chapter 1), but even more significantly, to develop as a human being. The stakes are high, as David Holbrook recognised fifty years ago. Like Dymoke, he chooses poetry as his example. This quotation from Holbrook has already been cited in Chapter 6, but it merits repeating here:

> Creative activity can ... become a gateway to the richness of civilisation which the teacher draws from the body of English poetry, as opportunity arises, to find immediately relevant examples to nourish the inward progress of each pupil as he [*sic*] strives towards insight.
>
> (1968: 13)

Perhaps one of the reasons you are reading this book is because, at some stage in your life, you encountered the kind of teacher of English described above by Holbrook: someone who was 'good at' making such life-changing assessment judgements – someone who introduced you to the right book at the right time, perhaps, or encouraged your writing, or gave you the confidence to find your voice.

## OVER TO YOU

### Activity 2

What Dymoke and Holbrook say about poetry here applies to all the modalities of English. As Richard Marshall (2009) puts it: 'Subject knowledge . . . should be at a premium, in order that as broad a construct of the subject as is possible be available to . . . communities [of teachers responsible for assessment]' (In Stevens, 2012: 105).

- Briefly review the activities undertaken earlier in the book which have invited you to reflect upon the strengths (and the inevitable gaps) in your subject knowledge. The activities in Chapters 1–3 are particularly relevant here.
- What further aspects of your own subject knowledge do you need to address in order to provide your pupils with 'as broad a construct of the subject as is possible'?
- Do you need to revise the subject knowledge targets and action plans established earlier in the book? If so, how? Who can provide you with additional support?

## Section 2: the reading/writing continuum

Suppose you were able to undertake with confidence the task I set you in Activity 1 because, actually, you are a reader who is very well versed in the subgenre of historical fiction which is the chosen medium of my written extract. Again, I might be happy with that response – but only if my purpose in presenting my writing to you for judgement was so that you could assess my *reading skills*.

## OVER TO YOU

### Activity 3

- Think of an occasion in your own education when you were invited to demonstrate your reading skills through the medium of writing. Do you feel the chosen assessment method gave you a fair opportunity to display those skills? What are the advantages and disadvantages of written approaches to the assessment of reading?

- If you do not feel that written assessment procedures alone can provide a full account of what a skilful reader knows, understands and can do, what other strategies might you use to provide more richly textured information?

Reading skills can be divided into two broad categories: *lower order* and *higher order*. Lower-order skills include basic decoding strategies such as the ability to blend letters into sounds or to divide words into patterned phonetic segments. You might feel that there would not be much benefit to be had in exploring the lower-order skills displayed in an extract written by someone who has been reading for sixty years. I chose the words in the extract after all: presumably I know what they mean and can read them.

## Activity 4

- Imagine, however, that I am in the room with you and you have asked me to read my written extract aloud. What would you expect my reading to sound like, if I am to convince you that I possess strong lower-order reading skills?
- Unfortunately, since I cannot be physically present for this exercise, you could alternatively record yourself reading the extract, or you could ask a friend to read it to you. This is not, of course, the same as hearing the author read. What might be lost by having to choose these alternative approaches and what are the implications for the way we should approach the assessment of reading?
- Imagine again that I am in the room, but now we are going to sit down together and you are going to interview me about the extract. What questions would you choose to ask and what further information would you hope to glean from those questions about my lower-order reading skills?
- Would there be anything to gain from inviting someone who is not the author to participate in the reading interview and to try to imagine what the author's responses might have been?

Higher-order reading skills include the ability to skim and scan when reading for essential information; to make inferences, deductions and predictions from and to ask pertinent questions of a text; to 'read between the lines'; to draw conclusions about what is *not*, as well as what is, written down; to understand how written texts attempt to position readers and to demonstrate the autonomy needed to be able to accept or reject textual intentions.

## Activity 5

- Study the three paragraphs of my written extract again. What evidence of higher-order skills can you identify?
- If you were to run again the assessment activities described in Activity 4, but this time looking for evidence of higher-order skills, how, if at all, would you modify those activities and what further evidence of reading attainment would you hope to collect?

Clarke notes the importance of 'learning to see writing as a reader sees it' (2010: 61); and indeed the assessment information gleaned from the tasks set in Activities 3 and 4 above could help me as the author to reflect upon and, if necessary, revise my three paragraphs – particularly if the comments I receive raise questions about the way I have tried to embed elements of research into the story. However, I think Clarke's observation needs to be taken further because, as Johnston puts it (the emphases in the quotation are his own):

> There is an exciting paradox in what reflection involves in English. While teaching students to reflect on their *writing* involves teaching them to *read* it in the role of the audience, teaching students to reflect powerfully on their *reading* involves teaching them to approach texts in the role of a *writer*.
>
> (1987: 105)

Helpful though it is to receive assessment information about my reading skills, what I would really welcome are your thoughts about the extract as a piece of *writing*. I am afraid that I am only prepared to take those comments from you if I know that you are a writer too. Strange though it may sound, this is partly a matter of self-esteem, even self-preservation. It is very difficult to disentangle a response to the writing from a response to the person – criticism of the former can imply criticism of the latter. If someone who has been a writer for sixty years can feel such unease, imagine what it is like when the author in question is a vulnerable adolescent whose need for 'self-respect and dignity' is particularly compelling (Gill and Thomson, 2012: 223). Johnston describes vividly the kind of psychological damage which can be inflicted on pupils by assessment procedures whose evaluative judgements fail to distinguish sensitively between the person and the work:

> Students are very familiar with assessment as a control mechanism and their experience of it affects how they think about themselves as learners. The most central issue is ... whether students' self-concepts as learners are based firmly in their own experience – or are mediated by and dependent on teachers' concepts of them.
>
> (Johnston, 1987: 15)

An assessor who has personal experience of the challenges writers face is more likely to lay aside what Fleming and Stevens memorably describe as the 'hissing and spitting red pen' (2004: 116). Of all people, English teachers willing to engage with a personal growth model of their subject need to find an approach to assessment which is capable of creating a 'mentoring dialogue' (Clarke, 2010: 59): an approach which caters for the needs of the *person behind the text* while at the same time providing focussed, practical and effective suggestions for purposeful development.

How do we achieve this delicate balance? 'What is needed', Black and Wiliam write, 'is a culture of success, backed by a belief that all can achieve' (1998: 141). Clarke notes that 'required and *deserved*' [my italics] feedback on writing should offer 'confirmation to the writer of the positive achievements of the piece' (2010: 60). When engaging with assessment as with other elements of the subject, deficit models of English are not to be encouraged.

## OVER TO YOU

### Activity 6

- Gill and Thomson suggest that 'feedback does not necessarily have to be accurate and truthful in order to reinforce (or feed back) into a process' (2012: 219). What do you think they mean by this and do you agree? Is what Clarke calls 'confirmation' the primary purpose of feedback?
- Choose a piece of assessed writing completed by you at some stage of your education in English. Think about the feedback – both written and, if you can still remember it, oral – that you received. If you can

choose two contrasting pieces, one positive in tone, one perhaps more negative, so much the better.

- Did the feedback reflect the principles espoused above by Black and Wiliam and by Clarke? How did you feel about it at the time and how do you feel about it now? If you selected two contrasting examples of feedback to consider, which did you find more or less helpful and why?

## Activity 7

- What positive comments could you make about the three paragraphs of my story opening? And how might I, as a writer, benefit from reflecting upon those comments?
- Are there any criticisms of my writing which you feel I should hear? What are they? How might you share them with me in a positive and sensitive manner?

By this stage of the book, it should be clear that, with assessment, as with all other elements of English teaching, our guiding principle should be to encourage what Erik de Corte calls teacher fade (Chapter 1, page 20). The aim of our 'mentoring dialogue' is to invest pupils with such confidence, motivation and skills that they are able to assess their own work for themselves, liberated from 'teachers' concepts of them', as Johnston put it.

## Section 3: the importance of questioning

Skilful and sensitive questioning, designed to promote powerful reflection, lies at the heart of this process. When choosing those questions, we need to make sure we get our wording right. As Gill and Thomson observe: '"How well are you doing?" is a very different question from "What needs to change?"' because the former 'looks for an evaluation, and for some kind of measurement, whether quantitative or not' (2012: 219).

## OVER TO YOU

## Activity 8

Pupils are often taught to consider *What, Why, When, Where and How?* questions. In the next task, I would like you, ideally, to experiment with all five.

Imagine that you and I are holding another interview about my writing, as in Activity 4.

- Using each of the words above in turn as the first word of the question, prepare **two interview questions per word** which you feel would make useful contributions to the writing interview. The first of the two questions should have the verb *did* as the second word. The second of the two questions should have one of the following verbs as its second word: *could, might, should, would.*

For example:

How did you . . .?

How might you . . .?

- Try to design the questions in such a way that they are both supportive and appropriately probing.

You might have wondered why I insisted on your using those particular verbs in that exercise. My intention was not to be pedantic, but to emphasise the importance of Gill and Thomson's point. I want the writing interview to provide opportunities for *reflection* on what has already been achieved (hence the insistence on *did*). I want also to *look forward* by encouraging the possibility of informed choice in future writing – be that a revision of the current three paragraphs or a development of the story (hence the selection of conditional verbs).

Imagine that one of your interview questions to me was: *How did you solve the author's age-old problem of creating an engaging opening to your story?* I would respond positively to a question like that because first of all it gives me confidence by suggesting that I have already achieved something (I solved a problem); second, because its attention is appropriately shared between writer and writing (how do storytellers 'hook' their audience?); and third, because by suggesting that I am an 'author', the questioner not only declares an intention to take me seriously but also helps me to feel part of a tradition and a community of fellow writers. Imagine, however, that your initial *did* question was: *Why did you make such a hash of your opening paragraph?* Both questions employ the personal pronoun *you*; but where the first one includes, this one excludes – by suggesting that I have failed to make it into what now seems like an indifferent if not openly hostile club. Asking me to account for my failure not only strikes at my sense of 'self-respect and dignity', it also leaves me nowhere to go in terms of reflection and possible development. I did not deliberately set out to make a 'hash' of the opening paragraph – I thought it must have been at least halfway decent or else I would not have submitted it for evaluation. To be told that I am so wildly off the mark in my judgements leaves me floundering for a response.

## OVER TO YOU

### Activity 9

- Consider the following conditional verb questions in the light of the discussion above.
  - How might you develop the relationship between the narrator and Philo as the story continues?
  - How might you revise your description of Philo to make him more credible?
- What is the likely impact of these two questions on me as the writer of the assessed extract and how successfully might those questions encourage purposeful reflection?
- In the light of the discussion above, review the questions you designed for Activity 8. Do any need modifying? If so, why and how?

### Activity 10

- Reread the examples of your own assessed writing which you explored for bullet points two and three of Activity 8, bearing in mind the issues we have considered above.
- Can you adapt any or all of your *did* and *conditional* verb questions so that they provide sensitive yet thought-provoking prompts to help you identify and reflect purposefully upon the achievements and the developmental needs revealed in that piece of writing?

If skilful questioning can provide a powerful stimulus to *formative* assessment – assessment which is designed to encourage the development of learning – then it can also play a decisive role in *summative* assessment – assessment designed to judge what learning has taken place by the end of a particular learning programme. An assessment response can only be as good as a question will allow it to be. Imagine that my three paragraphs of narrative fiction were written in response to a summative examination question for a creative writing course. Here is the question:

---

Create the opening three paragraphs of a historical novel set in third-century Roman Britain. Your novel opening should include:

- A narrator writing in the first person
- References to a specific geographical location
- Creation of tension and atmosphere
- Establishment of a relationship between the narrator and at least one other character

Your novel opening should be no more than 250 words.

---

This question raises so many fundamental issues about the assessment of English that it is difficult to know where to begin. A good place to start might be with this quotation from Fleming and Stevens:

> Reliability and validity are key concepts in understanding the tension at the heart of assessing English for they tend to pull in opposite directions.
>
> (2004: 118)

If I were to receive a question like the one above in an examination, I would be (*relatively* – see later) pleased for two reasons. First, it plays precisely to my personal interests and allows me to 'show off' the research into Roman history which I undertook before writing my novel opening. In that sense, the question could be deemed a *valid* way of allowing me to demonstrate what I know, understand and can do in this context. But could the same question be considered a *reliable* instrument for assessing summatively the knowledge, understanding and skills of my equally committed fellow course members – who have done no research into Roman Britain because the subject matter does not interest them in the slightest and who were hoping for a question on Magical Realism? This is a pressing issue for teachers of English, particularly those sympathetic to the personal growth model of the subject, because we are concerned, as D'Arcy (1995) so memorably puts it, with encouraging our pupils to write:

'from the inside', from that reservoir of recollections and speculations which are already a part of children's lives, related to their cultural experiences and to the values they hold.

(In Stevens, 2012: 100)

Yet, for reasons which will be explored further in Chapter 10, we are increasingly obliged to impose summative assessment procedures on our pupils which sacrifice validity on the altar of reliability in the belief that so-called standardisation will allow comparisons between pupils to be made nationally and internationally. So much for not judging the person when we judge the work: now we are judging whole nations, genders and cultures – as well as ethnic and social groups. If you are reading this in England and want further national proof of what I mean, just look online at the Standard Assessment Test (SAT) scores for eleven-year-olds and see if there is a correlation between the results for English and social deprivation or special needs. You can imagine how much more stark the tensions between validity and reliability become when the summative assessment procedures are conducted on an international basis. The Programme for International Student Assessment (PISA) initiative mentioned earlier in the book (Chapter 6 page 107) provides a vivid example. Squaring the validity/reliability circle with regards to reading, through the administration of a computer-based test to over half a million fifteen-year-olds from seventy-two counties and economies (OECD: 2016b), is quite some challenge. When you come to undertake the school-based activities described in Chapter 10, it would be interesting to ask your host teachers how helpful they find SATs and PISA data in planning to teach and assess their own pupils.

The other reason I *might* be pleased with the summative assessment question on Roman Britain is that it seems so easy. After all, how hard can it be to meet the question's bullet-pointed *assessment criteria*? All I have to do is use the pronoun 'I', insert a reference to a Romano-British settlement, have the narrator meet and interact with another character, abide by the word limit, and so on. I put 'might' in italics, however, because, as a candidate, I actually find the assessment question disappointing. If it is so easy to meet the brief, what chance do I get to demonstrate all the hard work that went into researching the background for the story or to thinking about characterisation and plot development? The suspicion arises that this summative assessment question is not really designed for the candidates to show what they can do – but actually to make the assessor's task easier. *First person narrator? Check. Two characters*

*introduced? Check. Geographical location? Check. Word limit? Check.*
Does the assessor – or any of the many interested parties who might stake
a claim to receiving assessment information – actually learn anything useful from such a tick box approach?

## Section 4: skimming or plunging?

This brings us to another issue fundamental to the assessment of English.
Do we assess only what we find easy to assess and do we shy away from
that which is complex and challenging? If so, can we then be surprised
if pupils emulate such an approach and, in Moffett's words (1981),
go 'skimming along in the froth instead of plunging into the current'
(In Johnston, 1987: 36)? Year after year, examiners – who, I am pleased
to say, do *not* approve of tick box assessment approaches – report
despairingly that school candidates concentrate in literature examinations
particularly on 'skimming along in the froth' of a text, instead of 'plunging
into the current' of its deep structural complexities:

> Perhaps the weakest approach ... is where the candidate has a list of
> characteristics that he/she trawls through. This type of answer finds
> examples of metaphors in each text, then similes, then alliteration,
> then rhetorical questions and so on. There is no attempt to probe
> how language has been used and very worryingly in this type of lim-
> ited response the students tended all to choose the same 'metaphor'
> and 'simile'.
>
> (WJEC CBAC, 2014: 32)

Would my creative writing summative assessment question allow candidates to get away with such a superficial approach? Not entirely. There is
one of the assessment criteria which differs from the others: *Creation of
tension and atmosphere.* Here is yet another important assessment issue
with which teachers of English need to engage. To what extent, Dymoke
asks, should we accept uncritically anything our pupils choose to present
us with in the sacred name of 'self expression' (2003: 148)? Three of my
chosen assessment criteria give me leave to express myself to my heart's
content without really being 'held to account' for what I actually write;
but that stubborn reference to tension and atmosphere demands something more: a capacity consciously and judiciously to *craft my material*
by making writerly decisions, not only about what information I should
include and what I should leave out, but also about the language and narrative sequence best suited to the story I wish to tell.

To include concepts such as tension and atmosphere in our assessment discourse is to acknowledge the importance of what Dewey called 'pattern and structure' (In Marshall, 2015: 193). Once we include pattern and structure as assessment criteria, we are entering the realm of aesthetics – somewhere those who have argued long and passionately that English is a language *art* (for example, Abbs, 1982; Stevens and McGuinn, 2004; Marshall, 2015) believe is its natural home. Is there any way that assessors committed to an aesthetic vision for English pedagogy could 'redeem' the bleakly mechanistic assessment question I imposed upon my three paragraphs of narrative fiction?

### Assessment weightings

One approach might be to signal to the candidates that certain of the assessment criteria are more significant than others by *weighting* them so that the most important (or most challenging?) are allocated bigger percentages of the *mark share* than the least important.

## OVER TO YOU

## Activity 11

• Imagine that you are responsible for weighting the four assessment criteria described on page 122. You have twenty marks to divide among the four. How would you do this? Would you simply allocate five marks to each assessment criterion or would you attempt to weight the allocation? If the latter, how and why? What can your decision tell us about your vision of English teaching and assessment?

Perhaps your response to this task was to allocate the 'heaviest' weighting to the *creation of tension and atmosphere* criterion. That would have been my decision – as I expect you thought it would. Refusing to opt for the easy tick box assessment strategy brings fresh challenges, however. How can we possibly assess elusive concepts like tension and atmosphere? If we consider the question too difficult to answer, we will find ourselves in good company. It proved too challenging for the Cox Committee to solve:

> The best writing is vigorous, committed, honest and interesting. We did not include these qualities in our statements of attainment because they cannot be mapped on to levels.

> (Cox, 1991: 147)

## Activity 12

- What is your reaction to this statement by Cox? What are its implications for the way that English is valued and assessed?

Strange though I find Cox's comment, I am going to try to consider it from the perspective of the committee members. Partly, the problem lies in the fact that judgements about *vigour*, *honesty* and *interest* and so on can be regarded as a matter of personal taste. If you *as a reader* (and you probably understand by now why I have put that phrase in italics) have no interest whatsoever in novels about Roman Britain, especially this one, and could not care less why my character 'Philo' wants to talk to the narrator in private, how can I expect you to come to an informed, let alone objective, judgement about the way I have tried to address the tension and atmosphere criterion? I have to appeal to you again to read the three paragraphs as if you were a *writer*. All writers of narrative fiction – irrespective of their chosen genre or subject matter – have had to grapple with this age-old question: *how can I make my writing interesting enough to engage my readers?* Writers have themselves faced the same challenges I faced here: they can read with a sense of fellow feeling and are therefore more likely to put aside issues of personal taste and to ask: *irrespective of whether I like it or not, does this work as a piece of writing?*

## Activity 13

- Look again at how you distributed the twenty marks among the four assessment criteria for my creative writing question. Assess the extract, allocating marks to each of the four assessment criteria. Total the marks out of twenty. How did I do?
- Write a brief report for me, explaining why you have allocated the marks in this way. Phrase the report from the perspective of a writer who is also a reader. Is it possible to write the report in such a way that it provides me with useful formative as well as summative information? (It is important to remember that the one need not exclude the other.)

There is no perfect solution to the assessment problem, of course. As Adams (1982) puts it: 'We *all* [original emphasis] know more than we can tell' (In Johnston, 1987: 112). You only had the words on the printed page to help you complete this activity. You cannot therefore have any real appreciation of the numerous writing decisions I had to make before I felt comfortable enough about presenting the extract for assessment. How can you come to an informed judgement about the writing unless you are privy to the thinking, the editing and the drafting that led to the version you see before you?

## An assessment system which works?

## Activity 14

Consider these five possible approaches to the assessment of English (think about all four modalities: speaking, listening, reading and writing).

1. Timed end-of-stage examinations marked by anonymous examiners. The school has a right to appeal if summative judgements are felt to be out of line with pupils' perceived progress throughout the course.

2. Continuous assessment throughout the course, based on the compilation of extensive and detailed records of the pupils' progress against all four modalities (including, for example, transcripts of talk, reading logs, writing portfolios). This material is marked by the pupils' teachers. Representative samples of the work are scrutinised by an external team of assessors in order to safeguard issues of standardisation and reliability.

3. A mixture of the above, with the end-of-course examinations weighted so that they are worth the most marks.

4. A mixture of the above, with the weightings reversed.

5. A mixture of the above, with equal weightings between end of course examination and continuous assessment.

- Which of these five alternatives most resembles your own school experience of assessment in English? How well did that assessment regime allow you to demonstrate what you knew, understood and could do?
- What are the advantages and disadvantages of the five alternative approaches? Is there ever a perfect solution? (Consider here the tensions between validity and reliability.)
- Which (if any) of the five summative approaches accommodates opportunities for formative assessment too?
- Which of the five alternatives would you prefer to work with (a) as a pupil and (b) as a teacher?
- Share your thoughts with an experienced teacher of English: which of these five alternative approaches are they familiar with? Which do they prefer and why?

Whichever assessment system we opt for (or have imposed upon us by external agencies) we have to acknowledge that English – as Chapter 6 suggested – is a particularly diverse, complex and wide-ranging subject area. It remains stubbornly and gloriously resistant to that *unweaving of the rainbow* which Keats describes in his poem *Lamia*. Unweaving the myriad individual strands of experience which combine to create the pen portrait rainbow would be practically impossible even if it were desirable. Richard Marshall (2009) warns, however, that this does not mean teachers of English should 'wallow in vagueness'. At the very least, basic human principles of equity and fairness demand that we help *all* our pupils gain full access to the skills, understanding and knowledge which we ourselves enjoy as proficient users of the language. Nor, however, Marshall continues, should we 'distort what is being assessed by stipulating vagueness away' (In Stevens, 2012: 104).

### A community of interpretation

Ultimately, we fall back on *configurational assessment* and *construct referencing* to inform our judgements. With the best will in the world, no matter how conscientiously you tried to follow the instructions for Activity 13, I suspect that your attempts at impartiality will have been distracted by a 'gut feeling' about the writing *as a whole*. Just as a bank note is valued not for the material it is composed of but for what it *represents*, so the mark or grade you will have given me is based on 'a *construct* [my italics] of what [you] think that grade looks like'. This construct represents a *configuration* of your various responses to the way in which my extract has or has not addressed the assessment criteria and other writing challenges (Marshall, 2007: 5, 4). The only practical way in which teachers of English can gain the confidence to make such judgements is by working alongside other teachers to create – through argument and debate – a shared community of interpretation.

## Section 5: curriculum backwash – positive or negative?

Assessment practices can exert a powerful degree of control – not only psychologically as described by Johnston on page 118 – but also in the way that they can condition our response to experience itself. Think about how, throughout the book, I have followed the English National Curriculum practice of referring to *Speaking and Listening*. Franks cites approvingly a question posed by a colleague: 'Speaking and listening?

What's wrong with *talk* [my italics]?' He suggests that one reason for the 'separation of talk into speaking and listening is to make a kind of an economy of the curriculum for the purposes of assessment' (2015: 153). Now the phrase is firmly embedded in educational discourse. Consider too the four criteria I included in the assessment question on my writing extract. Did they help or hinder your attempts to make an informed judgement about the text? Did they divert your attention from more pressing assessment issues and did you feel that there might be far more important alternative assessment criteria which could have been chosen instead? The issues played out here in my written extract can be observed at a national level – to such an extent that assessment practices can actually determine the kind of educational provision pupils receive. School subjects regarded as 'high stakes' in assessment terms can be afforded more resources and curriculum space than those which are not. White puts the point forcefully:

> A most powerful way of indoctrinating pupils is by so organising their studies that certain kinds of reflection ... are off the agenda.
>
> (1989: 62)

When you go into your host school to undertake the activities described in Chapter 10, you might find it particularly enlightening to discuss this point with teachers involved with the Arts generally and with English practitioners committed to Speaking and Listening or Drama in particular.

Assessment practices can exert a profound influence over curriculum content. Take my novel extract again as an example. If I had decided just to tinker around with a few creative ideas for my own private amusement, I could just have sat down at my computer one day and whiled away a few harmless and happy hours playing around with characters and plot line. However, my decision to offer this material for scrutiny in a public space means that I have had to take the enterprise far more seriously. As I hope the activities in Section 2 suggested, a significant amount of reading and research went into the preparation of the three paragraphs you see before you. I had, for example, to study Roman geography (were there links between the Romans and the people of the Indian subcontinent at this period of history?). I had to find out about Greek myths (the 'spinning sisters' who control human destiny); I had to investigate the rituals of the ancient Middle-Eastern religion of Baal – and so on.

In other words, assessment pressure obliged me to create a curriculum. If I had been serious about 'pitching' my novel to a publisher, that assessment pressure might have been all the more intense. A useful image for helping us to think about the influence which assessment can exert over what we learn is the metaphor of *curriculum backwash*. We have already considered above how this concept can be applied negatively. I want now to suggest how the term can be 'reclaimed'. The image of a ship pushing confidently forward against the waves of ignorance is attractive – leaving aside for the moment the reservation about progress narratives expressed earlier in the book – in that it evokes a sense of purposefulness. I am prepared to consider the metaphor in such a light – provided that *purposefulness* in this context means *personalised*. The curriculum I constructed in order to make my novel opening at least presentable to a critical and possibly hostile audience was entirely shaped towards my particular learning needs at the time. There was no occasion during my research when I found myself bored or disengaged or frustrated. Everything I studied had purpose or relevance for me – and one discovery led to another, pushing me beyond my immediate 'comfort zone' of history and literature into realms such as science and medicine which had seemed like *terra incognita* to me at school. One discovery led to another, even more fascinating than the last. You take my point? If used correctly, the assessment 'ship' can create an immensely powerful 'backwash': a rich curriculum experience which is tailored to the specific interests and learning needs of individual pupils. If applied in this way, imagine what exciting and engaged spaces classrooms might become!

## OVER TO YOU

### Activity 15

Before attempting the tasks which follow, you might find it useful to revisit your responses to Activity 1 in Section 3 of Chapter 5.

- What are your earliest memories of engaging with the modalities of language? (I am thinking of the home context, not school.) Can you remember, for example, being read to as a child? Or engaging with books for the first time? Or playing 'make believe'?
- Apply the metaphor of curriculum backwash (in its positive sense) to those experiences. How did the people closest to you – carers, siblings, relatives or friends – tailor their interactions with you to your specific learning needs?

- Think of a time in your life when you experienced an English curriculum of some kind. It might have been at school or in higher education – for example, a formal examination course, a module or a scheme of work. If you are currently training to teach English, you might want to consider the course you are taking now.
- Apply the same question about curriculum backwash to the course you have chosen for consideration. How does it compare with your early childhood experiences in terms of positive curriculum backwash?
- What lessons can you, in your role as teacher, learn from this exercise?

In Activity 1, Section 1 of Chapter 6, I 'nailed my curriculum colours to the mast' by describing what, in an ideal world, I believe that a pupil should be able to know, understand and do by the time they complete their compulsory schooling in English. I want to revisit those statements now and, for purposes of illustration, consider the first sentence of the first pen portrait, which has a focus on the modality we have not yet explored in as much detail as the others – *talk* (I am with Franks on this). Here it is:

> The pupils are able to listen sensitively and to speak fluently, tactfully and confidently in a range of repertoires, whether enjoying a night out with friends or responding to questions at a job interview.

In Activity 3, Section 2 of Chapter 3, we considered what a trainee teacher of English's successful developing practice might look like in the classroom. I would like us to attempt something similar here; but this time I want to think about what the pupils need to do to show their teacher or another assessor what they have learned.

I am going to focus on the *listening* element of the sentence statement.

> *Statement: The pupils are able to listen sensitively .... in a range of repertoires ...*

### Curriculum implications

As a teacher sympathetic to the personal growth model of English, my first response has to be to consider the needs of the whole person. Standard 7 of the current Teachers' Standards for England (see Chapter 2, page 30) states that teachers should be able to 'Manage behaviour effectively to ensure a good and *safe* [my italics] learning environment'. My declared aim of encouraging opportunities for sensitive listening in the classroom brings the issue of safety to the fore. If sensitive listening is to take place, it is imperative that the pupils believe not only that they can trust each other and me but also that that they believe sensitive listening is a skill worth learning and practising – not least within school.

In terms of curriculum content, therefore, I need to devote time to activities which build trust and which allow pupils opportunities to listen to a range of speakers on a regular basis. They may be reluctant to open up to each other about personal issues which require sensitive responses. One approach which might help us cater for *safety needs* could be to use Drama strategies as a means of creating fictionalised opportunities where sensitive listening might be practised at a protective distance from the personal. Whether or not I choose the medium of Drama to promote sensitive listening, the fact that I have committed my pupils to demonstrating these skills in a range of repertoires means that I cannot get away with simply devoting a 'one-off' lesson to sensitive listening.

The pupils need to show that they can listen sensitively to different speakers in different contexts. As well as providing opportunities for a range of contrasting dramatic improvisations, therefore, I might, for example, invite my pupils to watch and then deconstruct a television advert, listen to a charity appeal on radio which stirs the emotions, observe a professional dramatic performance which challenges the intellect, work with their peers on problem-solving tasks which require the demonstration of sensitive negotiation skills or analyse a persuasive speech delivered by the staff or by visiting speakers during a school assembly. If my pupils are to be equipped with the full range of skills expected of sensitive listeners, they need to appreciate how issues of status and context, as well as the deployment of non-verbal communication strategies, can influence the production and reception of talk, both on the part of the speaker and the listener.

### How will the pupils demonstrate that learning has taken place?

The statements described in the previous three paragraphs have significant implications for learning and teaching. I cannot expect my pupils to demonstrate success unless they have been *taught* the skills and content on which they are to be judged. To cite just one example, I cannot assess their listening skills through the medium of a Drama improvisation unless they know and understand what an effective Drama improvisation looks like.

The same points can be made about the references to television adverts, 'status play' in verbal interactions and so on. Perhaps the best way for the pupils to show what they have learned might be – taking the example of a Drama improvisation again as illustration – by asking them to reflect verbally and in writing on what they have listened to.

What seemed like a simple and straightforward 'wish list' statement about listening has opened up a whole range of teaching and learning possibilities which involve work in all four modalities and which embrace such diverse expressions of 'subject English' as media studies, sociolinguistics and Drama. I cannot imitate the members of the Cox Committee by shying away from complex assessment decisions. If I have declared that I want my pupils not only to be able to listen but to be able to demonstrate that they can listen *sensitively*, I need at the very least to help them recognise the difference between *sensitive* and *insensitive* listening. How far do I take this? Should I devise assessment criteria which can track progression from the negative to the positive extreme of listening? What would the criteria for *fairly sensitive* listening be?

## OVER TO YOU

### Activity 16

Having considered how we might plan for the teaching and assessment of listening, I would like you to think now about talk as production by focussing upon the speaking element of the 'partnership'.

- Read the statement below in the light of the previous discussion:

  o  The pupils are able . . . to speak fluently, tactfully and confidently in a range of repertoires, whether enjoying a night out with friends or responding to questions at a job interview.

- You have been asked to teach a sequence of **five lessons** designed to help pupils access and demonstrate the knowledge, understanding and skills implied by the statement above. The title of the sequence is Watch Your Language! (Please consider the significance of this title as you plan your work.)
- Use Table 7.1 to help you plan your sequence.
- Show your scheme of work to an experienced teacher and ask for their feedback.

*Table 7.1* A template for a scheme of work

| Lesson | What the pupils need to know, understand and be able to do | Activities | Progression from one lesson to the next | How will I know that learning has taken place? |
|--------|-----------------------------------------------------------|------------|------------------------------------------|------------------------------------------------|
| 1 | | | | |
| 2 | | | | |
| 3 | | | | |
| 4 | | | | |
| 5 | | | | |

# Part III

## Taking praxis into school

# Chapter 8

# Under the school microscope

## Observing and being observed

## Section 1: school experience – who can help and how?

It is six weeks into a teacher training year. The new recruits have started their full-time school placements. Just as the programme coordinator dares to congratulate herself that everything is going smoothly, she receives a troubling email. It comes from a young man who is confronting head-on one of those 'critical moments of perplexity and discrepancy' associated with the destabilised habitus described in Chapter 5. Such 'critical moments' can, as the quotation from Bruner in the same chapter suggested, stimulate learning; but if the experience is too extreme, critical moments can have negative consequences. That seems to be the case here. The young man says he is finding school life a huge 'culture shock' and is even having serious doubts about teaching as a career. Fortunately, his story has a positive ending. With skilful counselling and guidance, the young man in question settled down and started to find his feet. Now, a whole placement term into the programme, he feels much more positive and is glad that he decided not to quit.

Why should a potentially enlightening 'critical moment' have such a negative impact? A study of the young man's pre-course teaching experience revealed that this had consisted exclusively of some occasional, one-to-one work in a special school. That in itself is of course highly valuable. However, it did not prepare him sufficiently for the day-to-day reality of a full-time school placement: when the 'critical moment' occurred, it almost overwhelmed him.

I wanted to start with this anecdote to impress upon you the absolute importance of getting as much school experience as you can before you start your teacher training programme. Had the young man in question done this, he would have begun his placement with a much clearer sense of what life as a teacher, with its 'thousand or so interpersonal transactions in a single day', actually involves:

During any one day teachers may fill a variety of roles in carrying out their duties. These can include not only the traditional one of transmitter of knowledge, but also others such as counsellor (advising pupils about careers, aspirations or problems), social worker (dealing with family issues), assessor (marking children's work, giving tests, writing reports), manager (looking after resources, organising groups, setting goals), even jailer (keeping in school reluctant attenders or checking up on possible truants). As classroom life can be busy and rapidly changing, some teachers may fulfil several of these roles within the same lesson.

(Wragg, 1994: 95, 5)

Chapter 8 is written with the experience of the young man who nearly abandoned his training programme firmly in mind. You will have noticed that, throughout the first seven chapters of the book, reference is made to activities which involve school visits and observations. More will follow in this and the final two chapters. In the introduction, I suggested that you read through the whole book before engaging with the school-based activities. One of the reasons for this is to remain true to the principles espoused in Chapter 2: I want you to use that initial reading to establish an overview of the school-based tasks so that you can then work 'smartly' by thinking not only about how various activities from different chapters might be combined but also by deciding which context and mode of enquiry is best suited to helping you achieve the activities' objectives.

To help you get started, I have collated the school-based activities described in the book so far. I have limited the activities listed in Table 8.1 to what we have covered so far because I am using them for illustrative purposes. You will of course have your own ideas about how you might include the activities recommended in Chapters 8, 9 and 10 when setting an agenda for your time in school. The key principle is that you should use your time as 'smartly' and efficiently as possible.

Interestingly, the quotation from Wragg cited at the start of this chapter makes no mention of the roles teachers can play in professional training. The fact that, twenty-two years later, Table 8.1 contains so many references to various members of the school community – including carers and pupils – is a measure of the extent to which, in England as elsewhere during this period, teacher training has relocated from the university to the workplace. As the list indicates, there is clearly a wide range of people available in school to help you gain insights into teaching. How best then to make 'smart' use of your observation time without overtaxing the patience and goodwill of busy professionals?

Table 8.1 An overview of the school-based activities described in Chapters 1–7

| Location in book | Task | Possible school input |
|---|---|---|
| Chapter 1 Section 2 (pages 13–15). | Think about key questions relating to content, curriculum, pedagogical and professional knowledge. | English teaching staff (including support staff), pupils and their carers. |
| Chapter 1 Section 2 Activity 3 (page 20). | Map the information you have provided in your training application form in terms of content, curriculum, pedagogical and professional knowledge. | See details in the who or what can help column for Helen's worked example – note the references to pupils and carers as well as to school staff. |
| Chapter 2 Section 1 Activities 3–4 (pages 32, 33). | Create, 'blend' and date your own immediate, mid- and long-term targets following the Helen model. | See details in the who can help column as described in the Helen model (above). Note the references to pupils and carers as well as to school staff. |
| Chapter 2 Section 2 (pages 34–40). | Track Helen's baseline reviews. | School staff could help to monitor and review Helen's progress through discussions and observations – and of course could do the same for you. |
| Chapter 3 Section 1 Activities 1–2 (pages 44–45). | Share your suggested teaching practice folder with colleagues in school. | Staff and trainees involved in teacher training evaluate your folder and compare it with the examples used in school. |
| Chapter 3 Section 1 Activities 3–4 Worked examples 1 and 2 (pages 47, 50 and 47, 49). | Describe successful practice at beginner and experienced trainee level – Standard 7 of the current Teachers' Standards for England as an example. Consider the weighting of threshold descriptors between potential and efficacy. | Accounts of what successful classroom practice might look like - and of which threshold descriptors indicate progress - can inform subsequent lesson observations and discussions with relevant staff. |
| Chapter 3 Section 1 Activity 5 (page 50). | Share your incremental descriptions of successful practice and your tracking of threshold descriptors against Standard 7 with current trainees working in school. | Current trainees widen the discussion by sharing their thoughts about mapping progression against threshold descriptors. |
| Chapter 3 Section 2 Activity 7 (page 54). | Review the documentary evidence you have collected in response to the non-school-based activities you have completed as you have worked through the first three | A member of school staff involved in teacher training helps you review the evidence you have prepared. Together, you should come to a |

(continued)

Table 8.1 (continued)

| Location in book | Task | Possible school input |
|---|---|---|
| | chapters of the book. Map that evidence against the eight *teaching standards* headline statements on page 30, using the models on pages 52, 53–54 to guide you. | judgement about your current achievements and future targets. |
| Chapter 4 Section 3 Activity 5 (page 68). | Discuss the quotation from Aronowitz and Giroux with staff in school. | Trainee and experienced teachers of English compare their responses with yours. |
| Chapter 5 Section 3 Activity 3 (page 83). | Review your responses to any of the activities undertaken in the chapters so far which required you to think in some way about the theory and practice of teaching English. | Compare your reflections with those of a current teacher or trainee teacher of English and seek their advice about how you might develop your praxis. |
| Chapter 6 Section 3 Activity 4 (page 94). | Explore the ideological and pedagogic issues inherent in one of the five *Cox Models of English*. | Share your responses with a trainee and/or an experienced teacher of English. |
| Chapter 6 Section 4 Activities 7–9 (pages 102, 104, 106). | Discuss the comment from Kress about poetry, literature and creativity with staff in school and, in the light of this discussion, consider whether there is a future for English as an autonomous school subject. | Compare your reflections with those of a trainee, an experienced teacher of English and a member of staff responsible for literacy across the curriculum (preferably, a non-English specialist). |
| Chapter 7 Section 1 Activity 2 (page 115). | Briefly review the activities undertaken earlier in the book which have invited you to reflect upon the strengths (and the inevitable gaps) in your subject knowledge. The activities in Chapters 1–3 are particularly relevant here. Do you need to revise the subject knowledge targets and action plans established earlier in the book? If so, how? Who can provide you with additional support? | Members of English Department staff, including other trainees on placement. |
| Chapter 7 Section 4 Activity 14 (page 127). | Consider which of the five alternative approaches to assessment described in this section you would prefer to work with a) as a pupil and b) as a teacher. | Experienced teachers of English familiar with some or even all of the five assessment approaches. |
| Chapter 7 Section 5 Activity 16 (pages 133–134) | You have been asked to plan a sequence of five lessons. | An experienced teacher of English to provide feedback on your plan. |

## Section 2: working alongside the school community – planning strategically

This section of the chapter is designed to help you plan strategically, so that you can make the most effective use of the potential support available in school. Please note that I have tried in Table 8.2 to refine the somewhat general references to school staff found in Table 8.1. You should also bear in mind that Table 8.2's review of personnel who can offer assistance is probably most appropriate to trainees (like the young man whose experience of 'destabilised habitus' opened this chapter), who are already on placement in a school – not least because the host school is probably being paid to train them! In this context, too, it is important to remember that some of the school-based activities are intended for trainees already engaged on a training programme – and indeed, in some cases, for qualified teachers too. If you are a reader who has not yet begun a training programme, then remember: the more pre-course experience you can gain, the more confident and better prepared you will be. Whatever category of readership you belong to, *you will, of course, have completed all the requisite safeguarding checks before entering a school.*

### A worked example

As an example of how I might organise my time in school effectively, I am going to concentrate on activities which focus upon learning within the classroom. I suggest that the following extracts from Table 8.1 on pages 139 to 140 make a coherent and manageable grouping (I have numbered the various items so that you can see how the statements for each of the three headings link):

---

### Location in book

1   Chapter 1 Section 1 (pages 13–15)
2   Chapter 3 Section 1 Activities 3–4 Worked examples 1 and 2 (pages 47, 50 and 47, 49)
3   Chapter 3 Section 1 Activity 5 (page 50)

### Task

1   Thinking about key questions relating to content, curriculum and pedagogic knowledge.[1]

*(continued)*

*(continued)*

2    Describe successful practice at beginner and experienced trainee level – Standard 7 of the current Teachers' Standards for England as an example. Consider the weighting of threshold descriptors between potential and efficacy.

3    Share your incremental descriptions of successful practice and your tracking of threshold descriptors against Standard 7 with current trainees working in school.

## Possible school input

1    English teaching staff (including support staff); pupils and their carers.

2    Accounts of what successful classroom practice might look like – and of which threshold descriptors indicate progress – can inform subsequent lesson observations.

3    Current trainees widen the discussion by sharing their thoughts about mapping progression against threshold descriptors in general and about collecting evidence to address externally imposed criteria for teacher training.

These three tasks could feasibly be addressed in one lesson, largely through the medium of observation. When entering into negotiations – as here where, particularly if I have not yet started a formal training programme, I am asking the school community to do me a considerable favour – it is useful to have a wish list and a fallback position. The ideal arrangement for me in this example would be to observe how a current trainee or recently qualified teacher of English addresses the questions associated with content, curriculum and pedagogic knowledge described on page 14 of Chapter 1 when teaching Mary Shelley's *Frankenstein* to an age-appropriate group – on page 14, I suggested fifteen-year-olds.

In addition, the same observation would, ideally, provide me with an opportunity to 'fine tune' my exploration of the questions relating to pedagogic knowledge by observing what successful practice with regards to Standard 7 of the current Teachers' Standards for England might look like in a real classroom. Pushing my luck, I might ask, for good measure, if I could shadow a pupil or small group of pupils during the lesson, so that I might gain some understanding of the problematic relationship between what teachers think they are teaching and what pupils think they

Table 8.2 What the school community can offer: an overview

| Member of the school community | Advantages | Points to consider | When and where? |
|---|---|---|---|
| Head teacher | Strategic overview of the school's aims and of its place in the various communities it serves. Networked to other head teachers across the sectors and to educational policy makers. Informed on national education initiatives. Able to advise on management issues and career development. | Opportunities for regular contact may be limited. Possibly – but not necessarily – more concerned with the 'big picture' than with details. Perspective may be nuanced on account of 'political' considerations. | Whole and departmental staff briefings. Formal meetings with trainees. Possibility of informal conversations. |
| Governors | Community perspective on the service provided by the school. Individual governors may have a specialist brief. Governors from different working backgrounds bring a 'fresh pair of eyes' to the education service. | Opportunities for regular contact may be limited. Individual governors may have an 'agenda'. School code of contact needs to be consulted before individual contact with governors is considered. | Formal meetings with trainees. Possibility of shadowing a governor during a fact-finding visit to the school. Individual briefings may be possible – if the school code permits. |
| Senior management team | Teaching expertise across a range of specialisms. Can advise on key elements of school life including policies (for example, on special educational needs, safeguarding or English as an additional language) as well as on educational initiatives for which they hold a specialist brief. A particularly useful contact will be the member of the team responsible for trainees and or for the induction of new staff. Networked to colleagues nationally, regionally and locally. Can advise on management issues and career development. If not English specialists, may offer a fresh perspective on pertinent issues such as literacy across the curriculum. | Opportunities for regular contact may be limited. Perspective may be nuanced on account of 'political' considerations. | Whole and departmental staff briefings. Formal meetings with trainees. Possibility of shadowing. Possibility of informal conversations. |

(continued)

Table 8.2 (continued)

| Member of the school community | Advantages | Points to consider | When and where? |
|---|---|---|---|
| Teacher training coordinator | Expertise in working with trainees across subject specialisms. Networked to other training coordinators in schools and universities. Can advise on generic teaching skills. Can advise on various routes into teaching and on how best to prepare for the training year. Expertise in teacher training initiatives. Can liaise with subject mentor and other staff involved in training. Can encourage trainees to work together within and across subject specialisms. Responsible for checking on the quality and coherence of teacher training within the school. May liaise with programme's external examiners as appropriate. | Responsibility for teacher training may be just one of their school roles (see Wragg quotation on page 138) so cannot be expected to be always accessible. Trainees will be expected to move towards teacher fade (see Chapter 1, page 20). May not be able to advise on subject-specific issues. | Formal meetings with trainees across subject specialisms. Individual interviews, lesson observations and debriefings. Review of trainee progress throughout the placement. |
| English mentor | Expertise in working with trainee teachers of English. Expertise in teaching English. Networked with other mentors and, where appropriate, university staff across a teacher training partnership. Liaises with teacher training coordinator, other subject mentors and English department staff. Monitors, evaluates and reports on trainees' progress throughout the placement. | Will expect regular, daily contact with the trainee; but the same provisos apply as for the teacher training coordinator. May be committed to a particular vision of English teaching to the detriment of other approaches – especially if experiencing pressure from senior managers to conform to a specific 'vision' for the school. | Individual interviews, lesson observations and debriefings. Paired work on planning and assessment. Review of trainee progress throughout the placement. Departmental meetings and training sessions. Team teaching, particularly in initial stages of the placement. Supporting at parents evenings and with other additional contractual duties. |

| Members of the English department | Can offer a diverse range of experience, particularly if they are well established in the school or hold positions of responsibility within the department. Colleagues who have worked in a range of schools can offer a number of different perspectives on English teaching. Newer members of the department may themselves have trained recently and may therefore be particularly sympathetic to the challenges faced by current trainees. May be responsible for significant areas of the curriculum which apply across the whole school community – for example, special educational needs, English as an additional language or library provision. May be networked to colleagues nationally through their membership of professional associations or service on examination boards. Different colleagues may possess expertise in different areas of the English curriculum, such as language, media, Drama or national assessment requirements. Colleagues who are not in an official supervisory role may prove easier to approach for advice. Some colleagues may run clubs and societies to which a trainee can contribute. Some colleagues may have themselves been mentors in the past and are therefore particularly appreciative of the challenges facing trainees. | Mentoring is not part of the job description of these colleagues, so trainees need to be careful not to presume too much on their goodwill. Some colleagues may not have been trained in the skills of observing lessons and providing feedback to trainees; they may therefore have unrealistic expectations. Colleagues who have not undertaken a mentoring role themselves may not appreciate the demands placed on trainees – for example, in terms of planning, assignment writing or compiling the kind of evidence described in Chapter 3. | Departmental meetings and training sessions. Paired work on sharing resources, planning and assessment. Regular, day-to-day contact in the departmental office and the staff room. Team teaching, particularly in initial stages of the placement. Supporting at parents evenings and with other additional contractual duties and extra-curricular events (such as theatre trips). Team-building social events. |
|---|---|---|---|

(continued)

Table 8.2 (continued)

| Member of the school community | Advantages | Points to consider | When and where? |
|---|---|---|---|
| Other members of staff | May be responsible for significant areas of the curriculum which apply across the whole school community – for example, special educational needs, safeguarding or English as an additional language. May be able to offer similar advantages to those of the members of the English department, but with the additional benefit of providing a different subject perspective. However, that perspective might not always accord with the specifics of English pedagogy. May have expertise in a range of generic teaching skills such as questioning, assessing progress, differentiation or classroom management. May be able to share important training advice and information from a different subject perspective. | Mentoring is not part of the job description of these colleagues, so trainees need to be careful not to presume too much on their goodwill. Some colleagues may not have been trained in the skills of observing lessons and providing feedback to trainees; they may therefore have unrealistic expectations. Colleagues who have not undertaken a mentoring role themselves may not appreciate the demands placed on trainees – for example, in terms of planning, assignment writing or compiling the kind of evidence described in Chapter 3. | Whole staff and inter-departmental training sessions. Possibility of shadowing – particularly of colleagues from other subject areas who have a specific pedagogic expertise or responsibility (for example, special educational needs, safeguarding or English as an additional language) and/or who teach the same pupils as the trainee. Regular, day-to-day contact in the staff room. Supporting at parents evenings and with other additional contractual duties and extra-curricular events (such as theatre trips). Team-building social events. |
| Support staff | May have established good working relationships with and understanding of a range of individual pupils (and their carers), particularly those pupils who might have special educational needs of different kinds. | Given the many claims on support staff's time across the whole school community, opportunities to plan and work together on a regular basis may require particular logistical effort. | Whole staff, departmental and inter-departmental training sessions. |

|  |  |  |
|---|---|---|
|  | May have expertise in particular areas of teaching, such as working with pupils who have hearing or visibility impairment, liaising with home communities or updating technology provision. | Possibility of shadowing – particularly of support staff who work with pupils taught by the trainee. |
|  | Can provide a valuable fresh pair of eyes in the classroom (in terms of monitoring learning and providing feedback) as well as offering additional support and expertise to the class teacher. | Regular contact in the staff room. |
|  | May work with the same pupils across a range of subject areas and thus be able to provide a more holistic view of their learning interests and needs. | Team-building social events. |
|  | May provide a valuable link with key teaching colleagues, such as special educational needs, safeguarding and English as an additional language coordinators. |  |
| Pupils | The core element of the school community. | Formal meetings agreed beforehand with the relevant school staff. |
|  | Can offer invaluable insights into teaching and learning – both in English lessons and across the whole school experience. | Whole class, small group, pair and individual discussions in lessons. |
|  | It should go without saying that any contact with pupils must adhere strictly to school safeguarding policies. It should only be undertaken with the full approval of the relevant staff and, if appropriate, the pupils' carers. | Appropriate informal conversations around the school (for example, at lunch times, on break duties, at after school clubs or on organised school outings). |
|  | Discussions with pupils involving teaching and learning in general and school life in particular should be conducted in a professional manner and should not make reference to individual members of staff. | Formal consideration of feedback from 'pupil voice' forums. |
|  | Before any discussions with pupils take place, the purpose and consequences of the discussion should be clarified by both parties. | Informal and formal assessment of pupils' work in English lessons. |

Table 8.2 (continued)

| Member of the school community | Advantages | Points to consider | When and where? |
|---|---|---|---|
| | | | Shadowing of individual pupils through the course of a school day. |
| | | | Discussions at parents evenings and other formal extra-curricular events. |
| Carers | Like the pupils in their charge, the core element of the school community. | They may well not have a professional educationalist's insights into and appreciation of current developments in teaching and learning. | Parents evening and other formal (and informal) extra-curricular events such as school plays. |
| | They can offer unique insights into the learning concerns of their children. | | |
| | Their concern for their children's welfare means that they are particularly committed to the success of the school and may have pronounced views on what its vision should (or should not) be. | Strong and transparent lines of communication with the home are needed, therefore, so that carers understand, appreciate and feel able to support the work of the school. | Through school-approved informal communications (for example, a postcard home praising a pupil's efforts or achievements). |
| | If supportive, can help teachers create a powerful learning community in which home and school combine to enrich the experiences and life chances of the pupils. | Some carers may have had negative experiences of education and thus may feel like Bourdieu's 'fish out of water' when revisiting a school community as adults. | Formal school approved meetings where appropriate. |
| | Can enrich the life of the school by, for example, contributing to fund-raising activities, serving on governing bodies and supporting extra-curricular initiatives. | As with pupils, meetings with parents should adhere to the professional guidelines issued by the school. | |

are learning. I said on page 142 that classroom observation could 'largely' help me address the three tasks described in the list above. However, it must be obvious that I could not simply walk into a lesson one day, sit down and just start watching what happens. Crucially, as the content, curriculum and pedagogic knowledge questions listed on page 14 and the description of the tasks on pages 142 to 143 suggest, there have to be pre- and post-observation meetings. These serve not only to organise the necessary permissions for and logistics of the observation visit itself, but – and this is crucial again – they provide an essential opportunity to gain an understanding of the context in which this particular example of teaching and learning is taking place.

## OVER TO YOU

### Activity 1

- Reread my lesson observation wish list described on page 142. Is there anything you would change or add?
- Review Table 8.2's bullet-pointed list of school personnel who might assist you during your time in school. Think about your pre-observation visit. Who would you need to contact in order to obtain the necessary permissions?
- In my account of the 'ideal' observation, I say that I would want to work with pupils and either trainee or newly qualified teachers of English. Which other school personnel might I approach for assistance?
- What observation fallback position would you propose if your ideal wish list could not be accommodated?
- Who and what would your post-observation visit involve? Think particularly about the tasks associated with Standard 7: what do you need to take into account when sharing with the teacher concerned your thoughts about their classroom practice?
- What can you contribute to the school, in return for the favour of being hosted by their community and of being allowed to observe and interview their staff and pupils?

### Activity 2

In Table 8.3 below, columns one and two describe the daily timetable for a secondary school. The third column describes the Friday teaching commitments of the teacher you have been told you can observe. For the

*Table 8.3* An example of a typical school day timetable

| Time | Description | Teacher's Friday timetable |
| --- | --- | --- |
| 8:25 a.m. | Warning bell | |
| 8:30 a.m.–9:30 a.m. | Period 1 | Year 10 (14–15-year-olds) |
| 9:30 a.m.–10:30 a.m. | Period 2 | Year 8 (12–13-year-olds) |
| 10:30 a.m.–10:45 a.m. | Break | |
| 10:45 a.m.–11:45 a.m. | Period 3 | |
| 11:45 a.m.–12:45 p.m. | Period 4 | Year 7 (11–12-year-olds) |
| 12:45 p.m.–1:25 p.m. | Lunch | |
| 1:25 p.m.–1:45 p.m. | Assembly or Tutor Time | |
| 1:45 p.m.–2:45 p.m. | Period 5 | Year 8 (12–13-year-olds) |
| 2:45 p.m. | End of school | |

purpose of this example, imagine that Friday happens to be the only day of the week which the school can offer for the proposed visits.

- Imagine that your host school has given you permission to visit for **one day** (it can only be a Friday) in order to address the three tasks described on pages 141–142. You have **half a day** for the visit itself and **half a day in total** to accommodate the pre- and the post-observation visits.
- Consider the timetable above. What are the advantages and/or disadvantages of a morning as opposed to an afternoon visit? (As well as considering the teacher's teaching commitments here, take into account the ages of the pupils whose classes could be available for observation.)
- Thinking particularly of the pre- and post-observation visits, what issues do you need to take into account when setting up meetings with staff and pupils?
- Create an agenda and a timetable for the Friday observation visit (half a day) and the Friday pre- and post-observation visits (half a day in total).

Not all of the school-based tasks described in Table 8.1 necessitate classroom observation. The two tables which follow are linked by the fact that both require quiet, reflective, professional discussion with one or more teaching colleagues. The first cluster of tasks explores principles of English praxis; the second is concerned with evidence-based assessment (for which see also Chapter 10). (As before, I have numbered them as a reminder of which task links with which location in the book and which example of possible school input.)

Table 8.4 Exploring English praxis tasks

| Location in book | Task | Possible school input |
|---|---|---|
| (1) Chapter 4 Section 3 Activity 5 (page 68). | Discuss the quotation from Aronowitz and Giroux with staff in school. | Compare your reflections with those of a current teacher or trainee teacher of English and seek their advice about how you might develop your praxis. |
| (2) Chapter 5 Section 3 Activity 4 (page 83). | Review your responses to any of the activities undertaken in the chapters so far which required you to think in some way about the theory and practice of teaching English. | Share your responses with a trainee and/or an experienced teacher of English. |
| (3) Chapter 6 Section 3 Activity 4 (page 94). | Explore the ideological and pedagogical issues inherent in one of the five Cox Models of English. | Compare your reflections with those of a trainee, an experienced teacher of English and a member of staff responsible for literacy across the curriculum (preferably, a non-English specialist). |
| (4) Chapter 6 Section 4 Activities 7–9 (pages 102, 104, 106). | Discuss the comment from Kress about poetry, literature and creativity with staff in school and, in the light of this, consider whether there is a future for English as an autonomous school subject. | Members of English department staff, including other trainees on placement. |
| (5) Chapter 7 Section 1 Activity 2 (page 115). | Consider whether you need to revise the subject knowledge targets and action plans established earlier in the book. | |

## OVER TO YOU

## Activity 3

- How might the requirements for the sets of tasks described in Tables 8.4 and 8.5 differ from those in Activities 1 and 2 in terms of logistics, personnel and dynamics?

- What would be on your ideal wish list when planning the agenda for your visit(s) with regards to these two sets of tasks and what would be your fallback position in each case? What could you offer the host school community in return?
- Your host community (the same school as for Activities 1 and 2) has said that you can come in again on any day of the working week to

*Table 8.5* Evidence-based assessment tasks

| Location in book | Task | Possible school input |
|---|---|---|
| (1) Chapter 2 Section 1 Activities 3–4 (pages 32, 33). | Create, 'blend' and date your own immediate, mid- and long-term targets following the *Helen* model. | See details in the *Who or what can help?* column of Table 1.2 for the *Helen* model. Note the references to *pupils* and *carers* as well as to school staff. |
| (2) Chapter 2 Section 2 (pages 34–40). | Track Helen's baseline reviews. | School staff help to monitor and review Helen's progress through discussions and observations – and of course could do the same for you. |
| (3) Chapter 3 Section 1 Activities 1–2 (pages 44–45). | Share your suggested teaching practice folder with colleagues in school. | Staff and trainees involved in teacher training evaluate your folder and compare it with the examples used in school. |
| (4) Chapter 3 Section 2 Activity 7 (page 54). | Review the documentary evidence you have collected in response to the non-school-based activities you have completed as you have worked through the first three chapters of the book. Map that evidence against the eight Teachers' Standards headline statements on page 30, using the models on pages 52 and 53–54 to guide you. | A member of school staff involved in teacher training helps you review the evidence you have prepared. Together, you should come to a judgement about your current achievements and future targets. |
| (5) Chapter 7 Section 4 Activity 14 (page 127). | Consider which of the five alternative approaches to assessment described in this section you would prefer to work with a) as a pupil and b) as a teacher. | Experienced teachers of English familiar with some or even all of the five assessment approaches. |

address these two sets of tasks with the relevant staff – provided you do so out of lesson time. What opportunities and/or constraints does this stipulation entail?

- Plan your agenda and timetable.

## Section 3: confronting the normalising gaze

I want to turn now to that set of questions (described on page 15 of Chapter 1) relating to professional knowledge which I did not address in the worked example on pages 141–142.

I wanted to reserve that particular area of concern for consideration in a separate section of the chapter because it raises issues relating to an important aspect of school-based activity which has not yet been addressed and which needs to be explored now. The quotation from Wragg cited at the start of the chapter listed in some detail the multiple roles played by teachers in the course of a day. In order to address effectively the tasks described in the lists above, trainees too have to play each of the roles named by Wragg – with the exception, possibly, of 'jailer'. Management skills are required to negotiate and successfully execute the school visits. Discussing the content, curriculum and pedagogic questions described on page 14 requires the transmission of knowledge – as do conversations about the praxis of English teaching, the planning of resources or the reviewing of baseline assessment progress. Observing someone teach requires the observer, for better or worse, to play the role of assessor (more on this below); and the very skilful and delicate art of sharing lesson feedback – or of asking sensitive professional questions concerning teamwork or individual teachers' views about the value system espoused by their school – demands the emotional intelligence of a practised counsellor or social worker.

Power dynamics are at play in each of these roles – and they need to be handled carefully. As I suggested above, this is particularly important in the case of lesson observation and feedback. It is significant to note that the most recent writing I could find on the subject (Page, 2017: 62–74) should cite a forty-year old text by Michel Foucault bearing the ominous title: *Discipline and Punish: The Birth of the Prison*. For Foucault, the act of observing is a highly charged ideological activity through which those in power assert their authority. They achieve this through what he calls 'hierarchical observation' which 'coerces individuals by making them clearly visible and keeping them under watch' (Schwan and Shapiro, 2011: 115). Particularly pertinent – and this is one of the main reasons why *Discipline and Punish* is cited in in Page's 2017 chapter – is Foucault's identification of 'normalizing judgement' (1977: 177) as 'one of the distinctive features of modern disciplinary control' (Page, 2017: 66). Schwan and Shapiro's gloss on this term is worth quoting at length:

> We are judged not based on our own achievements or transgressions but in relationship to what everyone else is doing.... This institutes a sort of constant paranoia where individuals can never stop comparing their actions and 'nature' to the perceived, or assumed, intangible norm. Yet because the group defining the norm is hard to see or comfortably know, since it is constantly fluid, we can never allow ourselves to rest in the secure knowledge that we have done the right thing. Since only the authority who can observe everyone is able to know what is the collective standard, we are left in a state of anxiety, wondering if our actions are sufficiently 'normal' or not.... This uncertainty makes us more dependent on authorities... to tell us if our actions, personalities and bodies are normal or not.

Perhaps the most insidious aspect of the 'penalty of the norm' (Foucault, 1977: 183) is the suggestion that the powerless actually learn to do the controlling work of the powerful for them:

> Additionally, we also begin to internalize the function of supervision, even in the absence of a supervisor, as we begin to interrogate our 'selves' to see if they are acceptably 'normal'.
>
> (Schwan and Shapiro, 2011: 120)

It is not difficult to see how these accounts of 'hierarchical observation' and 'normalising judgement' might be applied to the educational system. Indeed, Foucault regarded schools as one of the prime sites in which habits of '[h]ierarchized, continuous and functional surveillance' (1977: 176) are acquired and internalised. Teachers working within the current English inspection system of high stakes, short-notice and 'snapshot' school assessment visits conducted by itinerant and remote teams of inspectors might wince with a sense of bitter recognition at Schwan and Shapiro's references to norm-defining groups which are 'hard to see or comfortably know' – or to that post-inspection interrogation of the self which too often marks a collapse of professional self-confidence. Small wonder, therefore, that the entire edited book, of which Page's chapter is one of thirteen, represents a sustained protest against the 'graded lesson observation' schemes which, for 'almost a quarter of a century' within the English system, (Pearson, 2017: 152) have 'come to be used as a means of exercising power and control over what teachers do and how their professional worth is evaluated and subsequently valued' (O'Leary, 2017: 2).

It is important to bear this in mind before asking to observe a teacher at work in the classroom. A seemingly straightforward request to engage in an unproblematic example of what Bronfenbrenner might call an 'observational dyad' (see Chapter 5) could be interpreted differently by teachers, especially if they have been scarred by the way that adjectives like 'hierarchical' and 'graded' have been linked to the noun 'observation' – sometimes with significant professional consequences. Part of the problem is that, as Wragg observes – and as was discussed in Chapters 3 and 7 – such judgements are so 'highly subjective' as to call into question the validity of the whole process:

> Classroom observers seen to have a single fixed stereotype of what is 'good' may be met with scorn or contempt if [the views expressed] are out of harmony with those of the teacher being observed, or with fear and apprehension if [the observers] are thought to be in a position of power and influence.
>
> (1994: 103, 54)

On page 34 of Chapter 2, I tried to alert trainee teachers to the likelihood of their teaching performance being allocated a grade or a bluntly evaluative category. 'The act of teaching', Wragg points out, 'is inseparable from the whole person and to attack the one is to demolish the other' (1994: 91). Despite the sensitivity which informs this quotation, even Wragg is not immune from the temptation to conflate judgements about teaching ability and personality. He recalls how his teacher-training colleagues would use a five-point grading system based on the alphabet when assessing their trainees, with C+ representing 'some honest plodder who was conscientious but not too stimulating' (1994: 34). How would you feel if it were your efforts and your personality which were labelled in this way? Nor do the pressures imposed by graded observations end here. Page quotes a teacher's response to the news that government inspectors working within the English monitoring system had decided to change the criterion for a Grade 3 from 'satisfactory' to 'needs improvement':

> I think [grading] is really bad. Before, if you got a grade three, you felt fine about that; you would prefer better, but it was ok to get a three. Now, it's not ok to get a three, it's like getting a grade four now, isn't it? Really, you're aiming for a two now ... If somebody gets a three or four, all of a sudden they've no confidence. They don't want to go to lessons. They think they are failing their students.

For Page, the concerns expressed above are a graphic illustration of Foucault's concept of 'normalising judgement'. The criteria associated with a 'normal' teacher (2017: 67) have suddenly – for some reason probably unknown to the interviewee – become more demanding, leaving her scrambling in vain pursuit of those 'highest levels' which, Wragg suggests, 'can be such that even gifted teachers may pale at the thought of trying to achieve them, and all of us feel guilty when we do not attain them' (1994: 103). Clearly, pupils are not the only members of the school community subjected to deficit models of education. Being allocated a grade at those 'highest levels' brings its own problems. It would be a rare teacher indeed who, day after day, lesson after lesson, was able to sustain that standard of achievement. It is not hard to imagine the kind of pressure an observation (of any kind, never mind one undertaken by an official inspector) would impose on such a teacher – no less than on Page's interviewee desperate to be regarded as 'normal'. In the words of another of Page's research participants: 'You set yourself standards and once you get a grade one you can't get any higher. The only way is down' (2017: 66).

There is a world of difference, of course, between a trainee's request to observe a teacher's lesson and a government inspector's demand to do the same. Teachers are mature professionals; they understand this. Nevertheless, making judgements and comparisons is something that human beings do throughout their daily lives – and, as Bethan Marshall pointed out in Chapter 7, people who are 'good at' English probably do it even more. Even the most determinedly neutral classroom observers cannot fail to form an evaluative opinion about what they see – in fact, if an observing trainee emerged from such an 'observational dyad' with no informed comments to make about what they had experienced, one would seriously question whether the teaching profession was right for them. We need, however, to bear in mind Shulman's suggestion that classroom teaching is – and I apologise for not sharing this earlier in the book – 'perhaps the most complex, most challenging, and most demanding, subtle, nuanced, and frightening activity that our species has ever invented' (2004: 258). Observing and commenting upon the practice of the people who engage in such a 'frightening activity' needs to be conducted with professionalism, empathy and sensitivity, so that the 'territory of the classroom' is seen as a 'rich and informative learning environment rather than a replication of the inspection arena' (Taylor, 2017: 20). Bronfenbrenner argues that it is impossible to understand behaviour 'solely from the objective properties of an environment without reference to its meaning for the people in the setting' (1981: 24). A first step towards transforming an 'observational' into a 'joint activity dyad' of the kind Taylor might welcome is to try to imagine how *we* would feel if *we* were to be observed and evaluated.

## OVER TO YOU

## Activity 4

There are numerous examples on television and social media of individuals – from aspiring dancers to chefs to entrepreneurs – attempting some act of skill under the critical gaze of a panel of expert judges who then provide feedback.

- Choose one or more of these examples to watch. Consider body language as well as what is said. How do the contestants behave under scrutiny? Does their behaviour suggest a sense of inhibition or excitement? Do the contestants 'play it safe' in an effort to give the judges what they think will please them; or do they attempt a 'high risk' approach which will either succeed or fail spectacularly?
- How do the judges respond? What feedback do they provide and how do they deliver it? Are the judges unanimous in their verdicts or is there disagreement? If there is, how are these differences of opinion resolved?
- How do the contestants respond to the feedback they receive?

## Activity 5

Your turn now.

- Choose a trusted critical friend and ask them to observe you attempt-ing an activity which requires skill and with which both you and your critical friend feel familiar enough to provide informed feed-back – examples might include a sports activity, cooking, a singing audition, 'do it yourself', an acting performance, a piece of writing and so on.
- Perform the activity for your critical friend and ask them to give you feedback.
- How did you feel about the way the feedback was delivered? Why did you feel like this?
- Was the feedback useful? Will it change the way you practise the skill in question? Why or why not?

## Activity 6

- Rerun Activity 5; but this time, reverse the roles. If your partner chooses an activity different from yours, how, if at all, does this affect the way you observe and the feedback you provide?
- Compare your responses to the questions with those of your partner.
- Use the information arising from your discussion to construct, together if possible, a list of key principles which need to be borne in mind when observing and evaluating or giving and receiving feedback on an activity.
- How appropriate would your list be in a school context? Does it need adjusting or refining in any way? If so, how and why?

## Section 4: locating the school community within its context

Towards the end of the last section, I brought Bronfenbrenner back into the discussion in order to emphasise again just how crucial it is for educationalists, of all people, to consider that 'what matters for behaviour and development is the environment as it is *perceived* [original italics] rather than as it may exist in "objective" reality' (1981: 4). This is as true for teachers and trainee teachers as it is for pupils. I want to cite Bronfenbrenner once more to suggest a link between that quotation and a second key point he makes about another core concept which has featured throughout the book: the importance of appreciating context. Bronfenbrenner writes:

> [T]he environment defined as relevant to developmental processes is not limited to a single, immediate setting but is extended to incorporate interconnections between such settings, as well as to external influences emanating from the larger surroundings.

Thinking in terms of Bronfenbrenner's conception of the '*ecological environment*' [original italics] as 'a nested arrangement of concentric structures, each contained within the next' (1981: 22), I want to continue our preparation for school observations by 'zooming out', as it were, from the 'dyad', the 'basic building block of the microsystem', to consider how the school as a community is situated within the outer rings of mesosystem and exosystem (see pages 75 and 81–82 of Chapter 5 for a reminder of how Bronfenbrenner defines these terms).

Chapters 4, 5 and 6, particularly, have explored the ways in which exosystemic influences such as curricular and other educational policy initiatives might influence your experience and behaviour as a teacher (and Chapter 10 will revisit the issue); so I want here to focus on the mesosystem and consider how a school community might be situated within its immediate social setting.

## OVER TO YOU

### Activity 7

At the click of a mouse, we can discover a wealth of information – ranging from household income to house prices to crime statistics – about the communities which our schools serve.

- What statistical information can online research provide about the community served by the school you wish to visit?
- How might this information help to inform your thinking about the content of the English curriculum and the way that you might teach it?

### A worked example

Table 8.6 shows some examples of the kinds of statistical information which could be collected for two communities, X and Y. They lie some ten miles apart from each other. I have chosen to compare two communities because I want to encourage you to think about the sometimes dramatic differences in quality of life and opportunity which can exist between people living in geographical proximity. I have fictionalised the communities; but the data presented is compatible with that which can be found in the statistical profiles of many English towns and cities today.

How did my selection of statistical categories compare with yours? Some of my choices might seem more obvious than others. Information about first language use is clearly extremely important to teachers of English; but so also, I would argue, are the statistics about religious faith, not least because they serve to sharpen the focus upon those questions regarding the purpose, content and ownership of the English curriculum which have been explored throughout the book, particularly in Chapter 6. Clearly, too, it helps to have information about the size of the potential school population; but what about those statistics regarding family backgrounds? Is that intrusive – or does it remind us as teachers not to make assumptions and to be sensitively attuned to the habitus of individual pupils, particularly if we might wish to explore with them the personal growth model (page 90 and 95, Chapter 6) of English?

Table 8.6 Statistical information for two contrasting communities

| Topic | Community X | Community Y |
| --- | --- | --- |
| Total population | 19,900 | 14,790 |
| Percentage aged 0–17 years | 30% | 21% |
| Main first language spoken (as a percentage of the population) | 56% English | 99% English |
| Main occupation | 21% jobs requiring basic skills only | 61% managers, professionals and associate professionals |
| Main religion | 67% Muslim | 67% Christian |
| Couple with children | 25% | 22% |
| Single parent with children | 9% | 5% |
| Average yearly household income | £19,000 | £38,000 |
| Average property price | £64,000 | £382,000 |
| Domestic gardens and green spaces | 27% | 79% |
| Number of reported crimes per 1000 people | 442 | 49 |

I have included statistical information about the employment and the financial profiles of the two communities because, as a teacher, I find Bourdieu's account of 'cultural capital' (Chapter 5) helpful. In fact, for me, that particular data set gets to the heart of the matter. What do I hope to achieve by teaching English? Is my task to 'drum into' my pupils – to borrow Althusser's metaphor from page 65 – 'a certain amount of "know-how" wrapped in the ruling ideology' so that they learn to conform to the current social status quo? Or is my task to focus on a cultural analysis model (pages 97–98, Chapter 6) of English, in order to expose the weaknesses and injustices of the current system with the intention of sweeping them away? In Section 1 of Chapter 6, I described the success criteria for my particular vision of English pedagogy. Should I have the same set of expectations for pupils from both communities X and Y? Or should I tailor my curriculum provision to match the communities' economic profiles? I remember a fifteen-year-old pupil telling me once that he saw no purpose in studying the poetry of Alfred, Lord Tennyson – a topic for his class that term – because he had a job lined up on his uncle's building site. Does he have a point? On page 102 of Chapter 6, I quoted Kress's uncomfortable question: 'How many school-leavers will be called on to become "creative" users of language?' Should we, as Kress suggests, 'reset the aims of language education more modestly'? Bluntly: is my task ultimately to shut my ears to Althusser's silent music? Must I resign myself to helping the pupils of community X attain jobs requiring only 'basic skills', and the pupils of community Y to move into the professions? I am being deliberately provocative here; but I hope you can see how a consideration of Table 8.6 above has thrown into sharp relief again so many of the core ethical, ideological and pedagogic issues explored throughout the book.

Why have I included statistics about domestic gardens and green spaces in my table? Part of the reason for their selection is due to my reading of a book, first published in 2010, called *Teaching Secondary English as if the Planet Matters*. The author, Sasha Matthewman, argues that 'English has a powerful part to play in responding to the environmental issues that face us in the twenty-first century'. Whether describing, for example, how pupils can be encouraged to write about links between landscape and identity, or to take Coleridge's *Rime of the Ancient Mariner* as a starting point for exploring how the image of the albatross has become 'one of the most potent symbols of man's wanton destruction of nature', or to consider how 'clear air' can be perceived as 'a trope of health and heaven' in Shakespeare's *Macbeth*, Matthewman argues that different models of the English curriculum can provide imaginative opportunities for engagement with this most pressing of contemporary concerns (2011: 1, 11, 13). Knowledge about the host community's access to gardens and green spaces can help me to gain some appreciation of the interplay between the natural and man-made world in my pupils' lives and thus attempt, at the very least, to tailor my teaching of environmental issues appropriately.

While working on this section of the chapter, I happened to come across a school's mission statement. It reads: 'Every child deserves to be happy, safe and successful'. Thinking about these words in terms of Bronfenbrenner's outer or macrosystemic circle, (Chapter 5, page 78) none of us is going to be happy, safe or successful if we do not attend, as a world community, to the issues so graphically described by Matthewman. However, for me as a teacher of English operating within the mesosystem of a school located within a particular community, statistics about gardens and green spaces also matter because that information helps to focus my attention on the psychological and physical wellbeing of the pupils I teach. Do they breathe unpolluted air? Can they hear natural as opposed to man-made sounds? Do they have access to traffic-free spaces where they can play and – an activity beloved of adolescents – just be together away from adult surveillance? The figures in Table 8.6 suggest that here, as elsewhere, the pupils attending schools in Community X have a harder time of it than their counterparts in Community Y – and when the crime statistics are taken into account, the differences in quality of life become all the more stark.

These statistics matter. A recent report published by Public Health England makes disturbing reading in this context. It suggests that approximately 695,000 children aged between five and sixteen in England – the country in which Communities X and Y are located – 'have a clinically significant mental health illness', the main manifestations of which are 'conduct disorder', 'anxiety', 'depression' and 'attention deficit hyperactivity disorder'. Equally concerning is the information that approximately one in seven fifteen-year-olds in England 'reports low life satisfaction'. Particularly pertinent to pupils attending schools in Community X is the knowledge that young people from the most socially disadvantaged sectors of society, as well as those from Black and Asian communities, report the highest levels of 'low life satisfaction'. There are significant regional variations in the figures. London has the highest level of reported 'low life satisfaction' (15.5%) while the North East, Yorkshire and the Humber have the lowest (at 13.1%, still far too high) – something again to bear in mind when considering that Communities X and Y are just over ten miles apart (2016: 12, 11, 11).

Contemplating these bleak statistics reminds me that our word *school* comes from the Ancient Greek *skhole* which can be translated somewhat surprisingly as: 'spare time, leisure, rest, ease; idleness; that in which leisure is employed; learned discussion' (*Online Etymology Dictionary*). Seeking an explanation for the seemingly improbable links between the words *school* and *leisure*, I turned to Abraham Maslow's ground breaking paper, *A Theory of Human Motivation*. Two quotes come particularly to mind: 'For the man who is extremely and dangerously hungry, no other interests exist but food'; and: 'Practically everything looks less important than safety' (1943: 374, 376). Maslow argues that it is only when our basic 'physiological' and 'safety' needs have been met that we can become, in Guditus' telling phrase (2013), 'available for learning'. Maslow writes:

> The healthy, normal, fortunate adult in our culture is largely satisfied in his safety needs. The peaceful, smoothly running, 'good' society ordinarily makes its members feel safe enough from wild animals, extremes of temperature, criminals, assault and murder, tyranny, etc.

Children especially, he continues, need the world to be 'predicable' and 'orderly'. They feel 'anxious and unsafe' if 'injustice, unfairness, or inconsistency' threaten that sense of order (1943: 378–379, 377). A *school* – and indeed an English classroom – becomes a *skhole* when it creates a safe space in which pupils feel sufficiently relaxed and *at leisure* to concentrate on acquiring the civilising knowledge, understanding and behaviours essential to Maslow's 'good' society.

Reflecting on Bronfenbrenner's image of the 'three-legged stool' (page 79, Chapter 5) I suggested that teachers of English are 'gatekeepers to culture, to life chances, to emotional wellbeing'. Contemplating the human stories which lie behind the statistical information available about the communities our schools serve, must help us to look with compassion and increased understanding at the *individual* pupils who troop through our classroom doors. All, except for a very unfortunate few, will be infinitely precious to somebody – a carer, a sibling, a relative, a friend. As English teachers especially, we must learn from this experience to be particularly mindful about what we choose (perhaps *need* is a more appropriate word) to talk, read and write about in our lessons and why we choose to do it.

## OVER TO YOU

### Activity 8

* With the information provided by the worked example in mind, review your responses to the activities undertaken for Chapter 5. Focus particularly on Section 3, Activity 1 (page 79). Do the views you expressed there still hold good; or have they been changed in any way?
* Focus again now on the particular school you wish to visit. What information about the school can you glean from its website? How does the school seek to present itself?
* Read what online reports you can find about the perceived 'health' of your chosen school and of its relationships with the community it serves. (If your school is in England, you could start, for example, by reading its latest Ofsted report.)
* Review the work you undertook for Activities 1 to 3 of this chapter in the light of the additional information gleaned from the tasks undertaken for Activity 8. Is there anything you might now want to change about your wish lists or your dealings with staff and pupils? If there is, say what you would change and why.

## Section 5: lesson observation – reclaiming the territory

The title of the 2017 text from which I quoted in Section 3 of this chapter is *Reclaiming Lesson Observation: Supporting Excellence in Teacher Learning.*

All the words in the title have been selected carefully; but the choice of that opening present participle is particularly significant. The intention of the authors is to reclaim those sites of education which, forty years previously, Foucault suggested had been colonised by the powerful so that they could create an 'apparatus of observation, recording and training' that would enable a 'single gaze to see everything constantly' (1977: 173). If 'vision' for Foucault has become 'the medium through which our actions can be constantly judged' (Schwan and Shapiro, 2011: 118), then other senses must be foregrounded to contest its potentially malign influence upon teacher and lesson observation. Martin, for example, proposes *hearing* as a counterbalance to *seeing*. She argues that 'an intuitive depth of listening and empathic use of silence' should form an essential element of any 'conversation' between observer and observed (2017: 108). Foucault regards 'schoolrooms with doors that allow for passing teachers to look in at the classroom at any time' (Schwan and Shapiro, 2011: 115) as a particularly potent example of how observation can be used to 'make people docile and knowable' (Foucault, 1977: 172). An understandable response would be for teachers to shut their doors – literally and metaphorically – against this perceived threat in a display of 'institutional guardedness' (Challis-Manning and Thorpe, 2017: 38). The authors of *Reclaiming Lesson Observation*, however, regard the open classroom door as a metaphor for professional enhancement. Stevens, for example, describes an initiative in which teachers established something which might have seemed abhorrent to Foucault – an 'observation classroom' complete with soundproofed viewing area where colleagues could watch and comment on each other's lessons. She notes:

> At first, most teachers used it [the observation classroom] mainly to record themselves teaching, which they then watched in their own time. Since then, it has taken on a more communal focus and [it] has become much more commonplace for staff to observe their peers teaching live.
>
> (2017: 144)

Foucault regards the act of recording information about teacher activity as a manifestation of 'the micro-economy of a perpetual penalty' (1977: 181). The 'apparatus of writing' transforms the individual into 'a case' that 'has to be trained or corrected, classified, normalised, excluded' (190, 191). Here again, O'Leary and his fellow authors attempt to reclaim the territory. Haines and Miller, for example, describe how *Video Enhanced Observation* (VEO), far from being a surveillance tool, can instead provide fruitful opportunities for 'continuous review, reflection, sharing and discussion' by tagging 'key moments' in a lesson and exploring the pupils' perspective on what is happening in the classroom (2017: 139, 135).

What gives such potency to this fightback against the dystopian world of control envisioned by Foucault is the fact that it is informed by one key principle: lesson observation should be a *'doing with'* rather than a *'doing to'* [original italics] (Taylor, 2017: 21). To put it another way: the prefix *per* needs to be detached from the word *formative* so that the person being observed no longer feels they have to give a special, high stakes 'performance' and the observer no longer feels they have to pronounce a possibly career-changing judgement on what they see. With a flurry of acronyms, the authors of *Reclaiming Lesson Observation* present a series of alternative, dialogic, non-judgemental approaches – from LEAP (Learning, Engagement, Attributes and Progress) (Taylor) to CHAT (Cultural Historical Activity Theory) (Lahiff) to QFF (Questions, Favourites, Feelings) (Stevens) to – a particular mouthful – GROW (Goal setting, Reality checking, Obstacles, Options and alternative strategies, What is to be done, When, and by Whom) (Martin). No matter what the acronym, all these approaches to lesson observation share the same deeply held belief that teachers must not be dismissed – to borrow again Bandura's phrase from Chapter 2 – as 'neurophysiological computational machines' who will, when left to their own devices without regular surveillance, underperform or worse. If treated as professionals, the counter-argument runs, teachers will respond *as* professionals, demonstrating a capacity to reflect upon and develop their practice with all the 'forethought' and 'perseverance' which Bandura regards as the essential qualities associated with personal agency. Thus, the approaches advocated by O'Leary and his fellow authors describe ways in which observer and observed might sit down together and engage in a reflective, professional and mutually informative dialogue which is focussed, not on the personal qualities of the teacher observed, but on the actual and potential learning opportunities which arose in the lesson under discussion.

## OVER TO YOU

### Activity 9

'When the observation process is taken for granted it is assumed that observation "just happens". In other words that it is just a matter of watching what takes place' (Lahiff, 2017: 53). By this stage of the chapter, it should be clear to you that when an experienced teacher educator like Ann Lahiff makes a statement like this, she intends her readers to raise a quizzical eyebrow.

- Look again at the activities you undertook for Sections 1–3 of this chapter and for the final bullet point of Activity 8. In the light of your reading of Section 5, are there any final adjustments you wish to make to your observation agenda and wish list?
- No matter how educational policy towards teachers in post might change, the fact remains that you, as a trainee, will be subjected to some kind of grading system which determines whether you pass or fail your training course. Consider how, in the light of your reading of Section 4 particularly, you might prepare yourself psychologically for the experience of summative, evaluative grading.

## Note

1 I have deliberately left out professional knowledge here, for reasons which will be explained later.

# Chapter 9

# Classroom observation
## The practicalities

## Section 1: quantitative observation methods

Although it is now over twenty years old, Ted Wragg's *An Introduction to Classroom Observation* remains one of the most accessible and comprehensive texts on the subject and I recommend that you get hold of a copy if you can. Wragg characterises two basic approaches to classroom observation: 'part-learning' at one extreme and 'holistic' at the other:

> The extreme part-learning stance is taken by some supporters of competency-based teacher education who believe that the teaching can be atomised into hundreds of discrete mini-acts which can be systematically learned and appraised, and the extreme holistic stance is adopted by those who contend that teaching is an art, and to seek to segment it, is to destroy it.
>
> (1994: 134)

The training system currently operating in England is a 'competency-based' model. That is the model cited most often throughout the book; and at this point, it might be worth rereading Section 1 of Chapter 3, where I describe the kinds of classroom activities and behaviours an observer might look for when trying to compile, for example, evidence for Standard 7.

## OVER TO YOU

### Activity 1

• Reread Sections 1 and 2 of Chapter 3, focussing particularly on my two worked examples and on your responses to Activities 3 to 7. Remind yourself of what you learned there about the opportunities and challenges posed by competence-based assessment in general.

- Look at Table 9.1 below. See also Chapter 3 pages 47 to 49.
- What evidence for successful practice would it be possible (and not possible) to collect from a lesson observation? (Assume that this is not the teacher's first lesson with this class.)
- What kind of activities would the observer need to engage in to collect this evidence?

### A worked example

Let us consider first what evidence could be collected during a lesson observation and how we might collect it. We cannot find evidence to address the content of the first sentence in Table 9.1, because this is not the teacher's first lesson with the class (one more instance of that vital contextual information we need to collect before we attempt an observation). Here is a list of the examples of 'successful practice' which I feel would be relatively straightforward to identify:

- A list of behaviour rules is prominently displayed on a classroom wall.
- Clear guidelines regarding key routines are established . . . for example, entering and exiting the classroom; taking the register . . . setting and collecting homework.
- Potential disruption is dealt with quickly before it can develop.
- Transitions between lesson activities take place smoothly and efficiently.

*Table 9.1* Identifying successful practice: a second look

| Criterion | What successful practice might look like |
| --- | --- |
| *Have clear rules and routines for behaviour in classrooms* | When first meeting the class, teacher explains clearly and authoritatively what is expected from the pupils in terms of behaviour. These expectations are reinforced – and respected – in this and subsequent lessons. A list of behaviour rules is prominently displayed on a classroom wall and referred to by the teacher and pupils as appropriate. Clear guidelines regarding key routines are established from the start: for example, entering and exiting the classroom; taking the register; managing talk; setting and collecting homework. A cheerful, well-ordered and working atmosphere prevails throughout lessons. Potential disruption is dealt with quickly before it can develop. Transitions between lesson activities take place smoothly and efficiently. |

*Quantitative analysis: a useful observational tool?*

An observer could tell at a glance whether a list of behaviour rules is displayed on the classroom wall. Similarly, it is fairly easy to see whether pupils enter and exit a room in an orderly fashion, or whether the register is taken or whether homework is set and collected. These are all cases where *quantitative analysis* might play a useful part in lesson observation. An observer could come into the classroom equipped with a pre-prepared ticklist and simply note whether the activity had or had not taken place. In Table 9.2, I am imagining that I am observing a lesson which starts at 9:00 a.m. and lasts for an hour.

*Table 9.2* Collecting quantitative evidence: an observation checklist

| Example of successful practice | Identified | Time |
|---|---|---|
| A list of behaviour rules is prominently displayed on a classroom wall. | ✓ | Not applicable |
| Clear guidelines regarding key routines are established . . . for example, entering the classroom. | ✓ | 9:05 |
| Clear guidelines regarding key routines are established . . . for example . . . taking the register. | ✓ | 9:08 |
| Clear guidelines regarding key routines are established . . . for example . . . collecting homework. | ✓ | 9:15 |
| Clear guidelines regarding key routines are established from the start: for example . . . setting . . . homework. | ✓ | 9:56 |
| [Behaviour] expectations are reinforced – and respected – in this [lesson]. | ✓ | 9:12 |
| | ✓ | 9:32 |
| | ✓ | 9:46 |
| | ✗ | 9:50 |
| | ✓ | 9:57 |
| Potential disruption is dealt with quickly before it can develop. | ✓ | 9:44 |
| | ✗ | 9:50 |
| Transitions between lesson activities take place smoothly and efficiently. | ✓ | 9:17 |
| | ✓ | 9:34 |
| | ✗ | 9:50 |
| Clear guidelines regarding key routines are established . . . for example . . . exiting the classroom. | ✓ | 10:04 |

This ticklist might seem like a blunt instrument; but, especially when a *Time* column is added, it can actually provide some useful pointers to what is happening in the lesson and to how well the teacher has implemented the 'guidelines' mentioned in the checklist as a key indicator of successful practice. For example: if the lesson is meant to start at 9:00 a.m., why did the pupils not enter the room until 9:05? Once the pupils were in the room, the register appears to have been taken and homework collected in a timely fashion – which again suggests that 'guidelines' have been explained clearly and then adhered to by the pupils. 'Transitions' – where the teacher signals a move to a new phase of the lesson – seem to have been managed well in two out of three recorded instances. But what was happening at 9:56? Setting homework with only four minutes to go does not look like effective practice. Three sets of checklist data appear to *triangulate* a critical incident of some kind which occurred at 9:50 and had significant negative consequences for the rest of the lesson. It is relatively straightforward to identify instances where the teacher reinforces behaviour rules – and whether the pupils appear to 'respect' those rules or not. Keeping a checklist of the number of times reminders had to be issued is therefore a feasible use of quantitative observation strategies. It can also, in this instance, help to provide a quick overview of the 'general health' of the lesson. The fact that only five reminders about behavioural expectations were delivered in the course of an hour – and that only two instances of 'potential disruption' seem to have occurred – appears at first glance quite promising. At 9:50, however, an act of potential disruption was not successfully checked and this prompted the teacher to issue a reminder which was, as my use of crosses on the checklist indicates, also not 'respected' for some reason. The situation seems to have been restored seven minutes later; but could the 9:50 incident provide a clue as to why homework was set so late and, as a 'knock-on' effect, why the pupils were only dismissed four minutes after the lesson was meant to have ended?

As I imagine you will already have begun to suspect from your refresher work for Activity 1 above, there are limits to the information quantitative data can offer an observer. There may, for example, be positive or negative reasons for the pupils' late entrance into the classroom. Perhaps the teacher was demonstrating her firm management skills by refusing to let the class enter until everyone had shown him or her self to be, as Guditus put it in Chapter 8, 'available for learning'. On the other hand, the pupils may have been late to class because the teacher was having trouble getting them to behave and to listen to her instructions. Again, as currently constituted, Table 9.2 does not tell the reader what strategies the teacher used to reinforce behavioural expectations. Were the reminders always verbal? Perhaps on occasions body language was used instead: a finger placed to the lips to indicate silence, perhaps, or the shake of a head to indicate disapproval.

The instances where I have used quantitative observation techniques in the chart above have all been focussed upon particular, clearly identifiable moments within a lesson: entrance into and exit from the room, for example, or an occasion where the teacher has to say or do something to reinforce behaviour. There are two examples from the worked example extract, however, where successful practice cannot be so easily isolated and identified because their presence is, or should be, a constant throughout the lesson: the 'management of talk' (recall the discussion about this term in Chapter 7) and the maintenance of a 'cheerful, well-ordered and working atmosphere'.

Would it be possible to construct a serviceable, quantitatively focussed table to identify and record useful information about the management of talk? First of all, I would want to classify the *kinds* of talk which might be observed in a classroom. There is a clear difference between the language a teacher might use when issuing a reprimand and the language they might use when encouraging a pupil lacking in confidence to make a contribution in class. Then, I would want to think about one of the cornerstones of every teacher's practice which we explored in Chapter 7 – the use of questioning. What kinds of questions are asked? *Lower order* questions testing factual recall (*What is the date of the Battle of Hastings?*) or *higher order* questions designed to stimulate thinking (*Why did King Harold lose the Battle of Hastings?*)? Who gets to answer the questions and why? Different individuals? The same particularly enthusiastic pupil again and again? Pairs or small groups of pupils? Taking this point further, I would want to know who speaks throughout the lesson as a whole and for how long. What is the balance between teacher and pupil talk and listening? Bearing in mind Shulman's comment (quoted on page 108 of Chapter 6) about 'the set of rules for determining what is legitimate to say in a disciplinary domain and what "breaks" the rules', I would want to note what kinds of discourse are permitted in the classroom, particularly the *English* classroom.

I have made an attempt to construct such quantitative observational tables (9.3 and 9.4 below). There are a number of contextual points to add so you can see how I might use them. Consulting a class register, I would assign a letter and a number to each pupil in the class – *B1* for the first boy on the register, *G1* for the first girl, and so on. I would use *P* for *pair*, *SG* for *small group* and *WC* for *whole class* interactions (and again, I could classify these groupings by gender: BP1, GP1, BSG1, or *MG 1* for *mixed group*). Every time the teacher addressed a particular individual, for example, I might write *B1* or *G1* (or whatever the number happened to be) in the *Individuals* column. You get the idea. I have identified six types of questions in an attempt to distinguish between lower and higher order examples – the allocation of just a single row to such an important element of classroom practice would be so broad as to be virtually useless.

The row titled *Use of metalanguage* is particularly important. It gestures towards another of those characteristics of powerful learning environments identified by Eric De Corte (see also Chapter 1, pages 13, 15, 20): effective learners know how to use the technical language associated with their chosen discipline. I want to get some sense of how often teachers and pupils engage with metalinguistic terminology during the course of the lesson. (For example, if I were observing an English lesson on poetry, I might be looking out for instances of the use of words like *verse*, *rhyme*, *rhythm*, *imagery*, *tone*, *diction*.)

Thinking in terms of Bronfenbrenner's classifications again, I would hope that a classroom is a site in which *joint activity*, not merely *observation*, dyads exist. I would hope to see plentiful examples of *reciprocity* taking place in a multiplicity of dyads – dyads established between teacher, individual, pair and small groups of pupils, as well as the dyad established between the teacher and the class as a whole. Finally and – bearing in mind the quotation from Martin on page 164 of Chapter 8 perhaps most

*Table 9.3* Talking and listening: a teacher checklist

| Type of talk | Whole class | Pairs or small groups | Individuals |
|---|---|---|---|
| Relationship building | | | |
| Managing behaviour | | | |
| Lecturing | | | |
| Discussion | | | |
| Reprimanding | | | |
| Use of metalanguage | | | |
| *What* questions | | | |
| *When* questions | | | |
| *Who* questions | | | |
| *Where* questions | | | |
| *Why* questions | | | |
| *How* questions | | | |
| Listening | | | |

*Table 9.4* Talking and listening: a pupil checklist

| Type of talk | Whole class | Pairs or small groups | Individuals |
|---|---|---|---|
| Relationship building | | | |
| Managing behaviour | | | |
| Lecturing | | | |
| Discussion | | | |
| Reprimanding | | | |
| Use of metalanguage | | | |
| *What* questions | | | |
| *When* questions | | | |
| *Who* questions | | | |
| *Where* questions | | | |
| *Why* questions | | | |
| *How* questions | | | |
| Listening | | | |

importantly – I want to know what *listening* takes place in a lesson, why it takes place and who listens to whom. Mapping and comparing the pupils' and the teacher's activities against the same headings is especially important and illuminating, not least because it helps the observer get a sense of whether or not the joint activity dyad of the lesson is actually, as the quotation from Bronfenbrenner on page 76 of Chapter 5 put it, 'effecting a gradual transfer of power' from teacher to pupils so that the latter take more and more responsibility for their behaviour and their learning.

## OVER TO YOU

## Activity 2

- Review your response to Activities 4–6 of Chapter 8 so they are fresh in your mind.
- Invite a group of friends round for a social evening. The deal is that you will provide the hospitality if they will agree to help you test the usefulness of my talking and listening observation table.
- One of your friends is to teach something to the rest of the group while you observe and use the checklist to note the interactions between teacher and taught. The 'lesson content' should be fun and should not

take more than ten minutes – or at least long enough for you to gain a reasonable impression about whether the table is practical and useful or not. The 'lesson' should also be substantial enough for you to be able to test the relevance of the categories I have suggested, including the metalanguage category (what metalanguage, for example, might be needed for a first lesson in how to play the guitar?).

- Before the 'lesson' – or even perhaps the social evening – starts, consider what contextual information should be shared between you, the 'teacher' and the 'pupils'. Here are some prompt questions to guide you:

    o Are you clear in your own mind what each of the checklist categories means and about how you will identify examples of that particular behaviour or activity?

    o Should you let the 'teacher' and/or the 'pupils' discuss the table and its categories with you before the 'lesson' or not? Do you need to take into account the so-called Hawthorne Effect – 'the theory that when people in their natural surroundings are aware of being observed, their behaviour alters' (Page, 2017: 67)?

    o Are there any measures you can take to encourage 'teacher' and 'pupils' to behave as if 'in their natural surroundings' – even though they are being observed by someone with a checklist?

## Activity 3

- Observe the 'lesson' – or more than one, if your friends are willing.
- Evaluate the checklist forms. The following questions might prove useful:

    o Is the checklist practical?

    o Are the categories relevant? Do any need changing, replacing or removing?

    o Would it be possible to use a checklist like this for a 'real' school lesson – perhaps one lasting forty minutes or even longer?

    o If the answer to the previous question is 'no', and you decided to use the checklist selectively, for a short burst of time, what might be the crucial points in a lesson that you would wish to focus on and why?

    o Were there important aspects of the lesson which the checklist was not able to capture?

    o How did the pupils' and the teacher's responses compare? Share and discuss the two checklists with the participants. Should pupils and teachers have separate checklists, rather than sharing the same categories as here?

    o Based on your experiences, does quantitative data collection have a place in lesson observations or not?

## Activity 4

- If you feel that quantitative data analysis does have a useful part to play in lesson observation, devise a checklist for either a reading or a writing lesson. If you have the time to create a checklist for both, so much the better.
- What categories might remain the same? What, if any, new categories might you include?

## Section 2: qualitative observation methods

### Lesson observation: a holistic approach

I should now come clean and say that, as someone who has observed hundreds of lessons over the past twenty-five years, I incline more to Wragg's 'holistic' as opposed to the 'part-learning stance'. When I observe in the classroom I – like many of my colleagues, according to Wragg (1994: 65) – write a narrative account of what I see. (Having learned to touch-type at evening classes over forty years ago has proved to be one of the most enduring transferable skills I ever acquired.)

Here is the opening section of a typical lesson narrative. The complete account is six pages long. In terms of contextual information, what I want to tell you for the moment is that the extract describes the first ten minutes of a lesson scheduled to begin at 11:50. The lesson opens with the teacher settling the class with a 'starter' activity. The pupils are required to study a quotation projected onto the classroom screen (a quotation, interestingly enough, from our old friend *Frankenstein* which seems to be a teacher favourite at the moment) and to note down any words in the quotation which strike them as interesting or unusual. To provide differentiated support, the pupils have been given individual copies of what the teacher refers to in the extract as a *word cloud* – a cluster of key words from the extract. They also have pens and white-boards on which to jot down their answers. The aim of the starter activity is to help the pupils to begin to engage with the tropes associated with the horror genre. The extract concludes as the teacher begins to initiate discussion of that topic.

The class consists of approximately equal numbers of boys and girls aged eleven and of mixed ability. The lesson takes place towards the end of the pupils' first term in secondary school. Pupil B1 has significant reading difficulties and has been assigned the support of a teaching assistant. In my account, the letter *T* stands for *Teacher*. I have used the labelling system described in the previous section on quantitative data collection to code the pupils mentioned in the extract. Words spoken by the teacher are in italics. My comments on what I see – sometimes written as a reminder for myself and sometimes addressed directly to the teacher who is the sole audience of this particular narrative text – are placed in brackets. Factual statements about what I witnessed during the lesson are in regular font.

---

11:50

T greets the class at the door.

Computer has logged off – which is difficult for T.

T has to wait for it to come on again (she keeps calm!).

T: *All you need at the moment is a whiteboard, a whiteboard pen and a word cloud.*

T reminds the class that this is an independent task: the only person they should talk to is a teacher – (good attempt to encourage independent learning).

T reminds the class that she will write on the board the name of anyone who misbehaves and that these pupils will have to *wow her* to get their names removed. She will also write up the names of those who misbehaved in the previous lesson, so that they have a chance to 'redeem' themselves.

11:55

T repeats the demand for silence.

T: *Thank you, much better.*

T deals with logistical issues patiently.

11:56

Register taken – *good morning!* (A pleasant and polite way of starting the lesson.)

T: *You have thirty more seconds to think about the word cloud.* (But I wonder if the instruction to 'think about' something is a bit vague for pupils of this age and range of abilities.)

(You have constructed useful power point slides for the class. I think you need to make more explicit reference to the information on them. For example, the instructions for the task are clearly set out and the pupils should be encouraged to refer to them if they need reminding of what they are meant to be doing. It would also be useful to invite a pupil to read the instructions on the slide, to check that everyone has understood what they have to do.)

11:59

T now puts on the board the names of pupils who misbehaved in the previous lesson.

T: *Pupil B1, which word were you drawn to and why? Have a look – you have written loads.* (Interestingly, Pupil B1 is confused by the use of the metaphor 'drawn' and thinks you have asked him to *draw* something. Much of his 'writing' was transcribed by the teaching assistant.)

Pupil B2 is invited to help B1 explain why the choice of the word 'work' from the *Frankenstein* slide and word cloud might be significant.

Pupil B3 is then invited to contribute – he introduces the idea of *work* being a negative experience and suggests the idea of not liking school as an example. (Is this something to build on?)

Pupil G1 is asked to say why she chose the word *black* from the word cloud.

T to the class: *Stop waving your hands at me – we are practising no hands up –* (good attempt to encourage more pupils to participate).

T to G1: *Pick a word that you are drawn to.*

T teases out the connotations of the word *black* selected by Pupil G1 and relates these to the horror genre.

*(continued)*

*(continued)*

T: *Pupil G2: when would you wear all black?*

Various pupils suggest Halloween and funerals.

T tells the class that the colour *black* can be associated with the idea of *death*.

## OVER TO YOU

## Activity 5

- How many of the points made in the narrative account above might have just as easily been recorded on a quantitative checklist?
- What information does a narrative account like this one provide, which a quantitative checklist might not?
- If you were being observed, would you prefer to receive, as part of the post-lesson debrief, written evidence collected on a quantitative checklist or in narrative form – or as a mixture of both?
- Are there any disadvantages to the narrative approach towards lesson observation?

### A worked example

Clearly, there are a number of activities recorded in the narrative account above which could have been recorded by ticks and timings on a quantitative checklist. For example, the pupils' entrance into the room; the taking of the register; the number and gender of the individual pupils who were invited to answer questions. A narrative account, however, allows me as observer to add 'flesh' to factual 'bones'. For instance, recording the teacher's verbal reaction at 11:55 when the pupils obeyed her request for focussed, quiet work, tells me far more about her management skills and strategy than a tick against the phrase *Behaviour expectations are reinforced and respected* ever could. Even more (perhaps most) importantly: keeping a narrative account encourages a focus on critical incidents involving *learning*. The interaction with Pupil B1 provides a particularly compelling example of what I mean. Acting from the best of motives, the teacher praised him for his contribution to the starter activity: *you have written loads*. However, when I went over to discuss Pupil B1's work with him, I found that the writing had actually been undertaken by the teaching assistant. Invited by the teacher to share what he had done, the pupil was thrown into confusion by her use of the word *draw*, which he interpreted literally and therefore felt that he should have presented the teacher with a picture. Thus, Pupil B1 chose to keep silent for fear of looking foolish in front of the rest of the class (who were, of course, aware that he needed special support from the teaching assistant).

I hope you agree with me that this brief and perhaps easily missed exchange offers a powerful opportunity for teacher and observer to engage in professional dialogue about a range of important pedagogic issues. This one critical incident alone has given me at least four items which I would wish to bring to our post-observation discussion:

- What kind of language should we use in the classroom?
- How might the inclusion of figurative language in classroom discussion encourage or inhibit learning?
- What strategies can we implement to try to ensure that there is a match between the teacher's and the pupils' understanding of a lesson's intended learning outcomes?
- How do we as teachers differentiate our material and our pedagogy so that our lessons become truly inclusive for all our pupils, regardless of ability and habitus? (Pupil B1 experienced a moment of destabilised habitus here and must have felt like a 'fish out of water'. I suspect he nodded in agreement when Pupil B3 made that anti-school comment later in the lesson.)

It is particularly important to note here that we have, in effect, drawn up a substantial agenda for discussion while – and this is a key principle – avoiding making the individual teacher and her personal teaching style the focus of attention. The discussion might steer well clear of personal issues; but this does not prevent the agenda from being specifically tailored to the consideration of learning concerns which are particularly pertinent to the professional development of this individual teacher. A lesson delivered on the same topic to the same class by a different trainee might well suggest a totally different discussion agenda.

In this context, the comments I placed in brackets within the narrative account serve as useful reminders of points I noted at the time about a range of critical incidents and which it might prove useful to feed into the discussion so that our dialogue does not slip away into generalities but stays focussed on the learning of *these* pupils, *this* teacher and, not least, *this* particular observer. The notes addressed to the teacher are written in acknowledgement of Bronfenbrenner's observation that the 'reciprocity' characteristic of an effective 'joint activity dyad' can be maintained 'even when [the participants] are not together' (see page 77, Chapter 5). When the observation is completed, the narrative account remains as a testament to and a means of continuing the professional dialogue – not least if the opportunity for further observations provides the participants with the opportunity to take up the discussion from where they left off.

No observation schedule is perfect. Interesting though it would be, this is not the place to launch into a philosophical discussion regarding those questions about the nature of reality or perception which all acts of narration invite. However, as I suggested in Section 2 of Chapter 5, teachers of English should have a particular interest in the way that the world is mediated through language and story. We, of all people, appreciate that a lesson narrative account is a text shaped and constructed by its author to a particular agenda. Consider the first two entries in the exemplar extract above. I chose to begin it with the words *T. greets the class at the door.* I could have begun – to take just one of many possibilities – by writing *When I arrived in the room before the lesson began, T. greeted me warmly and presented me with a copy of her lesson plan, together with resource materials and contextual information about the class.* All of which is equally true and important. Next, with a dexterous use of montage worthy of the pioneering Russian film director Sergei Eisenstein, my 'camera' 'panned' to the dysfunctional computer. I am very aware that one of the dangers of a *phenomenological* approach to classroom observation, as Wragg warns, is that 'We often interpret events as we wish to see them, not as they are' (1994:54).

How to mitigate these disadvantages? First, I suggest, is the need to be robust about the process as a whole by endorsing Dymoke and Harrison's point that observation offers 'a chance for questioning . . . often taken-for-granted assumptions' and 'to see one's own practice through the eyes of others' (2008: 8). The key point is that those 'others' must be trusted to observe in a compassionate but still clear-eyed manner informed by expertise and a concern for the professional welfare of, in this case, the trainee teacher and eleven-year-old pupils. The reason I chose to make my second recorded narrative entry a reference to the 'frozen' computer is because I felt that the trainee's calm response to a technical hitch that might have thrown another person into a panic said a lot about her professionalism and her ability to 'think on her feet'.

A second defence of the 'holistic' approach would be to acknowledge that all acts of narration are selective. To attempt a narrative account of a lesson so detailed that it included everything which took place, recorded from every point of view, would be impossible and pointless. Consider for example the issue of talk in the classroom. Wragg (1994:77) notes that teachers and pupils can speak at a rate of between 100 and 150 words per minute – or more. No wonder I, a touch-typist, only managed

to quote eight instances of teacher talk in the time covered by the narrative extract above. Wragg suggests that, realistically, it is possible to focus
on three critical incidents in a lesson (1994: 70). If this is the case, then
the writer of a narrative lesson observation report needs to be able to
demonstrate high skills of conceptual knowledge, defined by Krathwohl,
in words reminiscent of Bronfenbrenner's account of the ecological environment, as an understanding of the 'interrelationships among the basic
elements within a larger structure that enable them to function together'
(2002: 214). Why the focus on the dysfunctional computer or Pupil B1's
interpretation of the word *draw*? And – applying further skills of *synthesis, evaluation* and *analysis* – which critical incidents should be selected
for exploration in a time-limited post-lesson observation discussion?

## Activity 6

- In the worked example above, I have tried to demonstrate skills of
  synthesis, evaluation and analysis by selecting one out of several critical incidents to focus on. If you were to use my narrative account
  as the basis for a post-observation discussion, what other incident(s)
  might you choose to discuss and why?
- What strategies would you implement to ensure that the debrief was
  dialogic rather than inquisitorial?

## Section 3: sharing the information – who needs to know what?

If left to my own devices and bearing in mind all the points cited from
*Reclaiming Lesson Observations* in Chapter 8, part of me would be content to limit the post-observation discussion to a sharing in private of the
lesson narrative and a discussion of the learning issues it raised. I might go
further by following the example of an esteemed former teacher-training
colleague. He ingeniously and compassionately avoided the inquisitorial,
judgemental possibilities associated with a lesson observation by dividing
his narrative accounts into two simple sections: *Things you did well* and
*Things to think about.*

I said that 'part of me' would be happy to return to that report-writing
system which I too adopted when I started teacher training over a quarter
of a century ago. However, although I might agree with this approach
with regard to qualified teachers (unless they had been judged to be grossly
incompetent or unprofessional) I feel differently about colleagues who
are *training* to become teachers. If I were in hospital waiting for a major
operation, I would want to know that my surgeon had not only been

officially declared competent but, actually, was an outstanding practitioner. I think that a case can be made for applying what Wragg calls the 'competency-based' model to teacher training. I believe that there is a wider audience beyond the dyad of observer and trainee teacher which can legitimately expect me, as a trainer, to act as a 'gatekeeper' into the profession, declaring whether or not, in my professional opinion, a trainee has what it takes to become a competent teacher fit to be let loose on the nation's children. That audience can legitimately expect to have access to the lesson reports I write. (I will return to this issue in Chapter 10.)

## OVER TO YOU

### Activity 7

- Which members of a host school community (if any) should have access to a lesson observation report written about one of the trainees in their care? Why should they have this access and what would you expect them to do with the information provided?
- Is there an audience beyond the immediate community of the host school who should have access to lesson observation reports? (You might consider, for example, the case of an academic institution working in partnership with the host school, or of other schools in a 'cluster' that shares responsibility for the training of the teachers in question.)

### Activity 8

How should information about a lesson observation be shared with a wider audience?

- Look again at the extract from the narrative account in Section 2, pages 176 to 178.
- Are the format and language used appropriate for distribution to a wider audience (one which was not present during the actual lesson being described)?
- If you feel that the report needs to be rewritten before it 'goes public', could you rewrite it in such a manner which allows you to remain true to the principles described in Chapter 8 by O'Leary et al., while at the same time acknowledging the claim of a wider audience to know – bluntly – whether or not the trainee teacher is 'up to the job'?

## *A worked example*

The teacher in question here is training within the current English version of what Wragg calls a 'competency-based' model. This means that when I revised my narrative account for a wider audience – I suspect your answer to the second bullet point question for Activity 7 was *yes* – I had to rewrite and restructure it in terms of the eight Teachers' Standards (described on page 30 of Chapter 2). In the extract from the formal report below, I have chosen as exemplar material my comments for Standard 7 and Standard 1 because these are the two sections in which it is easiest for you to see how I have reworked the writing in the extract from the narrative account of the lesson opening studied earlier. The second paragraph of the entry for Standard 1, particularly, gives you some more contextual information about the issue of using metaphor and simile in the classroom.

---

### (Standard 7) Manage behaviour effectively to ensure a good and safe environment

It was very useful to be able to discuss the context for this lesson. I learned that you have only recently taken on this class, having originally worked with a different Year 7. You are therefore still in the process of establishing your relationship with them.

It is clear that you are working hard at establishing routines for behaviour. I was impressed by the way today that you dealt with unforeseen logistical challenges: not being able to get into the classroom to set up before the lesson began; the logging off of the computer. You responded calmly and well. You greeted the pupils at the door and you settled them to their starter activity efficiently: 'All you need at the moment is a whiteboard, a whiteboard pen and a word cloud.' It was good to see you remind the class that you intended to follow up on the instances of poor behaviour from the previous lesson and that you would record on the board the names of the pupils involved. You insisted on silence for the individual writing activities during the lesson. You dismissed the class efficiently and you followed up on the behavioural issues as you promised.

*(continued)*

*(continued)*

## (Standard 1) Set high expectations which inspire, motivate and challenge

I think you set high and challenging expectations today, especially given the range of ability within this mixed-ability grouping. The 200-year-old extract from *Frankenstein* contains a number of quite complex words (like 'endeavour') with which young people of this age may not be very familiar. It was interesting in this context that the example from the text which the pupils chose to share with you later in the lesson was the phrase 'straight black lips'. I wonder if this was because those were the words they found easiest to understand?

Some of the technical terms you used – *semantic field*, for example – need to be introduced carefully, not least because, as Pupil B1's response to your use of the word 'draw' suggested, pupils are not always clear about metaphors which we as English graduates might take for granted. *Field* is a case in point here – and later on, the phrase *'layers* of meaning' was employed.

## OVER TO YOU

## Activity 9

- Compare this formal account of the lesson opening with the narrative version explored earlier. In what ways are they similar and different? (Consider such issues as intention, tone of voice, use of personal pronouns, sense of audience, etc.)
- If this were your lesson I was reporting on, which of the two accounts would you prefer to read and discuss and why?
- Do you think this extract from the formal report strikes a successful balance between remaining true to the principles espoused by O'Leary et al. while at the same time making evaluative, 'quality assurance' judgements for a wider audience?
- How successfully – or unsuccessfully – does this extract from the formal report demonstrate and apply what Krathwohl describes as 'conceptual knowledge'?
- Draw up a list of **five** rules for compiling and sharing a formal lesson observation report.

## Section 4: classroom observation – points to consider

### Pre-observation

1   Ensure that you are fully aware of and compliant with your host institution's code of practice regarding lesson observation. If you intend to record pupils in a classroom situation, it is *essential* that you seek all the necessary permissions beforehand.

2   Liaise with the host teacher whose lesson you are going to observe. Make sure that the teacher clearly understands the nature and purpose of the observation and is able to convey this information in an appropriate form to the pupils.

3   Make sure that you and the host teacher are in agreement about what you can and cannot do during the observation. Is the host teacher happy for you to move around the room so that you can inspect the work of individual pupils and talk to them about the lesson? Should you observe for the whole lesson or only part of it? Is the host teacher happy for you to discuss the observation with a third party?

4   If you are going to hold a post-observation discussion with the host teacher, agree beforehand, where possible, what the agenda and the etiquette for that discussion should be. Agree, too, on when and where the discussion will be held and on how long it should last.

5   Gain as much information as you can from the host teacher about the *context* of the lesson. What is the topic of study? How far into the study sequence does the lesson you are going to observe occur? What have the pupils done in the previous lesson and what will they do in the next one? What information would it be helpful to know about the pupils you are going to observe? Is there confidential information that you should not be privy to? What are the learning outcomes for this lesson? Is it possible for you to have a copy of the teacher's lesson plan and to discuss it before the lesson itself?

6   I suggested in Chapter 8 that you might encourage a host school to welcome you into its community by offering something in return. One way to do this would be to act as an 'extra pair of eyes' for the host teacher during the observation. The teacher might ask you, for example, to give feedback on their use of a particular teaching or behaviour management strategy. They might ask you to shadow an individual pupil or a group of pupils in whom they have a particular professional interest. If the teacher does wish you to provide specific feedback like this, it might be worth seeing if you can hold the lesson in an 'observation classroom' of the kind described in Chapter 8 by Stevens – provided

your host school has one. Alternatively, this might be the occasion on which to experiment with VEO as described by Haines and Miller in the same chapter. Do *not* forget to secure the necessary permissions! It is important, too, that observer and teacher agree when the filming will occur during the lesson, as well as what and who will be filmed. They should agree, too, about how the pupils will be informed.

7    If possible, inspect the classroom before the lesson. How attractive is this room as a site dedicated to the promotion of *skhole* as described in Chapter 8? Does it have access to natural light, fresh air and an appropriate degree of warmth? How are the seats and tables arranged? What kinds of interaction does this layout encourage or discourage? What technical equipment is available for teacher and pupils to use? How might the physical setting influence the way teacher and pupils respond in the lesson?

### During the observation

Here are some approaches you may wish to take (having secured the necessary permissions):

1    Plan beforehand to focus on routine critical moments which form elements of all lessons. These include, for example: entrances and exits; points of transition; the sharing and assessment of learning outcomes.

2    Alternatively, observe with an 'open' agenda and see what critical incidents – or examples of silent music – present themselves (for instance, Pupil B1's misinterpretation of the word *draw*).

3    Focus on one or more particular strategies employed by the teacher. These might include: use of figurative language and/or metalanguage; tone of voice; questioning; demonstration of subject knowledge and exposition of learning points at a level appropriate to the developmental level of the pupils; sensitivity towards and ability to correct misconceptions; management strategies; ability to build a rapport with the class; ability to differentiate material so that all pupils can participate; sensitive consideration of pupils who have special educational needs or who are not yet fluent in English; awareness of gender, equality and social justice issues in the classroom.

4    Is there evidence, from this lesson, that the teacher is working as a team member, sharing and implementing the overall vision of the English Department and of the school?

5    Focus on a particular group of pupils. Who is vociferous in class? Who 'keeps their head down' and contributes little? Who seems to be suffering from peer pressure or cleft habitus? Does anybody seem

bored or antagonistic? Who is 'a fish in water'? Who appears to be struggling? In terms of the lesson topic, what do the pupils already appear to understand, know and be able to do? What progress do they make in the course of the lesson and how do you know?

6   If the host teacher is happy for you to move around the classroom and to talk to pupils, make the most of this opportunity when it is appropriate to do so (do not disrupt the flow of the lesson). What is it like to participate in the lesson from different points around the room – the back row, for example? Are the pupils who are seated there still within the teacher's sight line? Can they see the board properly and can they hear what the teacher is saying? If there are pupils with a hearing or visual impairment in the room, where are they sitting? Are pupils allowed to sit in friendship groups? If not, how is the seating plan arranged and why? Does the teacher remain rooted at the front, or does he or she 'own the space' by moving around and addressing the class from different positions in the room?

7   When shadowing particular pupils, see what they are writing and listen to what they have to tell you about their work. Be on the lookout for clues which reveal how the pupils are responding to the lesson. If the class has been given a writing task to complete, for example, are all the pupils working at the same speed? Has one pupil written a page while another is still struggling to complete a sentence? If the class has been allocated a task involving talk, is everybody contributing? What group dynamics are at play? What kind of questions do pupils ask and what kind of answers do they give when they are questioned? What range of vocabulary and registers do they use when they speak in lessons? What range of reading tasks are undertaken during the lesson and how well equipped are the pupils to cope with them? Are some pupils singled out for regular attention by the teacher and others seemingly neglected or ignored? Are boys and girls and pupils from all ethnic and social backgrounds given equal opportunities to participate in class?

8   If teaching assistants and/or other support staff are present, what kind of working relationship do they have with the teacher? How do they engage with the class? Do they work with designated individuals according to a pre-arranged plan, or do they engage with groups of pupils and even, on occasions, the whole class?

## Post-observation

1   The first question on every teacher's mind at the end of an observation of any kind is, naturally enough, *How did I do?* It would be rather insensitive of an observer to leave the observation without

saying an immediate word of encouragement to put the teacher's mind at rest. However, if a post-observation discussion has been agreed, it is most important that this takes place in a comfortable, private space after enough time has elapsed for both parties to draw breath and to reflect – but not of course so long after the event that memories and responses are no longer fresh and vivid. Agreements made before the observation about discussion etiquette need to be revisited. For example, the discussion should focus on 'spotlight questions' (Barrell, 2017: 36) concerned with illuminating learning, rather than on the kind of adversarial 'hyper questioning' (Wright, 2017: 82) normally associated with a court of law.

2   VEO can come into its own here. Observer and observed can watch and review critical moments from the lesson together. They can 'freeze' and replay particularly significant shots. They can study the accompanying sound track and analyse extracts of classroom discourse. The camera can capture those important elements of body language and tone of voice which are virtually impossible to convey in written reports. If appropriate, filmed material can be archived and reviewed on different occasions and even with different audiences for purposes of comparison, identification of progress and future training. For a trainee, it can make a significant contribution to the portfolio of evidence described in Chapter 3.

3   Following on from the previous point, teacher and observer need to decide what is going to happen to any print, visual or audial data collected for the observation. Both parties might wish to write a reflective response to the experience in order to enhance their future practice. Such pieces need to be written in a professional manner and, if the writing is to be presented to a wider audience, references to school, teachers or pupils should be anonymised. As with research data, confidential material needs to be disposed of appropriately after an agreed period of time determined by school policy.

4   Is there going to be any follow-up to the observation and subsequent discussion? Would the teacher be willing to host other observations so that the observer can gain a more detailed and informed understanding of the teacher's practice and the pupils' development? Would it be worth seeing if other colleagues might also be willing to host an observation? Perhaps the observer could observe the same set of pupils working with different members of staff in other subject areas. Is there anybody else who needs to know about the observation and the discussion which followed? Have teacher and observer agreed on who needs to know and on what they should be told?

# Chapter 10

# Assessment revisited

## The school context

## Section 1: two stories about assessment

I want to begin this final chapter by recounting two recent school experiences. The first occurred on a visit to a shiny new academy in an economically disadvantaged area of England. The member of staff responsible for trainee teachers of English was showing me the academy's state of the art intranet. I was impressed. There was a wealth of lesson plans, schemes of work and teaching resources available at the click of a mouse for sharing among staff. Pride of place, however, went to the assessment folder. Here, my host informed me, was stored all the assessment data for each of the academy's pupils. We could track in detail their progress across all the modalities of English. We could make predictions about the grades they might achieve in their final national examinations. Not least, my host continued as we explored minutely plotted colour-coded charts and graphs, the academy could scrutinise the performance of its teaching staff. Which pupils seemed to be making steady progress? Which seemed to have 'stagnated' or even fallen back since arriving at the academy? Which teachers were responsible for the English education of these pupils? How come Class X had done so well when Y taught them but seemed to be producing disappointing work now that they were in the care of Z? Might it be time, the implication went, for the academy's management team to consider 'letting Z go'?

The second incident occurred during an English lesson observation. A class of fifteen-year-olds had been asked to create a piece of writing which contained an extended metaphor. They were to imagine an encounter between the sea and a struggling swimmer, drawing upon images of battle to create their extended metaphor. I went round the room, discussing with the pupils their chosen approach to the task. Everybody had written from the point of view of the swimmer – everybody except one boy. He had decided to write from the point of view of the sea and had produced something far more interesting and arresting than anyone else had managed. I asked him to tell me about how he had come to make this writing choice. 'I thought', he replied, 'I would gain more marks.'

## OVER TO YOU

### Activity 1

- What is your response to these two stories? How do they relate to issues explored earlier in the book, and particularly in Chapter 7?

I wanted to open the chapter with these two stories because I think they illustrate graphically how attitudes towards assessment have changed in the forty years since I first trained to become a teacher of English. The fresh-faced new recruit I describe at the start of Chapter 6 would have been bewildered and, yes, disheartened to read these two stories. I might even go so far as to say that, had he been able to see into the future, he might have decided not to bother becoming a teacher at all. The academy story would have seemed to him like an extreme expression of the kind of surveillance regime described by Foucault in *Discipline and Punish* and explored in Chapter 8. The story about the fifteen-year-old writer might have disheartened him even more. The extended metaphor task was not selected by a group of young writers eager to explore this technique as part of their development. It was imposed by their teacher because she knows her pupils might well be asked to create an extended metaphor as part of the national examination they will have to sit in a year's time. The results of that examination will be subjected to internal and public scrutiny – and the teacher does not want to find herself in the same position as 'Teacher Z' in the first anecdote. The response of the young man to my question is equally disheartening. As Gill and Thomson might put it, school is teaching him the lesson of 'operationalism' – in other words, to confuse 'the means of measurement with the underlying valuable learning process'. His writing skills, his imagination, his creativity, are not celebrated as joyous and valuable in themselves, but rather they are transformed into something of 'instrumental value' (2012: 209, 213, 227) which, like money, can be bartered for material success.

## Section 2: assessment and accountability – who needs to know?

How did we get into this situation and is it as bleak as the opening paragraphs of Section 1 might suggest? Identifying the precise moment when a major shift in educational thinking occurs is always problematic. However, a useful starting point, certainly as far as my own experience of working as a teacher within the English system is concerned, might be October 1976, the month I began my teacher training course and, more to the point, the date which is now widely regarded as marking the start of a so-called 'Great Debate' about public education. On 18 October of that year, the Labour Prime Minister of the United Kingdom, James Callaghan, delivered an important policy speech at Ruskin College, Oxford, in which he issued a blunt warning to educationalists, not least to those working in schools:

> To the teachers I would say that you must satisfy ... parents and industry that what you are doing meets their requirements and the needs of our children.

Callaghan felt justified in issuing such a warning because he was the democratically elected representative of the taxpayers who paid for state education:

> I take it that no one claims exclusive rights in this field. Public interest is strong and legitimate and will be satisfied. We spend £6bn a year on education, so there will be discussion.

Those forthright verbs marked a serious declaration of intent. Once the principle of accountability had been conceded, the taxpayers – or in this case their political representatives – felt empowered to ask a series of uncomfortable questions about the curriculum. The questions Callaghan posed still sound sadly familiar today. He wanted to know, for example, why so many graduates 'have no desire to join industry', why 'such a high proportion of girls abandon science before leaving school', why, in higher education, 'humanities courses' are 'full' while 'science and engineering' are undersubscribed. It was not only the outcomes of the curriculum which Callaghan subjected to scrutiny. He noted 'the unease felt by parents and others about . . . new informal methods of teaching', questioned whether there was 'sufficient thoroughness and depth' of curriculum content and – particularly pertinent to the concerns of this chapter – speculated about 'the proper way of monitoring the use of resources in order to maintain a proper national standard of performance' (Gillard: 2010).

## OVER TO YOU

### Activity 2

- What do you make of Callaghan's argument here? To what extent (if at all) should teachers be accountable to the taxpayer for the educational progress made by the pupils in their care?
- The term 'taxpayer' covers a wide and disparate range of people in any community. Who exactly might have a legitimate right to scrutinise assessment information about pupils – and at what level of detail? What about people who, for one reason or another, are not taxpayers? Do they have a right to hold teachers to account in this way?
- Make a list of the groups or people whom you feel might legitimately claim access to some form of assessment data about pupils.

I wonder if James Callaghan really appreciated just how many people he was inviting to participate in his 'Great Debate'? When I attempted the task described in the third bullet point above, I found that ten minutes of thinking time gave me a list of some forty people or groups drawn from society as a whole who might stake a legitimate claim to assessment data in one form or other. If you look back at Table 8.2, you will see that a similar exercise conducted there – but limited to the immediate school community – produced only ten individual people or groups. I hope this comparison gives you some idea of just how momentous a change in accountability Callaghan initiated on 18 October 1976.

### Activity 3

I noted in Chapter 8 that Foucault considered school to be a prime site of '[h]ierarchised, continuous and functional surveillance'.

- Did the creation of your list incline you to be more sympathetic to Foucault's point of view?
- How do you feel, knowing that so many different people beyond the immediate school community believe they have a right to scrutinize the assessment data related either directly or indirectly to your teaching?

It is important that we hold our nerve here and resist the temptation to succumb to Foucault's nightmare vision. To protect our sanity, we need to place Callaghan's crowd of eager debaters in an orderly queue. One positive first step might be to see if we can organise them into broad interest groups.

### A worked example

Table 10.1 represents my list, organised into broad interest groups. Note where it resembles or differs from Table 8.2.

## OVER TO YOU

## Activity 4

- Compare my list with yours. Did we come up with a similar account of possible claimants to assessment data? Did you include any I missed, or vice versa? Were you surprised by any of the people or organisations I included in my list?
- What do you think of the way I have tried to organise my list into broad interest groups? Do any of the headings surprise you? Could you work with them or do you feel you need to change some or even all of the categories? If so, organise your list into the broad interest categories which you feel would work best for you.

Let me explain some of what may seem like the more unusual choices of broad interest groups in my list. I began with a category which I have called *People*, not because I want to sound precious, but because I am mindful of an issue raised in Chapter 7 and posed here by Noddings as a question: 'Is education aimed at the student's development as a whole person?' (In Gill and Thomson, 2012: 233). Having read Chapter 7, I hope you agree with me that the overriding aim of assessment should be to contribute positive answers to that question on behalf of the pupils – and the people who care about them – for they are absolutely at the heart of the whole enterprise of education. Teachers of English, especially, should be sensitive to the intimate links between assessment and self-esteem. We have seen throughout the book – not least when we explored instances of Althusser's 'silent music' in Section 3 of Chapter 4 or when in Chapter 7 I confessed to feelings of trepidation about sharing an extract of my attempt at fiction – just how problematic the encounter between habitus and what Foucault calls 'normalising judgement' can be.

Table 10.1 Who needs to know about assessment?

| People | Teaching professionals working 'at the chalk face' | Teaching professionals with a wider remit for pupils' welfare | Teaching professionals with an overall responsibility for assessment data | Pastoral support outside school | The world of work | Non-governmental agencies concerned with education | Governmental agencies concerned with education | Political bodies |
|---|---|---|---|---|---|---|---|---|
| The person being assessed. | The teacher responsible for educating the pupil being assessed. | Staff at transfer schools and/or colleges (for pupils who move between educational establishments for various reasons, including cross-phase transition). | Head teachers. | Welfare agencies. | Employers at a local level. | Academics involved in educational research. | School inspection agencies. | The elected government. |
| Parents and carers. | Teaching colleagues within a school department. | School consortia (for example, schools who work together within a cluster, as in the current English educational system). | Senior management teams in school. | Educational support staff outside school. | Employers at (inter)national level. | Teaching unions and professional associations. | Government researchers and statisticians. | Opposition political parties. |
| Family members such as siblings or grandparents. | Teaching colleagues within a school responsible for pastoral welfare. | Higher education admissions staff. | Teacher trainers. | Police liaison officers. | | Political pressure groups. | Educational policy makers and review committees. | Elected politicians at national level. |
| Other school pupils in the class. | Educational support staff within school. | | | Referral units. | | Educational trusts and charities. | | Elected politicians at local level. |
| School governors. | Trainee teachers. | | | Young offender institute staff. | | Compilers of online data about local communities (as described in Chapter 8). | | |
| Parent/teacher associations. | | | | Health workers. | | Commercial publishers of educational resources. | | |
| | | | | Teachers working outside the school system (for example, teaching pupils who are in hospital). | | Staff who work for examination boards. | | |

Johnston offers two particularly poignant reminders in his account of two Australian pupils' responses to the statement: 'What Failure in English Means to Me'. One commented that 'it sort of grows on one – like a fungus'. The other was more specific:

> I think, perhaps, that to fail English is, in a way, to fail as a person of [sic] society ... because English is concerned with how well you can explain things, the way you talk, how to interpret something, how well you understand, using your initiative, how much insight a person has, to show your ability at reading, writing and talking, to show how creative you can be and many other things that can tell what sort of person you are.
>
> (Johnston, 1987: 4)

My choice of a category called *Pastoral support outside school* is also designed to emphasise the human dimension of assessment. As the references to mental health in Chapter 8 suggested, pupils are vulnerable. Their lives might take a wrong turn. They can suffer from illnesses which may be serious and even life-threatening. Should they encounter the justice system or a welfare agency during the course of their school careers, what assessment information about the pupils would you, as a teacher, feel justified in sharing with such organisations?

I hope that the crowd of demanding voices invited by Callaghan to 'put [their] oar in', as he phrased it, (Gillard: 2010) is now appearing to form a more orderly and manageable queue, even if that queue is four times larger than it was in Chapter 8. If you are still feeling somewhat overwhelmed by the size of it, please keep a sense of proportion. Remember that different members of the education profession will have different obligations and priorities to address in terms of collecting and sharing assessment data. My principal concern in this final chapter is to explore the issues of assessment data collection and accountability primarily from the perspective of someone considering or embarking upon a secondary English teacher training programme. If I were considering those issues from the perspective of a head teacher or a school governor or a police liaison officer, say, the section which follows would read differently.

## Section 3: exchanging assessment information – privileges and obligations

I am going to revisit the list of people and organisations arranged in my broad interest categories, therefore, by focussing now on those with whom the primary audience for this chapter needs to have regular contact. In each of the examples explored, writing as if I were the trainee concerned and thinking again of Bronfenbrenner's joint activity dyads, I want to identify opportunities where I might learn about assessment procedures and the interpretation of data. In the interests of reciprocity, I also want to draw attention to those occasions where there is a corresponding obligation upon the trainee to act as a creator and provider of assessment data for other interested parties. Before reading on, it might be worth revisiting Section 2 of Chapter 8, which prepared the ground for much of what follows.

## People

### Individual pupils

The needs of the individuals I am teaching and assessing lie at the heart of the educational enterprise. They are the reason I am in the classroom. Those individuals therefore have a right to expect me to give them regular feedback on their progress. I might assess them informally – not only on a daily basis but also throughout a lesson – by monitoring individual learning behaviours and attitudes across all modalities of English. I will do this by, for example, questioning, explaining and encouraging. I will listen carefully to what individual pupils say to me and to each other in – and, where appropriate, beyond – the classroom. I will include regular opportunities for reflecting with my pupils on what they think they are learning. Does it accord with what I think I am teaching? During these periods of reflection, I will be particularly alert for any misunderstandings which I might need to correct and for critical moments of insight which provide me with the opportunity to push individual pupils' thinking further. On a more formal basis, I will set and mark written work according to my host school's assessment policy, encouraging my pupils to play an active part in the assessment process by explaining to me, where appropriate, how they intend to respond to my requests for improvement and also by encouraging them to help their peers to assess their own work. *Crucially, as discussed in Section 5 of Chapter 7, I will use this regular supply of informal and formal assessment information to plan and structure future lessons so that they are focussed upon the personalised learning interests and needs of the pupils in my care.*

### Parents, carers and family members

Parents, carers and other family members have a right to know how their children are progressing at school. I might provide this information on an informal basis – for example, by sending home a postcard commending good work undertaken in class or, if appropriate, by providing this information through a phone conversation. More formally, I will share appropriate information with representative family members at parents evenings and other community-based events organised by the host school. If individual pupils develop a particular learning or pastoral need, I might be expected to contribute to a meeting between family members and staff from within and beyond the immediate school community. Parents and carers will also receive formal written assessment information regarding their children's progress judged according to school-based and national criteria at times determined by the school or the government.

### Other school pupils in the class

For pupils, just as for teachers, the urge to know 'how we are doing' in comparison with our peers is an understandable human characteristic. That way, however, lies *norm referencing*: the placing of a class of pupils in a rank order of achievement, with all its attendant consequences for motivation and self-esteem. Those at the top of the list may become complacent; those near the bottom may find themselves, in Johnston's telling phrase, 'alienated from their own resourcefulness' (1987: 21) and stop trying. Rather than making comparisons with their peers, I want my pupils to focus on their individual learning needs and their individual progress. Of course, this does not mean that I as a professional responsible for the overall welfare of the class will not want to utilise all the assessment data of the kind I saw at the academy described in the opening of the chapter, in order to make comparative judgements about the pupils as a group of learners. As well as the examples of formal written assessments described earlier, such data might include information provided by the 'feeder' schools responsible for the initial stages of my pupils' education, or by colleagues who are teaching them now in other subject areas or have taught them English in earlier years at secondary school. It might include data provided by tests of reading or spelling or cognition. Target grades may have been set for each of the pupils, predicting what they might be expected to achieve in English by the time they leave school.

My purpose in analysing this data is not to make personal judgements about whether X is 'better' at English than Y. Which of us is 'good at' every aspect of the subject – or indeed, as the teacher interviewed by Page in Chapter 8 implied – consistently 'good at' something all of the time? Equally importantly, as Johnston notes: 'no-one is always bad at every task that English involves' (1987: 16). What I am interested in is finding out how best this assessment data can help me to *personalise* the learning for my pupils in subsequent lessons. It must be clear by this stage of the book that I am impatient with deficit models of education which focus on what pupils cannot do, instead of starting from the premise that, as proficient users of language, they bring a wealth of skills and experiences to the English classroom.

The assessment data I am describing here can help me to harness the talent in the classroom as efficiently as possible, by, for example, organising pupils who share similar learning interests and needs into 'trusted pairs' (Clarke, 2010: 61) or small groups who, by working together for a shared purpose, can in Vygotsky's famous words, 'grow into the intellectual life of those around them' (1930/1978: 88). It can help, as Holbrook reminded me in Chapter 7, identify critical moments of potential growth in that 'intellectual life'. Might the boy described at the start of the chapter who created an extended metaphor from the point of view of the sea, enjoy engaging with the magical realist writing of Isabel Allende or Gabriel García Márquez? Might a young reader who was moved, say, by the quotations from William Blake's poem 'The Schoolboy' in David Almond's novel *Skellig*, enjoy discovering the *Songs of Innocence and Experience*? Perhaps these two learners are representative of a substantial number of pupils in the class who would be receptive to a scheme of work in English which enables them to explore ways of representing the world beyond the 'naturalistic' confines of the television soap opera or the 'realistic' novel? 'The class', Clarke writes, 'has to show that it knows and can think . . . before it is allowed to move on' (2010: 57). Pupils who feel that they cannot demonstrate such knowledge and thought will not find the classroom a safe and stimulating place to be – and they are more likely to express their sense of confusion and lack of confidence through disengagement or worse. Sensitive interpretation of assessment data can help a teacher to, as Petty puts it, 'find faults, fix, then follow up' where necessary (2004: 455) so that the whole class can move forward confidently together as a community of learners.

### Teaching Professionals working 'at the chalk face'

In choosing this title for one of my broad-interest categories, I am thinking of those colleagues who share with me the day-to-day work of the school.

## The teacher responsible for educating the pupil being assessed

As a trainee or potential trainee teacher of English, I would hope to be assigned to a 'mentor' or other experienced colleague whom I would be allowed to observe and then work alongside in the classroom. From these colleagues, I would hope to gain invaluable assessment information not only about the pupils' academic development as explored earlier in this section, but also, thinking again of the quotation from Noddings, about the pupils as human beings. Which of their peers do they work well with – or not? If someone enters the classroom in a negative frame of mind, what is the best way of helping that person to engage? Who struggles in English? Who might have behavioural issues or a specific learning need? Thinking again of the report from Public Health England considered in Chapter 8, is anybody facing a particular challenge in their personal lives that I should know about and if so, how should I take this information into account when interacting with them during lessons?

As a trainee, I, in my turn, need to be aware that my host teachers are placing a significant amount of professional trust in me, first by letting me observe their teaching and, later, by allowing me to take increasing responsibility for the progress of their pupils – pupils whom they will have to 'take back' after I have moved on. In terms of the assessment data I might provide for these colleagues, then, I need to be sensitive, professional and respectful in the way that I comment on their teaching. Once I start taking responsibility for their classes, I need to be sure that I submit my lesson plans for scrutiny, leaving enough time for the host teacher to check them and to suggest revisions if necessary. I need to keep the host teacher fully informed of the assessment data I compile while responsible for their classes and I need to make sure that I conduct this assessment in full compliance with school and departmental policies. My host teachers will observe my lessons and provide me with verbal and written feedback. I need to be able not only to receive this assessment feedback in a professional manner but also demonstrate that I have absorbed the advice given and acted upon it.

## Teaching colleagues within a school department

Informal daily contact with colleagues who also teach English can help me acquire more nuanced and holistic assessment information about pupils. For example, Teacher A tells me that Pupil B, who seems disengaged in my lessons, used to be enthusiastic and alert when she taught him last year. What can I learn from this? By observing and interacting with my colleagues at work, I can also gain insights into the skills of leadership and teamwork needed to create a shared and effective vision for the teaching of English. Using words pertinent to this entire chapter – and which we shall explore in detail later – Bethan Marshall writes: 'it is the interpretation of evidence that is crucial' (2011b: 28). By attending more formal meetings with my English colleagues, such as moderation and training sessions, I can learn how this core principle is put into practice by teachers who need to feel confident about the high stakes, national assessment judgements they have to make on behalf of the pupils in their care. Such confidence is only gained through the establishment of those 'communities of interpretation' described in Section 4 of Chapter 7. Those communities are built, in turn, upon a thorough knowledge of how particular examinations are structured, how their requirements might be addressed through engaging learning activities and, finally, how those requirements should be assessed.

In return for receiving such invaluable assessment training from my English colleagues, I need to reciprocate by, first, marking alongside and sharing assessment judgements with more experienced teachers. As my confidence grows, I should assume increased responsibility for marking work on my own. I need to write comments which make it clear to the pupils exactly how their assignments might or might not have met specified assessment criteria. It is also important that those pupils understand how *assessment informs future learning* – that the two are 'looped' as Petty has it (2004: 455). To this end, I need to provide very clear guidance about what, *if anything*, they need to do in order to develop as writers.

### Teaching colleagues within a school responsible for pastoral welfare and educational support staff within school

I am going to consider these two groups together because I want to foreground again the importance of the question posed by Noddings and cited in the first section of the chapter. That question speaks clearly to the personal growth model of English which emphasises 'the relationship between language and learning in the individual child, and the role of literature in developing children's imaginative and aesthetic lives' (Hardman, 2001: 14). If English is to flourish as a school subject, it is essential that its practitioners have an understanding of the emotional, intellectual and psychological pressures their pupils encounter as they attempt, through the medium of language, to find a place for themselves within the world. How can I expect someone to tell me honestly why a work of literature has moved or upset them, or, through writing, to confide in me their thoughts and feelings about life's most profound experiences, unless they feel that I will make a trusted and compassionate listener and reader?

Like my host teacher of English described earlier, pastoral staff can help me to establish a more rounded, human understanding of my pupils and this in turn will help to create the sense of trust so essential to the joint activity dyads I am seeking to create with them. The information might be seemingly trivial. Pupil A is a fanatical football supporter: we begin each lesson with some banter about how well her team did or did not do over the weekend. Sometimes the information is more sombre. Pupil B is up at 5:00 a.m. each morning in order to care for his disabled mother before heading off for school: how do I take this into account when planning my lessons? To cite again the phrase taken from Guditus in Chapter 8, how 'available for learning' will he be by the time I try to teach him English at 3:00 p.m. on a Friday afternoon?

Specialist staff can offer expert guidance on how I might accommodate particular learning needs – remember Pupil B1 (described on pages 177 and 184 of Chapter 9) and the confusion he felt when he was asked which words he was *drawn* to? Perhaps a pre-lesson discussion with the teaching assistant who works with Pupil B1 on a regular basis would have helped the trainee responsible for teaching the class to tailor her verbal and written resources more appropriately to his needs. While revisiting that particular lesson here I am going to mention another member of the same class who, like Pupil B1, needed specific – though different – support in order to engage with the challenges of *Frankenstein*. Pupil G3 had just arrived from Turkey and spoke almost no English. One of the issues the trainee and I discussed after the lesson observation described in Chapter 9 was how in future we might help Pupil G3 to be 'available for learning' without us falling into the deficit trap of focussing exclusively on what she cannot do. With the help of the members of staff responsible for supporting pupils for whom English is an additional language, we might, for example, devise a series of non-verbal strategies to help her engage with her teacher or peers; and, thinking of the lesson's theme, we might find appropriate stories about monsters from Turkish literature and folk culture which could be shared in the classroom to the mutual enjoyment and benefit of all the pupils.

What should a trainee teacher of English do in return for the privilege of accessing this kind of assessment data and expertise? Fundamentally, they must demonstrate a willingness and ability to put such information to practical use. They must show that they can apply what they have learned, not only to a specific situation such as the one described in the previous paragraph, but also to all the future lessons that they will teach throughout their careers. Teachers who know how to use assessment data to maximum effect not only create lesson plans which are constructed to meet *the specific learning needs of individual pupils* but also – and this is most important of all – they translate those plans into powerful, personalised practice which secures learning.

### Non-governmental agencies concerned with education

#### Academics involved in educational research

I have chosen this group as my final example of people who can contribute productively to an exchange of assessment data information with trainee teachers of English, for two reasons. The first reason is because – certainly if you are training or thinking of training within the current English system – you are very likely to undertake a programme which is affiliated in some way to an institute of higher education. You might, like the trainee I described at the start of Chapter 4, feel that connection is nothing more than a tiresome distraction from the practical business of teaching. By this stage of the book, you should be very clear about what I think of such a response! I hold passionately to the belief that, if teachers are to be regarded as autonomous professionals rather than unthinking doers of the state's bidding – and we saw in Chapter 4 where such acquiescence can lead – then they must be receptive to and capable of demonstrating informed praxis. One of the reasons I devoted so much space in Chapter 8 to the work of O'Leary and his colleagues is because I believe they provide a stirring, contemporary example of how thinking professionals can 'reclaim' the territory as they put it – in that instance by pushing back against the use of lesson observation as the kind of punitive surveillance device Foucault abhorred.

Throughout the book, I have turned to academics for two kinds of assessment data. On the one hand, there are works of empirical research, commissioned by government bodies or other organisations mentioned in my list earlier such as educational trusts and charities, political pressure groups, teaching unions and professional associations. Examples cited in the book so far include reports written for the OECD (Chapter 2), Stonewall (Chapter 4), the House of Commons Education Committee (Chapter 6) and Public Health England (Chapter 8).

The second kind of assessment data I would seek out from academics is equally important; and to explain why, I need to share another anecdote from my own teaching career. My first full-time employment as a teacher took place in a very large comprehensive school. The pupils were divided into two broad ability groups called, imaginatively enough, the A Band and the B Band. Fresh out of my university training course, I knew that pedagogically this was questionable practice; and on a basic, human level, I baulked at the thought that other human beings could be labelled in such a way. However, to my shame, within a couple of months at the school, I was using the same terms myself. What is perhaps even more concerning as I look back on that experience now is the fact that I was very happy working within that community and stayed there for four years!

Although I did not realise it at the time, I was encountering at first hand something Ellis describes as the 'continuity-displacement contradiction' (2007: 17). Taking his cue from Lave (1988), who continued and developed Bronfenbrenner's exploration of the relationship between the individual and the settings in which she or he operates, Ellis envisages the school as an 'arena' in which trainee and experienced members of a community engage in 'productive tensions' (2007: 22, 17). When the encounter is a positive one, 'the relationships and ways of knowing which characterise the community are reconfigured to accommodate both parties' (McGuinn and Naylor: 2009: 212). However, if the host community is unwilling to seek accommodation (why should Senior Management alter a major policy on the say-so of an inexperienced new recruit?) then somebody – the lowly incomer in my case – has to give ground. Such a community, Ellis continues, is in danger of becoming 'a closed, reproductive system and one where knowledge is understood as static and given' (2007: 17–18).

I could at this point cite the crudest of *extrinsic* motivations and remind you that, as a trainee affiliated to a higher education institute of some kind, you will be obliged whether you like it or not to complete written assignments which require you to link theory and practice by engaging at some level with academic writing and thinking. There is, however, a reason for doing this which far outweighs extrinsic considerations. I told you that I worked happily for four years within a school community which saw nothing wrong in using phrases like *A and B Band pupils* as part of its daily educational discourse. If your experience of your host school is a positive one, you, like me, will grow to cherish it as – in Lave's terms – a community of practice which sustains and nourishes you, not only intellectually and professionally, but emotionally and socially too. You will be tempted to regard the assessment feedback you receive from your host teachers – about your own progress, about the nature and purpose of education – as *sacrosanct*. Please, whenever you feel yourself becoming too comfortable within your community of practice, ask yourself one question: *Does teaching and learning have to be like this?* The 'assessment data' – I am using the term in its widest sense here – provided by academic research and thinking is your lifeline to the world's treasure house of thinking about education. Throughout the book, I have shared with you the ideas of some of the thinkers who have helped shape my vision of English pedagogy. The 'assessment trade-off' I suggest here is that you find your own inspirational guides and engage in a lifelong professional dialogue with them.

## OVER TO YOU

### Activity 5

- Look through my list of broad interest groups in Table 10.1. Choose **one or more** people or organisations from **two** different clusters which you feel might provide contrasting perspectives on the issues we have explored above. For example, I might select for comparison *Teaching professionals with an overall responsibility for assessment data* and *Pastoral support outside school*.
- In what situation might you, as a trainee teacher of English, need to establish a joint activity assessment dyad with members of these groups? What would be the nature of the reciprocal exchange of information between you and what issues (ethical and pedagogic) might be raised by this exchange?

### Activity 6

- Share the work and the thinking you have undertaken for the activities in the chapter so far with staff within and, if possible, beyond the immediate school community – for example, a teacher of English, a special needs expert or a police liaison officer.
- What do they make of the respective lists we have drawn up and their place in my suggested broad interest group categories?
- How do they see their role with regards to the reception and production of assessment data about the school community? What issues of accountability do they face and what core principles guide their response to those issues?

## Activity 7

- Review your host school's website. How are assessment issues presented to the site's 'visitors'? What information does your host school choose to share or not to share and why might this be?

I thought at first I might model the activities above for you as I have done on other occasions in the book. However, I decided not to because we are coming to the end of our time together and I wanted to conclude as I began, with a reference to Erik de Corte's concept of teacher fade. If the book has achieved its success criteria, and progression has taken place in terms of your ability to know, understand and do, you should feel confident and even excited about taking up the activities challenge by yourself. If you find it hard, remember what Beckett said about failing better; and be assured: your training programme will provide you with many opportunities to refine your planning skills.

And finally. Thinking again about teacher fade, before I wish you good luck as you head into one of the most important and rewarding jobs in the world, here are two last sets of activities for you to complete.

## Activity 8

- Reflect on the work we have done together for Chapters 7 and 10. Draw up a list of key assessment principles which you intend to apply during your teaching career.

## Activity 9

- Revisit the lists of people in and out of school who might help you to develop your thinking about assessment (see Tables 8.2 and 10.1).
- Devise a set of questions arising from our work on Chapters 7 and 10 which you feel would help you to develop further your understanding of assessment issues. Allocate the questions to the appropriate people from your list.

# References

Abbs, P. (1982) *English Within the Arts: A Radical Alternative for English and the Arts in the Curriculum*. London: Hodder and Stoughton.

Adams, P. (1982) Revealing more than we can tell and Speaking more truly than they know. In B. Johnston (1987) *Assessing English: Helping Students to Reflect on Their Work*. Milton Keynes and Philadelphia: Open University Press; Sydney: St Clair Press.

Althusser, L. (1971) *Lenin and Philosophy and Other Essays*. Translated by B. Brewster. London: NLB.

Andrews, R. (2001) *Teaching and Learning English: A Guide to Recent Research and its Applications*. London and New York: Continuum.

Aronowitz, S. and Giroux, H. (1986/2003) *Education Under Siege: The Conservative, Liberal and Radical Debate over Schooling*. London: Routledge and Kegan Paul.

Babbitt, F. C. (1927) (Trans.) Plutarch: *On Listening to Lectures*. Loeb Classical Library, Harvard University Press: Cambridge: MA. http://penelope.uchicago.edu/Thayer/E/Roman/Texts/Plutarch/Moralia/De_auditu*.html (accessed 23 August 2016).

Bandura, A. (1989) Human Agency in Social Cognitive Theory. *American Psychologist* 44:9, pp. 1175–1184.

Barrell, E. (2017) Grades Don't Count: Building Success from the Inside Out. In M. O'Leary (ed.) *Reclaiming Lesson Observation: Supporting Excellence in Teacher Learning*. London and New York: Routledge.

Beck, J. (2000) The School Curriculum and the National Curriculum. In J. Beck and M. Earl (eds) *Key Issues in Secondary Education*. London and New York: Cassell.

Bell, D. S. A. (2003) Mythscapes: Memory, Mythology, and National Identity. *British Journal of Sociology* 54:1, pp. 63–81.

Ben-Peretz, M. (2011) Teacher knowledge: What is it? How do we uncover it? What are its implications for schooling? *Teaching and Teacher Education* 27, pp. 3–9.

Bernstein, B. (1971/2003) *Class, Codes and Control*, I: *Theoretical Studies Towards a Sociology of Language*. London and New York: Routledge and Kegan Paul.

Bernstein, B. (2000) *Pedagogy, Symbolic Control and Identity: Theory, Research and Critique*. London: Routledge.

Bjork, R. A. (1994) Memory and Metamemory Considerations in the Training of Human Beings. In J. Metcalfe and A. Shimamura (eds) *Metacognition: Knowing about Knowing.* Cambridge, MA: MIT Press.

Bjork, R. A. (2016) How We Learn Versus How We Think We Learn. *120th Faculty Research Lecture delivered to the UCLA Department of Psychology.* Recorded on 17 February 2016 and first published online on 3 May 2016. https://www.youtube.com/watch?v=oxZzoVp5jmI (accessed 21 November 2016).

Black, P. and Wiliam, D. (1998) *Inside the Black Box.* Occasional Paper. London: King's College.

Blackburn, G. W. (1985) *Education in the Third Reich.* Albany, NY: State University of New York Press.

Börner, R., Groh, R. and Schnabel, P. (1938) *Guck in die Welt: ein Lesebuch für die Kleinen.* Leipzig: Friedrich Brandstetter.

Bourdieu, P. (1977) *Outline of a Theory of Practice.* Translated by R. Nice. Cambridge: Cambridge University Press.

Bourdieu, P. (1997) The Forms of Capital. In A. H. Halsey, H. Lauder, P. Brown and A. S. Wells (eds.) *Education: Culture, Economy, Society.* Oxford: Oxford University Press.

Bourdieu, P. (1998) *Practical Reason.* Cambridge: Polity Press.

Bourdieu, P. (2000) *Pascalian Meditations.* Cambridge: Polity Press.

Bourdieu, P. and Wacquant, L. J. D. (1992) *An Invitation to Reflexive Sociology.* Chicago: University of Chicago Press.

Bradshaw, J. (2013) *Programme for International Student Assessment (PISA) Results from PISA 2012: Country Note, United Kingdom, Key Findings.* http://www.oecd.org/unitedkingdom/PISA-2012-results-UK.pdf (accessed 19 November 2016).

Bronfenbrenner, U. (1981) *The Ecology of Human Development: Experiments by Nature and Design.* Cambridge, MA and London: Harvard University Press.

Bronfenbrenner, U. (1986) Ecology of the Family as a Context for Human Development: Research Perspectives, *Developmental Psychology* 22: 6, pp. 723–742.

Bruner, J. S. (1960) *The Process of Education.* Cambridge, MA: Harvard University Press.

Bruner, J. S. (1971) The Perfectibility of Intellect. In A. Gil (ed.) *The Relevance of Education.* New York: W. W. Norton & Company.

Burnett, M. T. (2007*) Filming Shakespeare in the Global Marketplace.* Basingstoke and New York: Palgrave Macmillan.

Calderhead, J. (1989) Reflective Teaching and Teacher Education. *Teaching and Teacher Education* 5, pp. 43–51.

Cazden, C., Cope, B., Fairclough, N., Gee, J., *et al.* (1996) A Pedagogy of Multiliteracies: Designing Social Futures. *Harvard Educational Review* 66:1, pp. 60–92.

Challis-Manning, S. and Thorpe, S. (2017) Introducing and Piloting a Model of Non-graded Lesson Observations: Chichester College as a Case Study. In M. O'Leary (ed.) *Reclaiming Lesson Observation: Supporting Excellence in Teacher Learning.* London and New York: Routledge.

Clarke, S. (2010) Assessment: Ticking All the Boxes, Even if Some are Difficult to Tick. In S. Clarke, P. Dickinson and J. Westbrook (eds.) *The Complete Guide to Becoming an English Teacher*. London: SAGE Publications.

Cope, B. and Kalantzis, M. (1993) (eds.) *The Powers of Literacy: A Genre Approach to Teaching Writing*. Pittsburgh: University of Pittsburgh Press.

Cox, B. (1991) *Cox on Cox: An English Curriculum for the 1990's*. London, Sydney, Auckland, Toronto: Hodder & Stoughton.

D'Arcy, P. (1995) Two Contrasting Paradigms for the Teaching and Assessment of Writing. In D. Stevens (2012) (ed.) *A Guided Reader for Secondary English: Pedagogy and Practice*. Abingdon and New York: Routledge.

De Corte, E. (ed.) (2003) *Powerful Learning Environments: Unravelling Basic Components and Dimensions*. Amsterdam, Boston: Pergamon Press.

DES (1985) *The Curriculum from 5 to 16: Curriculum Matters 2*. London: Her Majesty's Stationery Office.

DfE (2014) *Statutory Guidance: National Curriculum in England: English Programmes of Study*. https://www.gov.uk/government/publications/national-curriculum-in-england-english-programmes-of-study/national-curriculum-in-england-english-programmes-of-study#key-stage-3 (accessed 12 August 2016).

DfEE (2001) *Framework for Teaching English: Years 7, 8 and 9*. London: DfEE.

Dymoke, S. (2003) *Drafting and Assessing Poetry: A Guide for Teachers*. London: Paul Chapman Publishing.

Dymoke, S., Barrs, M., Lambirth, A. and Wilson, A. (eds.) (2014) *Making Poetry Happen: Transforming the Poetry Classroom*. London and New York: Bloomsbury Academic.

Dymoke, S. and Harrison, J. (2008) *Reflective Teaching and Learning*. London: SAGE Publications.

Eisner, E. (1984) No Easy Answers: Joseph Schwab's Contributions to Curriculum. *Curriculum Inquiry* 14:2, pp. 201–210.

Ellis, V. (2007) *Subject Knowledge and Teacher Education: The Development of Beginning Teachers' Thinking*. London and New York: Continuum International.

Fleming, M. and Stevens, D. (2004) *English Teaching in the Secondary School: Linking Theory and Practice*. London: David Fulton Publishers.

Foucault, M. (1977) *Discipline and Punish: The Birth of the Prison*. Translated by A. Sheridan. Harmondsworth: Penguin Books.

Franks, A. (2015) Talk and Drama: Seeing Voices. In S. Brindley and B. Marshall (eds.) *MasterClass in English Education: Transforming Teaching and Learning*. London: Bloomsbury.

Gill, S. and Thomson, G. (2012) *Rethinking Secondary Education: A Human-Centred Approach*. Harlow: Pearson Education.

Gillard, D. (2010) James Callaghan's Ruskin College Speech. *Education in England: the History of our Schools*. http://www.educationengland.org.uk/documents/speeches/1976ruskin.html (accessed 8 February 2017).

Giroux, H.A. (1985) Intellectual Labor and Pedagogical Work: Rethinking the Role of the Teacher as Intellectual, Part I, *Phenomenology and Pedagogy*, 3(1) (1985), pp. 20–32.

Goffman, E. (1974/1986) *Frame Analysis: An Essay on the Organization of Experience. With a new Foreword by Bennett Berger*. Boston, MA: Northeastern University Press.

Goldthorpe, J. H. (2007) 'Cultural Capital': Some Critical Observations. *Sociologica* 2, pp. 1–23.

GOV.UK (2011) *Teachers' Standards*. https://www.gov.uk/government/uploads/system/uploads/attachment_data/file/283566/Teachers_standard_information.pdf (accessed 10 March 2016).

Guasp, A., Statham, H., Jadva, V. and Daly, I. (2012) *The School Report: The Experiences of Gay Young People in Britain's Schools in 2012*. London: Stonewall.

Guditus, S. (2013) Maslow's Hierarchy of School Needs. *Reflections of an Educator: The Reflections and Thoughts of a Middle School Educator*. http://sguditus.blogspot.co.uk (accessed 11 January 2017).

Habermas, J. (1982) A Reply to My Critics. In J. Thompson and D. Held (eds.) *Habermas: Critical Debates*. London: Macmillan.

Haines, J. and Miller, P. (2017) Video-Enhanced Observation: Developing a Flexible and Effective Tool. In M. O'Leary (ed.) *Reclaiming Lesson Observation: Supporting Excellence in Teacher Learning*. London and New York: Routledge.

Hardman, F. (2001) What Do We Mean by Secondary English Teaching? In J. Williamson, M. Fleming, F. Hardman and D. Stevens, *Meeting the Standards in Secondary English: A Guide to the ITT NC*. London and New York: Routledge Falmer.

Harris, R. (2009) Speech and Writing. In D. R. Olson and N. Torrance (eds.) *The Cambridge Handbook of Literacy*. Cambridge: Cambridge University Press.

Hirst, P. H. and Peters, R. S. (eds.) (1970/2012) *The Logic of Education*. London and New York: Routledge.

HMSO (1975) *A Language for Life: Report of the Committee of Inquiry Appointed by the Secretary of State for Education and Science under the Chairmanship of Sir Alan Bullock F.B.A.* London: Her Majesty's Stationery Office.

Hoffman, M. (1999) *William Shakespeare's 'A Midsummer Night's Dream'*. New York: HarperCollins.

Holbrook, D. (1968) Creativity in the English Programme. In G. Summerfield (ed.) *Creativity in English: Papers Relating to the Anglo-American Seminar on the Teaching of English at Dartmouth College, New Hampshire 1966*. Champaign, Illinois: National Council of Teachers of English.

House of Commons Education Committee (2014) *Underachievement in Education by White Working Class Children: First Report of Session 2014–2015*. London: The Stationery Office.

Irish, T. (2011) Would You Risk it for Shakespeare? A Case Study of Using Active Approaches in the English Classroom. *English in Education* 45:1, pp. 6–19.

Johnston, B. (1987) *Assessing English: Helping Students to Reflect on Their Work*. Milton Keynes and Philadelphia: Open University Press; Sydney: St Clair Press.

Krathwohl, D. (2002) A Revision of Bloom's Taxonomy: An Overview. *Theory into Practice* 41:4, pp. 212–218.

Kress, G. (1985) *Linguistic Processes in Sociocultural Practice*. Geelong, Victoria: Deakin University Press.

Kress, G. (1989) Texture and Meaning, In R. Andrews (ed.) *Narrative and Argument*. Milton Keynes and Philadelphia: Open University Pressl

Kress, G. (1994) *Learning to Write*. London and New York: Routledge.

Kress, G. and Bezemer, J. (2009) Writing in a Multimodal World of Representation. In R. Beard, D. Myhill, J. Riley and M. Nystrand (eds.), *The SAGE Handbook of Writing Development*. London: SAGE Publications.

Lahiff, A. (2017) Maximising Vocational Teachers' Learning Through Developmental Observation. In M. O'Leary (ed.) *Reclaiming Lesson Observation: Supporting Excellence in Teacher Learning*. London and New York: Routledge.

Lange, M. (2011) Progress. *The Stanford Encyclopedia of Philosophy* (Spring 2011 Edition). http://plato.stanford.edu/archives/spr2011/entries/progress/ (accessed March 13 2016).

Lave, J. (1988) *Cognition in Practice, Mind, Mathematics and Culture in Everyday Life*. Cambridge: Cambridge University Press.

Legislation.gov.uk (1988) *Clause 28 of the Local Government Act 1988*. http://www.legislation.gov.uk/ukpga/1988/9/contents (accessed 12 August 2016).

Lindsay, G. and Desforges, M. (1998) *Baseline Assessment: Practice, Problems and Possibilities*. London: David Fulton Publishers.

Locke, T. (2015) Paradigms of English. In S. Brindley and B. Marshall (eds.) *MasterClass in English Education: Transforming Teaching and Learning*. London: Bloomsbury.

Marshall, B. (2007) Assessment. http://www.ite.org.uk/ite_topics/assessment/001.php (accessed 13 September 2016).

Marshall, B. (2011a) English in the National Curriculum: a Simple Redraft or a Major Rewrite? *The Curriculum Journal* 22:2, pp. 187–199.

Marshall, B. (2011b) Testing English: Formative and Summative Approaches to English Assessment. London and New York: Continuum.

Marshall, B. (2015) Progress in English. In S. Brindley and B. Marshall (eds.) *MasterClass in English Education: Transforming Teaching and Learning*. London: Bloomsbury.

Marshall, R. (2009) Epistemic Vagueness and English Assessment: Some Reflections. In D. Stevens (2012) (ed.) *A Guided Reader for Secondary English: Pedagogy and Practice*. Abingdon and New York: Routledge.

Martin, J. (2017) Embedding Coaching and Mentoring in Peer Observation. In M. O'Leary (ed.) *Reclaiming Lesson Observation: Supporting excellence in teacher learning*. London and New York: Routledge.

Maslow, A. H. (1943). A Theory of Human Motivation. *Psychological Review* 50:4, pp. 370–396.

Matthewman, S. (2011) *Teaching Secondary English as if the Planet Matters*. London and New York: Routledge.

McGuinn, N. (2014) The Challenges and Opportunities for Engaging with Poetry. In S. Dymoke, M. Barrs, A. Lambirth and A. Wilson (eds.) *Making Poetry Happen: Transforming the Poetry Classroom*. London and New York: Bloomsbury.

McGuinn, N. and Naylor, A. (2009) Hesitantly into the Arena: An Account of Trainee Teachers' and Sixth Form Students' Preliminary Attempts to Enter into Dialogue Through Email. *English in Education* 43:3, pp. 211–225.

Mengham, R. (1993) *The Descent of Language: Writing in Praise of Babel*. London: Bloomsbury.

Moffett, J. (1981) *Coming on Centre: English Education in Evolution*. Montclair, New Jersey: Boynton/Cook.

Morrison, K. (2001) Jürgen Habermas. In J. A. Palmer (ed.) *Fifty Modern Thinkers on Education: From Piaget to the Present*. London and New York: Routledge.

Nash, R. (1999) Bourdieu, 'Habitus', and Educational Research: is it All Worth the Candle? *British Journal of Sociology of Education* 20, pp. 175–187.

Noddings, N. (2003) *Happiness and Education*. Cambridge: Cambridge University Press.

OECD (2016a) *Education at a Glance 2016: OECD Indicators*. Paris: OECD Publishing.

OECD (2016b) *PISA 2015: Results in Focus*. Paris: OECD Publishing.

O'Leary, M. (2017) Introduction: Reclaiming Lesson Observation as a Tool for Teacher Learning. In M. O'Leary (ed.) *Reclaiming Lesson Observation: Supporting Excellence in Teacher Learning*. London and New York: Routledge.

Online Etymology Dictionary. School. *http://www.etymonline.com* (accessed 11 January 2017).

Page, L. (2017) The Impact of Lesson Observation on Practice, Professionalism and Teacher Identity. In M. O'Leary (ed.) *Reclaiming Lesson Observation: Supporting Excellence in Teacher Learning*. London and New York: Routledge.

Pearson, T. (2017) Using Lesson Observations to Promote Teacher Self-efficacy. In M. O'Leary (ed.) *Reclaiming Lesson Observation: Supporting Excellence in Teacher Learning*. London and New York: Routledge.

Petty, G. (2004) *Teaching Today*. Cheltenham: Nelson Thornes.

Pollard, A. (2002) (ed.) *Readings for Reflective Teaching*. London and New York: Continuum.

Public Health England (2016) *The Mental Health of Children and Young People in England*. London: Public Health England.

Reay, D. (2004) 'It's All Becoming a Habitus': Beyond the Habitual Use of Habitus in Educational Research. *British Journal of Sociology of Education* 25:4, pp. 431–444.

Reay, D. (2015) Habitus and the Psychosocial: Bourdieu with Feelings. *Cambridge Journal of Education* 45:1, pp. 9–23.

Robinson, M. and Ellis, V. (2000) Writing in English and Responding to Writing. In D. Stevens (2012) (ed.) *A Guided Reader for Secondary English: Pedagogy and Practice*. Abingdon and New York: Routledge.

Schwab, J. J. (1978) *Science, Curriculum and Liberal Education*. Chicago: University of Chicago Press.

Schwan, A. and Shapiro, S. (2011) *How to Read Foucault's Discipline and Punish*. London: Pluto Press.

Scott, D. (2016) Learning Affordances of Language and Communication National Curricula. *The Curriculum Journal* 27:1, pp. 46–61.

Shulman, L. S. (1986a). Those who Understand: Knowledge Growth in Teaching. *Educational Research* 15:3, pp. 4–14.

Shulman, L. S. (1986b) A Perspective on Teacher Knowledge. In A. Pollard (2002) (ed.) *Readings for Reflective Teaching*. London and New York: Continuum.

Shulman, L. S. (2004) *The Wisdom of Practice: Essays on Teaching, Learning, and Learning to Teach*. San Francisco, CA: Jossey-Bass.

Slade, P. (1954) *Child Drama*. London: University of London Press.

Stevens, D. (2012) (ed.) *A Guided Reader for Secondary English: Pedagogy and Practice*. Abingdon and New York: Routledge.

Stevens, R. (2017) Observing What Matters. In M. O' Leary (ed.) *Reclaiming Lesson Observation: Supporting Excellence in Teacher Learning*. London and New York: Routledge.

Stevens, D. and McGuinn, N. (2004) *The Art of Teaching Secondary English: Innovative and Creative Approaches*. London and New York: RoutledgeFalmer.

Tamir, P. (1991) Professional and Personal Knowledge of Teachers and Teacher Educators. *Teaching and Teacher Education* 7:3, pp. 263–268.

Taylor, L. (2017) Somewhere Over the Rainbow: Transitioning from Performance to Informative Models of Observation. In M. O'Leary (ed.) *Reclaiming Lesson Observation: Supporting Excellence in Teacher Learning*. London and New York: Routledge.

Vygotsky, L. S. (1930/1978) *Mind in Society: The Development of Higher Psychological Processes*. M. Cole, V-J. Steiner, S. Scribner and E. Souberman (eds.) Cambridge, MA and London, England: Harvard University Press.

Vygotsky, L. (1986) *Thought and Language*. Cambridge, MA and London, England: The MIT Press.

Wacquant, L. J. D. (2005) Habitus. In J. Becket and Z. Milan (eds.) *International Encyclopedia of Economic Sociology*. London: Routledge.

Westbrook, J. (2009) The Secondary National Strategy. In J. Davison and J. Dowson (eds.) *Learning to Teach English in the Secondary School: A Companion to School Experience*. London and New York: Routledge.

White, J. (1989) An Unconstitutional National Curriculum. In L. Bash and D. Coulby (eds.) *The Educational Reform Act: Competition and Control*. London: Cassell.

Wilson, J. (2000) Teaching a Subject. In A. Pollard, (2002) (ed.) *Readings for Reflective Teaching*. London and New York: Continuum.

WJEC CBAC (2014) *GCSE Examiners' Reports: English, English Language and English Literature (English out of Wales) 4203/01 English Literature*. Cardiff: WJEC.

Wragg, E. C. (1994) *An Introduction to Classroom Observation*. Second Edition. London and New York: Routledge.

Wright, V. (2017) Examining Lesson Observation Feedback. In M. O'Leary (ed.) *Reclaiming Lesson Observation: Supporting Excellence in Teacher Learning*. London and New York: Routledge.

# Index

 # Taylor & Francis eBooks

## Helping you to choose the right eBooks for your Library

Add Routledge titles to your library's digital collection today. Taylor and Francis ebooks contains over 50,000 titles in the Humanities, Social Sciences, Behavioural Sciences, Built Environment and Law.

**Choose from a range of subject packages or create your own!**

### Benefits for you

» Free MARC records
» COUNTER-compliant usage statistics
» Flexible purchase and pricing options
» All titles DRM-free.

 REQUEST YOUR **FREE** INSTITUTIONAL TRIAL TODAY

**Free Trials Available**
We offer free trials to qualifying academic, corporate and government customers.

### Benefits for your user

» Off-site, anytime access via Athens or referring URL
» Print or copy pages or chapters
» Full content search
» Bookmark, highlight and annotate text
» Access to thousands of pages of quality research at the click of a button.

## eCollections – Choose from over 30 subject eCollections, including:

| | |
|---|---|
| Archaeology | Language Learning |
| Architecture | Law |
| Asian Studies | Literature |
| Business & Management | Media & Communication |
| Classical Studies | Middle East Studies |
| Construction | Music |
| Creative & Media Arts | Philosophy |
| Criminology & Criminal Justice | Planning |
| Economics | Politics |
| Education | Psychology & Mental Health |
| Energy | Religion |
| Engineering | Security |
| English Language & Linguistics | Social Work |
| Environment & Sustainability | Sociology |
| Geography | Sport |
| Health Studies | Theatre & Performance |
| History | Tourism, Hospitality & Events |

For more information, pricing enquiries or to order a free trial, please contact your local sales team: www.tandfebooks.com/page/sales

Printed in Great Britain
by Amazon